Giftedness
Has Many Faces

Giftedness
Has Many Faces

Multiple Talents and Abilities
in the Classroom

Starr Cline, Ed.D.

The Foundation for Concepts in Education, Inc.
Florida ● New York

Copyright © 1999 The Foundation for Concepts in Education, Inc.
All rights reserved.
ISBN: 1-890817-94-5
Printed in the United States of America
Library of Congress Catalog Card Number: 99-64401

Dedication

This book would not have been possible without the unending support and encouragement of my husband Jerome Z. Cline and my children Adam and Larry, who have been by my side through my nineteen years of formal education. My husband helped me formulate the ideas and philosophies upon which this book is based. Always an active advocate of appropriate educational programs for students with all kinds of gifts, he has appreciated and applauded my interest in my students; his encouragement and patience have been unending.

Contents

Acknowledgments ix

Foreword xi

Introduction xiii

Overview xv

Chapter 1: Who Are the Gifted? 1

Chapter 2: Introducing the Cline Model 19

Chapter 3: Multiple Intelligences 53

Chapter 4: The Identification and
            Development of Giftedness .105

Chapter 5: Teaching Tools:
            Lessons, Records, Reports .139

Appendices 151

Bibliography 161

Index 181

Acknowledgments

This book is the result of working with children identified as gifted for more than twenty years. Formal education, research, and observations in the classroom have led me to formulate a philosophy which serves as the foundation of the book. There are many people who have supported me in my efforts. Dr. Abraham J. Tannenbaum, my professor at Teachers College, Columbia University has been especially instrumental. He has been my teacher, mentor and friend. His work has served as the cornerstone of mine. I have always counted on his wisdom and insight. Dr. Tannenbaum introduced me to Dr. A. H. Passow who also guided me through the years. Dr. Kathryn Hegeman and Dr. Michael Pyryt, both classmates of mine at Columbia University, as well as Dr. Rose Rudnitski, Dr. Rena Subotnik and Dr. Lannie Kanevsky, have been advisors and supporters of my endeavors.

I would also like to thank my friends on the AGATE Board (Advocacy for Gifted and Talented in New York State), especially Dr. Sandra Kay for her expertise in the arts, and Dr. Mary McKnight Taylor for her expertise on disadvantaged populations. There are many others whom I turned to for their expertise in specific areas. William Grabowski, Muriel Rosen, and Sid Rosen—art. Edward Rothgarber—music. Dr. Rose Rudnitski—cognition. Lotte Goslar, Barry Oreck, Sophia Semler, and Lance Westgard, dance. Mark Somer and Mary Kalisky—school psychologists. I would also like to thank the library staff at Adelphi University, Dr. Jeffrey Kane (now Dean of Education at C. W. Post). A special thanks to all of my family and friends who have helped to review the work from time to time.

To the staff members and parents at the Herricks School, a special note of thanks for providing me with the challenge and opportunity to grow as an educator through my work with the district's wonderful gifted children.

I would like to acknowledge with special thanks the staff at Winslow Press, and especially Diane Kessenich, President of The Foundation for Concepts in Education, Inc. She has had the wisdom, insight and courage to recognize the role of creativity in the education of children and appreciates the many gifts that children possess.

Foreword

Textbooks on gifted children usually emphasize either the nature of this population or its nurture, rarely both. Academic scholars write mostly about relevant theory and research, but they do not always have the training or experience as pedagogues to suggest ways for practitioners to educate the gifted. Teachers have to draw their own inferences from material that is often abstract and difficult to translate into day-to-day enrichment in the classroom. On the other hand, books on how to educate the gifted—without anchorage in scientific knowledge about the target population and how it functions—can amount to manuals on quality education for most children, not differentiated education for the gifted.

Starr Cline has produced a teacher-friendly book that is based on solid insight into how superior young minds function. Dr. Cline's career-long teaching experience, mostly in service to able children, relieves teachers from the burden of designing education for the gifted afresh or "reinventing the wheel," as it were. What qualifies Dr. Cline as a creator of enrichment programs is not only what she has learned from many years of service as a practitioner but her equally long immersion in relevant scholarly activity. This book reveals the benefits she has reaped from regular participation in professional conferences on giftedness, some of which she has organized and many of which have provided her with platforms to share her own thinking with equally dedicated colleagues. A clear example of how she combines an understanding of theory and of practice is her treatment of multiple intelligences. Even though Howard Gardner's model has come under criticism, mainly from psychometricians, Dr. Cline sees valuable applications of the theory in planning curriculum enrichment, and she elaborates on these possibilities.

In this book, Dr. Cline shares the wealth of her expertise as an educator who has always seen herself as a professional rather than just a routine classroom employee and is proud of it as the readers of this book should be.

Abraham J. Tannenbaum
Professor Emeritus
Teachers College
Columbia University

Introduction

Picture this—A seven-year-old second grader begins her day in an elementary school, where she meets with her second grade classmates until 9:45 AM. Then, until 10:30 AM, her schedule is as follows: Mondays she spends time with the librarian on independent research. On Tuesday, the District Mathematics Coordinator stops by to see if she needs any help with her mathematics class. Wednesday she spends the morning with her classmates. On Thursday she works with the computer teacher creating her own Web page for the Internet. On Friday the fifth grade music teacher gives her clarinet lessons.

She spends the rest of her morning reading. Last year her reading level was tested at a 12.9 level. Even though her comprehension is superior, her writing skills are not on the same level. She tires easily. She is guided by a resource room teacher who also works with students who have reading problems. She joins a group of fifth graders for a discussion of Junior Great Books. At 12:00 PM, she boards a minibus with an adult aide and is transported to the Middle School where she attends an honors mathematics course for seventh and eighth graders. It's time for the students in the class to take their quiz. Students look on in amazement as she receives her mark: a perfect score.

She returns to her elementary school where she spends time with students her own age, and some of the day with students three to four years older. She wants to learn more about the physical sciences. She was given the seventh and eighth grade physical science tests and "tested out." Next year she will go into ninth grade biology.

No, this is not fiction. It is happening today in a suburban elementary school. She is a second grade student who at seven years of age took the Johns Hopkins Talent Search exam and qualified as a state winner. She is a quiet child who enjoys being seven years old. She skips down the hall and admires her new shoes. Ideas from the Cline Model of Curriculum for the Gifted have been used to guide administrators and teachers in designing a program that will meet her needs. Her parents have been instrumental in helping educators to understand their daughter's unique profile.

This book has been written to introduce those who are entering the teaching profession as well as professionals in the field to the many faces of giftedness, how to recognize them, and how to plan programs that will meet their needs in ways that are cost effective. This model has been designed to serve as a guide to identifying and planning for the many faces of giftedness. It introduces and integrates new theories of intelligence and flexible programming into classroom practice.

Giftedness has many faces. It is color blind and is not limited to those without disabilities. This work addresses the need to provide all students with opportunities and experiences that allow them to reach their potential.

Overview

Chapter 1. Who Are the Gifted? Concern for gifted children and inconsistencies in current and previous attempts to serve this population are discussed. A timeline of the development of the IQ test as an indicator of giftedness as well as the controversies surrounding it is presented as are different conceptions of giftedness and inconsistencies in providing for the gifted from state to state. Issues concerning inclusion and the dilemmas facing educators today are discussed.

Chapter 2. Introducing the Cline Model. The Cline Model is presented. The model integrates multiple intelligence theory with curriculum differentiation that is appropriate for the gifted. Details of the model are presented in terms of content that is appropriate for all students so that giftedness can be expressed and identified. Strategies that differentiate the curriculum and programming or ways that services can be delivered are presented.

Chapter 3. Multiple Intelligences. Multiple intelligences in the classroom are described. This chapter explains the author's expansion and interpretation of Howard Gardner's (1983) theory of multiple intelligences, links them to the curriculum, and demonstrates how the curriculum can be used to identify gifts, replacing the IQ test that has posed an impassable "gate" or barrier for many able individuals. Each of the intelligences is described. Potential giftedness in each of the domains is defined in terms of advanced development. Anecdotes and samples of students' work that demonstrate potential giftedness in each of the domains are provided. Strategies are presented that can be used to differentiate the curriculum once gifts have been identified.

Chapter 4. The Identification and Development of Giftedness. The theory supporting the educational philosophies for the Cline Model and the factors that contribute to giftedness, which include definitions of intelligence, creativity, task orientation/motivation, knowledge/background of experience and external environment and/or opportunity are discussed. The role of cognitive and creative development is presented along with strategies that enhance their development.

Chapter 5. Teaching Tools: Lessons, Records, Reports. This chapter provides examples of how educators might design or modify existing units so that opportunities are provided to observe students with potential gifts in multiple domains. It addresses ways that "markers" of giftedness can be recorded, such as portfolios, anecdotes, and observations. Suggestions are made as to how to report student progress and involve parents in the education of their child.

Manifesto for Children

Don't be afraid to fall in love with something and pursue it with intensity
Know, understand, take pride in
Practice, develop, exploit and enjoy your greatest strengths
Learn to free yourself from the expectations of others
And to walk away from the games they impose on you
Free yourself to play your own game
Find a great teacher or mentor who will help you
Don't waste energy trying to be well rounded
Do what you love and can do well
Learn the skills of interdependence

E. Paul Torrance

Maybe we can be that special teacher or mentor!

Printed by permission. E. Paul Torrance, Morgan Henderson and Jack Presbury (1983).
Manifesto for Children. *Athens, GA: Georgia Studies of Creative Behavior.*

There are gifted children in every classroom.

Photo by Carole Meyers

Chapter 1
Who Are the Gifted?

Typical questions a classroom teacher might ask:

- How is giftedness defined?
- Does giftedness manifest itself in more than one way?
- What is the role of intelligence testing in the assessment of giftedness?
- What attempts have been made to meet the needs of this population?
- Should gifted children with disabilities be included in the regular classroom?

To answer these questions, this chapter includes:

- Different views on the identification of the gifted and the definition of giftedness.
- An overview of the development of the IQ test and the controversies surrounding it.
- An historical overview of attempts to meet the needs of the gifted child.
- The dilemmas facing educators of the gifted today.
- A definition of the concept of inclusion and appropriate practices.

Defining Giftedness

What Is Giftedness

What is giftedness? Is it something that can be measured on a test? Can it be distilled into a single score? Does a particular score on an IQ test determine who is gifted? Are IQ and giftedness synonymous? Is giftedness the result of someone's "intelligence"? What is intelligence? These are some of the questions that continue to plague us. Experts and researchers have addressed them in a variety of ways. Giftedness is a phenomenon easily observed once it has blossomed but difficult to define. In this work it is viewed as the culmination of an individual's intelligence and creativity that can combine to produce a product that is unique and valuable to society. Non-intellectual factors, such as task orientation and motivation, working in concert with an individual's background and the opportunities provided, allow potential talent to blossom.

In the past, intelligence was most often measured by an IQ test. More recently, the use of this test as the primary measure of an individual's potential has come into question. Current theorists are asking us to reexamine the way we view intelligence and have proposed that there are many ways in which one can be intelligent. The role of the school is not to predetermine possible future achievement but to provide students with opportunities that expose them to different domains, allowing them to express any potential gifts.

Through the years, we have claimed to recognize the need to identify and nurture gifted students, but we have vacillated historically in our quest for excellence—at times the emphasis has been on providing opportunities for the gifted, at other times, we have emphasized providing a "democratic education" for all students.

We have acknowledged the presence of gifted individuals in our society, but we have not agreed on how to properly identify or educate them. Two major reasons for our failure to do so include our inability to identify who the gifted are and our lack of attention to special populations of the gifted that have been underserved, i.e., gifted children with sensory, physical, and learning disabilities, ethnic minorities, young children, the exceptionally gifted females and the underachieving (Frasier 1992; Frasier, Garcia, & Passow, 1995; Passow, 1982b). Underserved populations suffer from neglect because opportunities to nurture, stimulate, and guide the full potential of their individual abilities are missing. As we address the need to include students of all abilities and disabilities in regular classrooms, we need to reassess how we view giftedness and to provide teachers with insights and strategies that reveal the many faces of giftedness in their students, including those from populations that have heretofore been neglected.

Recent theorists of intelligence and giftedness call into question traditional models favoring general intelligence as measured by intelligence tests. The IQ or intelligence test that has been used as the primary identifier of giftedness is now being seen as a "gate" that prevents children from reaching their potential. The limiting nature of IQ tests has served as an obstacle to identifying the gifted and developing appropriate educational opportunities for them. Current theorists have proposed that intelligence is pluralistic in nature. Pluralistic models broaden the lens through which giftedness is viewed, consider the many different ways in which children can be gifted, and question the extent to which tests can capture these diverse gifts. In essence, they ask educators to rethink how gifted students are identified as well as the instructional opportunities provided to them.

Frequently, the IQ tests that are used in schools to identify the gifted population are group tests, which can be highly inaccurate. Some school districts use the tests to place students in programs that provide special opportunities. As a result, gifted programs have come under attack as communities have become polarized (Sapon-Shevin, 1994). However, just as students at one end of the spectrum need to be provided with programs that meet their needs, children who exhibit potential gifts need to receive an education that is commensurate with their abilities.

Attempts to Measure Intelligence

Interest in intelligence and intelligence testing dates back to 2200 B.C. (Sattler, 1992). Although individual IQ tests can serve as valuable tools in educational assessments, there have been abuses. A review of the movement to test for intelligence and the controversies surrounding it reveals its evolution. The use of such tests is now being questioned. A timeline of the history of the movement appears at the end of this chapter to provide some insight into this continuing debate.

The development of quantitative instruments to test for intelligence began with Alfred Binet, who undertook the task of constructing mental tests that would discriminate between normal and mentally-deficient children. Binet's ideas led to the development of the Stanford-Binet Intelligence Scale, which yielded one composite score known as an "intelligence quotient" (IQ) or "g." Lewis Terman (1926), in his longitudinal studies of giftedness, used a high IQ as the measure of intelligence and giftedness. The Stanford-Binet Intelligence Scale (and other types of IQ tests) tap into abilities that are primarily logical/mathematical and verbal/linguistic. The tests are typically taken under stressful conditions. The resultant score reflects a snapshot of a moment in time of a limited set of abilities. These same tests have been used as the basis for entry into special programs for gifted children. Although they provide special opportunities for some, their narrow focus leads to the neglect of many potentially gifted students.

Identification of the gifted child is problematic. There is no single clear-cut method that can be used to identify gifted students, and confusion still reigns as to what "gifted" and "talented" mean. The debate on how IQ tests identify giftedness continues to rage. We cannot easily predetermine who will make contributions to society. Intelligence is, to some extent, an inherited characteristic (Blakeslee, 1990, 1995; Dehaene, 1998); however environment, too, plays a significant role (Campbell & Ramey, 1994, 1995; Ramey & Campbell, 1984). For example, researchers have found that children who have suffered from severe malnutrition tend to have lower IQ scores, poorer attention and memory, and lower school achievement (Galler, 1984; Lozoff, 1989). Whereas some have equated giftedness with a particular score on an intelligence test, others have conceptualized giftedness in global terms, in terms of development or behaviors, or in terms of potential future contributions.

Intelligence Is Multifaceted

Research Supporting the Existence of Specific Abilities. Through the years, researchers have observed the existence of multiple factors that influence intelligence. Thurstone (1947), when examining factors used to measure intelligence, identified those involved in memory and fluency as well as verbal, numerical, spatial, and reasoning abilities, along with a factor for perceptual or judgment speed, and a second-order factor dominated by inductive reasoning. Burt (1949) identified two main groups of abilities: a higher-order factor for reasoning as well as one for judgment or evaluation and a second group composed of artistic or aesthetic understanding. Vernon (1950,

1979) suggested that intelligence consisted of more than group factors and that verbal abilities could be separated from spatial and mechanical skills. Cattell (1971, 1987) identified two types of mental capacity: fluid and crystallized. Fluid capacity can be directed to almost any problem requiring adaptation. Crystallized capacity results from learning experiences acquired through education and daily life experiences. Guilford (1967) designed a model, "The Structure of the Intellect," in which he observed variations in the content and form of information processed. Using factor analytic statistical techniques, he attempted to identify or isolate each of the abilities that are a part of human intelligence. He maintained that every human ability has three dimensions and can be classified according to the sub-categories within each dimension: operations (evaluation, convergent production, divergent production, memory, cognition), product (units, classes, relations, systems, transformations, implications), and content (figural, symbolic, semantic, behavioral).

Despite attempts to define the facets and nature of giftedness, it has become increasingly obvious that the nature of intelligence is quite complex.

Different Conceptions of Giftedness. Although we know that giftedness exists in all segments of our population, we continue to embrace some and ignore other children with special abilities (Tannenbaum, 1979, 1983, 1993). Each of the extant views of giftedness can be defended and are not mutually exclusive. In fact, each lends insight into the nature of giftedness from different vantage points. In this section, we elaborate on some of the more salient attempts to define giftedness.

The impetus for the last wave of interest in the gifted occurred with the appearance of The Marland Report (see Marland, 1972). It did not attempt to quantify giftedness but recognized giftedness in a number of domains as follows:

> Gifted and talented children are those identified by professionally qualified persons who by virtue of outstanding abilities are capable of high performance. These are children who require differentiated educational programs and/or services beyond those normally provided by the regular school program in order to realize their contribution to self and society.
>
> Children capable of high performance included those with demonstrated achievement and/or potential ability in any of the following areas, singly or in combination.
>
> 1. General intellectual ability
> 2. Specific academic aptitude
> 3. Creative or productive thinking
> 4. Leadership ability
> 5. Visual and performing arts
> 6. Psychomotor ability (subsequently eliminated). (p. 2)

Renzulli (1977) did not define specific types of gifts but described giftedness as having three components, i.e., above average ability, task commitment, and creativity. He, thus, introduced the notion of an interplay of other factors in the development of gifts.

Gardner (1983) proposed a model of multiple intelligences in which giftedness can be evidenced in one or more domains. In his work with brain-injured and autistic individuals, he discovered that brain injury did not lead to decreased intelligence; rather, a specific kind of intelligence was affected. Based on his observations, he grouped intelligences into seven broad categories, i.e., mathematical/logical, verbal/linguistic, spatial, musical, bodily/kinesthetic, interpersonal, and intrapersonal. According to Gardner, traditional IQ tests tap into two symbol systems; i.e., logical/mathematical and verbal/linguistic, precluding the possibility of giftedness in other domains. He believed that individual profiles vary, with some individuals having gifts in one or more areas. His ideas have strikingly broadened the way we view giftedness, providing opportunities for strengths in all domains to be observed and applauded.

Tannenbaum's (1986) definition of giftedness reminds us of our role as educators, that is, that we are to provide opportunities appropriate to the domain and level of giftedness observed. He states that "Keeping in mind that developed talent exists only in adults, a proposed definition of giftedness in children is that it denotes their potential for becoming critically acclaimed performers or exemplary producers of ideas in spheres of activity that enhance the moral, physical, emotional, social, intellectual, or aesthetic life of humanity" (p. 3). Elsewhere, he states that

> Giftedness in children means different things to different people. But no matter what definition we accept, identifying it has to be counted among our inexact sciences, partly because the methods and instruments available for that purpose are imprecise. Besides, childhood is usually too early in life for talent to be fully-blown, so we have to settle for dealing with talent-in-the-making and keep in mind the uncertainties about the future. Identification is, therefore, a matter of locating children who possess high potential in comparison to other children, with no guarantees that they will eventually excel by universal standards as adults, even with proper nurturance. (Tannenbaum & Baldwin, 1983, p. 11)

In the Jacob K. Javits Gifted and Talented Students Education Act (1988), the Marland (1972) definition that saw the need to recognize giftedness in a variety of domains was reechoed:

> (1) The term "gifted and talented students" means children and youth who give evidence of high performance capability in areas such as intellectual, creative, artistic, or leadership capacity, or in specific academic fields, and who require services or activities not ordinarily provided by the school in order to fully develop such capabilities. (Section 4103. Definitions. 102 Stat. pp. 237-238)

Silverman (1993) saw the need to address the social and emotional aspects of giftedness and suggested using the following definition arrived at by the Columbus Group:

> Giftedness is asynchronous development in which advanced cognitive

abilities and heightened intensity combine to create inner experiences and awareness that are qualitatively different from the norm. This asynchrony increases with higher intellectual capacity. The uniqueness of the gifted renders them particularly vulnerable and requires modifications in parenting, teaching and counseling in order for them to develop optimally. (The Columbus Group, 1991, p. 36)

Gagné's (1995) definition acknowledges that children have potential in one or more areas that can be developed. He differentiated between gifts and talents, stating that individuals initially possess gifts in a variety of domains (i.e., intellectual, creative, sensorimotor, others) that are developed through a variety of catalysts and that these gifts lead to talent. "It follows from this relationship that talent necessarily implies the presence of well above average natural abilities; one cannot be talented without first being gifted" (p. 107). A critical factor affecting the identification and support of giftedness is the degree to which the gift or talent in question is valued by a society at a given time (Amabile, 1983; Gardner, 1983; Tannenbaum, 1983).

Cline (1989) elaborated on Renzulli's (1977) "three-ring" model of giftedness (above-average ability, creativity, and task commitment). According to Cline, the factors that work in combination include intelligence, creativity (internal and external states), task orientation and motivation, knowledge and/or background of experience, and the external environment or opportunity.

Robert Sternberg (1988) of Yale has also provided insight into the concept of intelligence. Sternberg saw intelligence as having three major aspects: analytical, creative, and practical. Conventional, good test takers tend to excel in analytical intelligence, but not necessarily in creative or practical tasks, he believed, because the latter are often discouraged in schools.

According to Coleman (1994), giftedness is evidenced in behaviors. His research revealed 18 primary identifiers of exceptional potential, grouped as follows:

I. Exceptional Learner (Acquisition and Retention of Knowledge)
    A. Exceptional memory
    B. Learns quickly and easily
    C. Advanced understanding of area

II. Exceptional User of Knowledge (Application of Knowledge)
    A. Exceptional use of knowledge
    B. Advanced use of symbol systems; expressive and complex
    C. Demands a reason for unexplained events
    D. Reasons well in problem solving: draws from previous knowledge
       and transfers it to other areas

III. Exceptional Generator of Knowledge
    (Individual Creative Attributes)
    A. Highly creative behavior, especially in areas of interest or talent
    B. Does not conform to typical ways of thinking, perceiving
    C. Enjoys self-expression of ideas, feelings, or beliefs

D. Keen sense of humor that reflects advanced, unusual comprehension of relationships and meaning

E. Highly developed curiosity about causes, futures, the unknown

IV. Exceptional Motivation (Individual Motivational Attributes)

A. Perfectionism: striving to achieve high standards, especially in areas of talent and interest

B. Shows initiative; self-directed

C. High level of inquiry and reflection

D. Long attention span when motivated

E. Leadership: desire and ability to lead

F. Intense desire to know (p. 66)

What becomes apparent in this brief review of how giftedness is defined is that we need to address the needs of all our students, including the highly able. It involves creating an atmosphere that allows multiple gifts to be expressed, identified, and nurtured, not with the aim of predicting or guaranteeing eminence in the future but with an eye to providing opportunities that allow gifts and talents to flourish and bloom in the here and now.

The Cline Model for Developing Curriculum for the Gifted, referred to hereafter as "The Cline Model," is an attempt to meet this need. In the model, new theories of intelligence have been integrated with existing concepts and strategies that are deemed appropriate for the gifted. The IQ test is seen as one tool that can identify specific abilities rather than as a predictor of giftedness. In the model, there is no specific distinction between talent and gift. Intelligence is seen as being of a pluralistic nature. Giftedness or talent is viewed as potential in multiple domains that surfaces when combined with creativity, task orientation, and motivation, and when an appropriate background of experiences and opportunities has been provided.

The Cline Model, presented in detail in Chapter 2, has been designed as a framework that encourages educators to permit potential giftedness to be expressed in a variety of ways, allowing the many faces of giftedness to emerge. In the model, the curriculum is the vehicle for ongoing assessment, a tool to be used to provide the background necessary to recognize multiple talents as they are expressed. The model includes suggestions for curriculum differentiation in and out of the classroom.

Previous Attempts to Serve the Gifted

It has always been recognized, in educational settings, that some students have superior abilities. Through the years, a variety of administrative options have been implemented to attempt to meet their needs. Beginning in 1869, programs were designed in the St. Louis schools to accelerate rapid learners and provide for flexible promotion (Bentley, 1937). In the 1900s, grade skipping came into vogue. Rapid Advancement classes and specialized schools were established in New York City. As IQ testing became popular, Leta Hollingworth (1926) began designing classes for gifted students, admitted on the basis of a Stanford-Binet test score ranging from 120 to 168.

In 1918, the Commission of Reorganization of Secondary Education issued its Cardinal Principles of Secondary Education (Tanner & Tanner, 1980). Educators began to question whether students should be accelerated, or whether they should be involved in gaining a deeper understanding of the curriculum. In programs that were developed after 1920, the wisdom of removing students from classes with their agemates was questioned. To avoid criticism, school districts began to offer ability grouping or enrichment, rather than acceleration (Bentley, 1937).

The 1950s brought a revival of sensitivities to the gifted and Tannenbaum (1983) and Khatena (1992) have highlighted the impact the launching of *Sputnik* as a critical factor. Crash programs in mathematics and science were implemented to counter the fears that the Soviet Union was gaining on the United States in technology and science. The "gifted bandwagon" of the 1950s and early 1960s slowed down considerably as attention was focused on other concerns, such as the civil rights movement, school integration, and the Vietnam War. The 1970s brought renewed interest in the gifted. In 1972, Sidney P. Marland, U. S. Commissioner of Education, presented a report entitled Education of the Gifted and Talented. The principal findings of the report acknowledged the need to address issues involved in educating gifted children. The National/State Leadership Training Institute received federal funds to assist state education departments to develop plans for programs for the gifted. However, during the early 1980s, the Reagan Administration reduced funding and abolished the Office of Gifted and Talented. Interest in the gifted was revived once more when Congress passed the Jacob K. Javits Gifted and Talented Education Act of 1988, which focused on the identification of economically disadvantaged students. The Act supported funding to stimulate research and development, personnel training, and the establishment of a National Center. Sometimes, it appears that we are still at the place where we began.

Inconsistencies and a Lack of Uniformity in the Treatment of the Gifted Remain

State of the States. In the United States, there is little uniformity or consistency in the attention to the gifted among its 50 states. When one reviews the *State of the States Gifted and Talented Education Reports*, issued periodically by the Council of State Directors of Programs for the Gifted (1991, 1994, 1996), inconsistencies can be noted. The number of states having mandates varies, as does those that require training for teachers of the gifted, or the amount of monies allotted to the gifted. Some of the findings reported are presented below, chronologically.

In 1991:
- 26 states had mandates for programs for the gifted.
- 17 states had requirements for teacher training.
- Concern existed that some of the states might be losing their mandates because of the current fiscal crisis.

In 1994:
- 33 states had mandates.

- 17 states required that teachers of the gifted have training.
- New York had allotted 25% of a State Director's time to the gifted.
- Arkansas had assigned 3 people at the state level to the gifted.
- New York allotted 13.3 million to the gifted.
- Texas, 50.6 million.
- Florida, 130.5 million.
- New York had no mandate. Children entering school had to be identified and parents notified, but schools did not have to provide services.
- Texas had a mandate that required that children in all grades had to be identified and served.
- In New York, 6% of the school population was being served.
- In Texas, 7% were being served.
- New York reported that its greatest strength was the leadership provided by coordinators of programs, its state advocacy association, and its summer institutes in math and science.
- Texas reported that its strengths included its mandate, its advocacy association with 7,500 members, and interest at the state agency level.

In 1996:
- 31 states had a mandate requiring gifted students be identified.
- 34 states allotted funds for the gifted.
- The number of people assigned to the gifted at the state level varied greatly, with Guam reporting 37, Texas 5, and most others reporting between 1 and 2. New York had lost its State Director.
- 44 states had a definition of the gifted and talented.
- 24 states had mandates to provide educational programs for the gifted.
- 25 states reported that the most powerful force negatively affecting delivery of services was the trend towards anti-ability grouping.

We are, indeed, a country of mixed messages. We would certainly not consider assembling football teams or orchestras of mixed ability. We are being pushed toward providing heterogeneous academic groups as we complain about not meeting world-class standards.

Still in Search of Excellence

In his latest report, *National Excellence: A Case for Developing America's Talent* (1993), Richard W. Riley, United States Secretary of Education, informed us that America is facing a "quiet crisis" in the education of gifted and talented students. Not only were the needs of this population not being met, but gifted students were not being identified. Significant findings of the report are that:

- Compared with top students in other industrialized countries, American students perform poorly on international tests, are offered a less rigorous curriculum, read fewer demanding books, do less homework, and enter the work force or post-secondary education less prepared.

- Not enough American students perform at the highest levels on National Assessment of Educational Progress (NAEP) tests, which are one of the few available indicators of how well our students are achieving.
- Gifted and talented elementary students have mastered 35 to 50 percent of the curriculum to be offered in five basic subjects before they begin the school year.
- Most regular classroom teachers make few, if any, provisions for talented students.
- Appropriate opportunities in middle schools are scattered and uncoordinated.
- High school schedules do not provide the flexibility needed to meet the needs of talented students.
- Most of the highest-achieving students in the nation included in *Who's Who Among American High School Students* reported that they studied less than an hour a day. This suggests that they get top grades without having to work hard.
- Only 2 cents out of every $100 spent on K–12 education in the United States in 1990 supported special opportunities for gifted students.

According to the report, in order to improve educational opportunities for America's top students we need to:

- Set challenging curriculum standards
- Provide more challenging opportunities to learn
- Increase access to early childhood education
- Increase learning opportunities for disadvantaged and minority children with outstanding talents
- Broaden the definition of giftedness
- Emphasize teacher training and technical assistance
- Have our students match world performance

In addition to these recommendations, we need to consider gifted education in the context of inclusion, i.e., including students with both abilities and disabilities in the regular classroom. Public Law 105-17 IDEA provides specific guidelines for educators regarding the identification and planning for students with disabilities, but is not clear about how to do so for students with above-average ability. As a result, the types and number of services provided for able students across the nation have been left to the discretion of individual school districts. Although some states mandate serving gifted students, others do not. And even among states with mandates, policies vary greatly (Passow & Rudnitski, 1993).

Where programs for the gifted exist, identification procedures vary widely and special populations are underrepresented. A student identified as "gifted" in one school may not be identified as such in another. Some programs rely on IQ tests, while others do not. Those that use IQ tests do not agree on a specific score that determines who the gifted are. Conventional IQ tests cannot provide accurate information for gifted students with disabilities. As a result, services are erratic, and the disabled, disadvantaged, and minority populations have been neglected. Existing opportunities are decidedly unequal.

What Is Inclusion? Inclusion is viewed not as a program but rather as a philosophy around which appropriate strategies must now be devised that meet the needs of all students in the regular classroom. It encompasses a belief system that emphasizes individual worth and value and promotes a sense of belonging for all members of our society. These ideas apply to all students, whether "disabled," "average," "gifted," or "disabled and gifted."

> One of the defining characteristics of an inclusive school is a "zero reject" (Lilly, 1971) philosophy—that is, the notion that no child will be excluded from general education classrooms because of a characteristic or trait such as gender, race, socioeconomic status, or a differing ability. A first step to take, then, when planning for individual student differences is to identify the unique characteristics, skills, strategies, and knowledge each particular student brings to different learning tasks and to identify likely educational mismatches. (Villa, Van der Klift, Udis, Thousand, Nevin, Kunc & Chapple, 1995, pp. 138–139)

Legal mandates driving inclusive education in this country date back to P.L. 94–142, the Handicapped Children's Education Act, passed in 1975. The law has been amended four times, in 1983 (P.L. 98-199), 1986 (P.L 99-457), 1990 (IDEA, P.L. 101-476), and 1997 (IDEA, P.L. 105-17). The Individuals with Disabilities Education Act (IDEA), passed in 1990, reauthorized P.L. 94-142. The law guarantees a free and appropriate education, a fair and nondiscriminatory evaluation, due process, an individualized education program, and education in the least restrictive environment. It states:

> To the maximum extent appropriate, handicapped children, including those children in public and private institutions or other care facilities, are educated with children who are not handicapped, and that special classes, separate schooling or other removal of handicapped children from the regular educational environment occurs only when the nature or severity of the handicap is such that education in regular classes with the use of supplementary aids and services cannot be achieved satisfactorily. (P.L. 94-142, Section 14-12 [5] [B]. Falvey, M. A., Gifner, C. C., and Kimm, C., p. 5)

Falvey, Gifner and Kimm (1995) claim that previous attempts to integrate students with disabilities, including mainstreaming and integration, have failed and have set out necessary conditions for successful inclusion programs:

Inclusion is not just for students with disabilities, but rather for all the students, educators, parents, and community members. Experience tells us that as communities and schools embrace the true meaning of inclusion, they will be better equipped to learn about and acquire strategies to change a segregated special education system to an inclusive service delivery system, with meaningful, child-centered learning. In the process, a society and world intolerant and fearful of difference may change to one that embraces and celebrates its natural diversity. (p. 3)

The authors point out that "inclusion" is still an elusive term, and refer to York's (1994, p. 3) definition that inclusion involves students' "attendance in the same schools as siblings and neighbors, membership in general education classrooms with chronological age appropriate classmates, having individualized and relevant learning objectives, and being provided with the support necessary to learn (e.g., special education and related services)."

Villa et al. (1995) point out that inclusive schooling does not "mean that children with gifts and talents will not receive focused attention in one-on-one or homogeneous group arrangements." They continue: "On the contrary, both will be options, as needed for any student. Capitalizing on the multiple intelligences notion of human difference and potential, homogeneous groups could be arranged along any number of dimensions of interest or 'intelligence' (e.g., musical preferences, recreational interests)" (pp. 143–145). Even though the philosophies guiding inclusion are sound, many obstacles need to be overcome before full inclusion can take place. These include limited resources, variability of student behaviors, teacher attitudes, inadequate teacher preparation, and a lack of systematic reintegration.

Advocates for special education fear that a continuum of services or cascade model (Reynolds, 1962; Deno, 1970), which includes placements in resource rooms, special classes, special schools and residential schools, will be replaced by a "one-size-fits-all" model. Proponents of inclusion have called for responsible inclusion. This involves building a vision, a restructuring of the roles and responsibilities of faculty, collaboration among schools, families, and community, and on-going professional development (Muscott, 1991). Responsible inclusion also means that schools should make individual case-by-case decisions. Failure to do so will lead to great dissatisfaction with public schools and will not serve the students and their families well.

An inclusive classroom is not possible without appropriate staff development, training, and support. For potential giftedness to surface, each student needs to be provided with the appropriate background and support. Once identified, gifted children need to have the benefit of interaction with their intellectual peers. In special cases, meeting the needs of the individuals involved might require segregated settings. The challenges faced by classroom teachers today require an understanding of the unique characteristics of the gifted as they build a repertoire of classroom strategies needed to address the educational needs of diverse populations both within and beyond the classroom walls.

Summary

Society has vacillated in its attempts to meet the needs of gifted students. Consequently, great inconsistencies exist in the services being provided. Identification of giftedness is not an exact science. The IQ test (a primary identifier of giftedness) has been used and abused and has come under attack. Different conceptions of giftedness and how it should be nurtured abound. Intelligence is now viewed as being of a pluralistic nature. Challenges today include providing for the gifted in the context of the inclusive classroom.

Attempts to describe and/or identify the gifted individual have served as grist for the mill as theorists and practitioners continue the debate. Teachers need to establish environments where giftedness in different domains is expressed, thus allowing them to observe student behaviors that reveal potential gifts.

Measures of intelligence have often been equated with giftedness. In this work, a multidimensional view of intelligence is adopted in which intelligence is seen as a component of interactive elements that combine in the life of individuals who achieve eminence in their fields. Giftedness in children is viewed as advanced development and superior reasoning skills, which may be domain specific and which need to be nurtured and challenged. The Cline Model, presented in Chapter 2, can be used to empower teachers in their quest for identifying, nurturing, and programming for the gifted child in the regular classroom and beyond. The timeline below outlines the development of the IQ test as well as the controversies regarding its use.

Measuring Intelligence: A Timeline of Its History and Salient Issues

2200 B.C.: Chinese emperors establish civil service exams (Sattler, 1992).

1834: E. H. Weber measures thresholds of awareness with regard to how observers detect differences between stimuli; G. T. Fechner gives the work mathematical form between stimulus strengths and strength sensations (Sattler, 1992).

1869: Galton's "Classification of Men According to Their Natural Gifts" links intelligence with heredity. He surveyed the achievement of males of distinguished British families and devised a statistical analysis of inherited characteristics (Galton, 1925).

1884: The Anthropometric Laboratory is established by Galton to study body measurements. Sensory discrimination and motor coordination are thought to be related to intelligence (Sattler, 1992; Sokal, 1987).

1880s–1900s: James McKeen Cattell develops procedures for testing physiological and psychological characteristics thought to be correlated with intelligence (Sokal, 1987).

1898–1901: Sharp and Wissler debunk Cattell's work (Postman, 1962; Sattler, 1974). Sharp reported that Cattell's tests were unreliable, inasmuch as they were measuring different functions. Wissler, using correlational methods, reported low relationships among test scores themselves.

1904: Binet and Simon are commissioned to find a procedure to determine how to segregate slow learners in Paris schools. Tests involve motor development, cognitive abilities, comprehension, memory, and divergent production. Binet believes intelligence can be improved (Sattler, 1992).
Charles Spearman develops a method of analysis to determine "g" (general intelligence) (Spearman, 1927).

1910: Henry Goddard brings Binet's work to the United States and favors using tests to categorize the feebleminded and categorize and classify children into groups. He advocates grouping children when they enter school—exceptionally intelligent, nervously brilliant, moderately bright, average, feebleminded, and imbeciles (Goddard, 1920).

1910–1917: Lewis Terman and Robert Yerkes, hereditarian eugenicists, attempt to improve upon Binet's work. Terman revises Binet's tests, and Yerkes develops a more sophisticated scoring system (Reed, 1987).

1913: Goddard uses intelligence testing at Ellis Island to exclude feebleminded immigrants from entering the country: 83 percent of the Jews, 80 percent of the Hungarians, and 87 percent of the Russians are found to be feebleminded (Goddard, 1913, 1917).

1917: Yerkes uses intelligence tests to classify and assign U.S. Army recruits during World War I. The average mental age of the draftee was only 13. Central to this effort was that the tests be used to categorize and classify students in school. Arthur S. Otis, then a graduate student at Stanford, saw a need for group testing and constructed a Scale for the Group Measurement of Intelligence, a precursor to multiple-choice and true/false items, enabling mass testing (Samelson, 1987).

1920: Yoakum and Yerkes promote using tests to categorize and classify individuals for use in schools. Students would be grouped as "superior," "intermediate," and "inferior." The test could be used to determine racial and environmental differences. "It seems within the bounds of reason to prophesy the development of methods that will finally aid in defining racial and environmental differences"(Yoakum & Yerkes, 1920, p. 193).

1920s: Carl Brigham uses data from Army mental tests to forecast that Americans will be less intelligent when blended with other cultures (Brigham, 1923):

> We may consider that the population of the United States is made up
> of four elements, the Nordic, Alpine and Mediterranean races of
> Europe, and the Negro. If these four types blend in the future into
> one general American type, then it is a foregone conclusion that this
> future blended American will be less intelligent than the present
> native born. (pp. 204–205)

1926: Terman publishes his study of mental and physical traits of a thousand gifted children. Terman believed that nothing is more important to individuals than their IQ, except possibly their morals (Minton, 1987). Participants in his study have been followed through 1995 (Burks, Jensen, & Terman, 1930; Cox, 1926; Goleman, 1995; Terman, 1926; Terman & Oden, 1947; Terman & Oden, 1959).

1947: L. L. Thurstone develops the Tests of Primary Abilities, which assess seven primary factors—Verbal Comprehension; Word Fluency; Number (computational fluency); Space (spatial visualization); Associative Memory; Perceptual Speed; and Reasoning (Thurstone, 1947).

1950: Philip Vernon suggests that intelligence has more than one facet and that verbal abilities should be separated from spatial and mechanical skills (Vernon, 1950, 1979).

1950s: Interest in Piaget's view of intelligence is revived, and intelligence is linked to developmental stages (Phillips, 1975; Pulaski, 1980; Sattler, 1992).

1953: Ann Roe links different abilities to different sciences (Roe, 1953).

1958: David Wechsler divides his test, the Wechsler Scale, into verbal and performance components (Wechsler, 1958).

1967: John Horn and Raymond Cattell develop their theory of fluid and crystallized intelligence. Fluid intelligence is defined as nonverbal and culture free, while crystallized intelligence is seen as involving acquired skills and as being culture dependent (Horn & Cattell, 1967).

1967: In his *The Nature of Human Intelligence*, J. P. Guilford asserts that intelligence is comprised of more than 150 factors (Guilford, 1967)

1969: Jensen proposes that genetic factors are strongly implicated in differences in intelligence between whites and blacks (Jensen, 1969).

1973: McClelland addresses the validity of so-called intelligence tests. He claims that even though intelligence may predict success in school, these tests are not related to any other behaviors of importance (McClelland, 1973).

1978: Donald MacKinnon studies 40 eminent architects and states that the influence of IQ is overestimated in creative achievement (MacKinnon, 1978).

1978: Lev Vygotsky's work on "Zones of Proximal Development" is presented (Cole, John-Steiner, Scribner, & Souberman, 1978).

1979: Reuven Feuerstein presents his theory of mediated learning and proposes that instrumental enrichment can increase intelligence (Feuerstein, 1979).

1983: Howard Gardner publishes *Frames of Mind: The Theory of Multiple Intelligences* (Gardner, 1983).

1984: James R. Flynn states that IQ scores increase over time (Flynn, 1984). C. T. Ramey and F. A. Campbell conduct research on "Preventive Education for High-Risk Children" and report positive cognitive effects as a consequences of early intervention in the Carolina Abecedarian Project (Ramey & Campbell, 1984).

1985: Benjamin Bloom claims that factors other than IQ, such as parental involvement and first teachers, lead to talent development (Bloom, 1985).

1988: Robert Sternberg presents his Triarchic Theory of Intelligence according to which intelligent behavior involves an interplay between environmental context, prior experiences, and cognitive processes. He found no relationship between scores on tests of practical intelligence given to business executives and scores on conventional tests of intelligence (Sternberg, 1988b).

1988: Marian Diamond demonstrates the impact of the environment on the anatomy of the brain (Diamond, 1988).

1992: Andrew Hacker claims that the types of IQ tests currently in use are creating *Two Nations: Black and White, Separate, Hostile, Unequal* (Hacker, 1995).

1994: Herrnstein and Murray claim in *The Bell Curve*, that IQ is inherited. They assert that those with low IQs are consigned to the ranks of the impoverished and that the cognitive elite will lead to cognitive partitioning (Herrnstein & Murray, 1994).

1995: Daniel Goleman asserts the importance of emotional intelligence (Goleman, 1995).

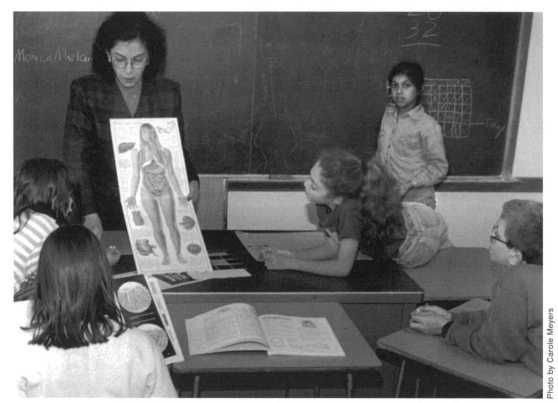

Photo by Carole Meyers

As children are introduced to curriculum, precocity is noted and appropriate differentiation implemented.

Chapter 2
Introducing the Cline Model

Typical questions a classroom teacher might ask:

- How might I identify the different types of giftedness in my room?
- How might I use the curriculum to identify students' gifts in my room?
- What is involved in curriculum differentiation?
- Once identified, how might I provide opportunities for the gifted child?

To answer these questions, this chapter includes:

- A rationale and need for a workable model.
- Content that is appropriate for all children.
- The relationships of multiple intelligence theory to content in the classroom.
- The academic foundations for a differentiated curriculum.
- Variations in curriculum differentiation depending on the domain or content involved.
- Ways that teachers can creatively program for the gifted.

According to the U.S. Department of Education (1993), gifted students may already know 35% of what is to be taught. Oftentimes, giftedness may not be recognized in classroom settings. When accurate assessments are not made, gifted students can lose interest, leading to underachievement and/or attention-seeking behaviors. If students are to meet their potential, once assessments are made, a curriculum needs to be provided that is challenging and allows for total involvement, stemming from intrinsic motivation (Csikszentmihalyi, 1990). Throughout, the guiding principle should be that giftedness can take many forms.

The Cline Model, the organizing framework for this book, was developed to provide a "road map" that teachers could use both to design classroom environments in which potential giftedness can be expressed and also to assist in identification and planning. The model grew out of "The Model of Human Potential" (see Figure 2-1) (Cline, 1989). The Cline Model integrates theories on differentiating curriculum with current research on the identification of gifted students.

The Model of Human Potential

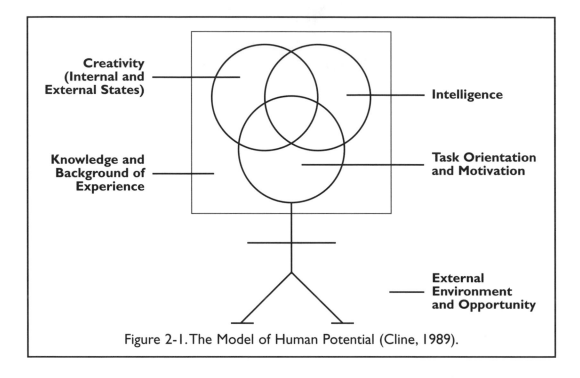

Figure 2-1. The Model of Human Potential (Cline, 1989).

Summary of Components

Giftedness is expressed when all of the elements come together in an interactive fashion.

Intelligence. An individual may be born with a genetic predisposition in one or more domains. In addition to a proclivity in a domain, the individual possesses the ability to exercise critical thought processes that allow for an understanding of the nature of the domain. Intelligence is not viewed as a unitary factor that can be measured on a single test. Cline (1989) postulates that intelligence is a combination of cognitive abilities that operate interactively in a particular domain. For giftedness to be expressed in one or more of the many domains, individuals need to be exposed to the domain(s). Students can exhibit signs of giftedness in one or more domains of intelligence. Potential giftedness is observed as students make connections in thinking that reflect complex critical thought processes. Nurturing for intelligent behavior is an important component in the development of potential giftedness. Relevant teaching strategies are described in Chapter 4.

Creativity. Individuals have the ability to exercise creative thought processes that allow them to create ideas or design products that are unique and make valuable contributions to society. Creativity needs to be stressed and modeled in the classroom. Creative thought processes are used in each of the domains and can be observed as students work in one or more content areas. Establishing an environment that fosters creativity as well as appropriate strategies for the classroom is covered in Chapter 4.

Task Orientation and Motivation. Given a suitable environment, individuals can be intrinsically motivated to devote energy to their work and to develop a passion for it. Behaviors indicative of task orientation and motivation are covered in Chapter 4.

Knowledge and Background of Experience. The importance of providing individuals with experiences which allow their gifts to be exposed and nurtured in the domain in which proclivities are present is covered in Chapter 4.

External Environment and Opportunity. The impact of early home and school environments on children's intelligence is covered in Chapter 4.

Gardner's (1983) theory of multiple intelligences enlightens previously held assumptions that intelligence is a numerical score on a test. His theory can be used as an umbrella for identifying intelligences that are linked to classroom curricula. Gardner proposed that intelligence has seven facets:

1. Mathematical/Logical—Facility with numbers and ability to reason and recognize patterns and relationships

2. Verbal/Linguistic—Verbal and written communication ability

3. Spatial—Seen in art work or in activities having to do with navigation

4. Musical—Performing and composing musical works

5. Bodily/Kinesthetic—Athletic ability and movement

6. Intrapersonal Intelligence—Knowledge of oneself

7. Interpersonal Intelligence—Sensitivity to others

Students need to be exposed to experiences in each of Gardner's domains of intelligence, so that their gifts can surface—whether in one or more domains. For some students, specific proclivities may not be evident, but giftedness may become apparent in the quality of their responses. Giftedness may be evidenced in the use of complex thought processes and in the speed in learning. For these students, the direction their lives may take may not become apparent early on, but they may be our future politicians, historians, and philosophers.

Morelock and Feldman (1997) also differentiate between levels and types of giftedness:

1. Individuals with an extraordinarily high IQ (omnibus prodigy) demonstrate performance in multiple domains and display passionate involvement in many. These individuals have exceptional abstract reasoning ability in logical and verbal/conceptual areas and a voracious appetite for academic knowledge.

2. The prodigy performs at an adult level and is passionately involved in one domain. Prodigies display extraordinary generalized abstract

reasoning ability and may demonstrate an intense desire to master academic knowledge.

3. Extraordinarily high IQ children display extraordinarily high generalized abstract reasoning capability. They may have domain-specific skills or may be drawn to a number of different areas. They may have difficulty committing to one and exhibit a voracious appetite for academic knowledge.

4. Prodigious savants are concrete thinkers who display islands of extraordinary advanced domain-specific gifts in one or more areas with little ability for abstract reasoning.

In the Cline Model, giftedness in each of the domains is seen as advanced development. We cannot predetermine who will integrate innate proclivities with other elements involved in achieving eminence in a field. It is the role of the school to introduce students to all of the domains, to advance development, and to continue to challenge students in the areas of giftedness noted. The school becomes a partner, providing the background and environment that assist able students as they strive to reach their potential.

If teachers are to provide instruction in inclusive classrooms, they need guidelines to assess ability in specific domains. Once potential giftedness is noted, they need to provide environments and use educational strategies that can differentiate the curriculum, depending on the ability noted. The Cline Model meets this need. Exposure and identification begin in the regular classroom. When extraordinary gifts are noted, educators need to go beyond the classroom walls to provide instruction that provides a level of choice, control, and challenge for their students.

The model (see Figure 2-2) has its roots in the Tannenbaum Matrix (1983) but has expanded on that matrix to include multiple intelligence theory as a way of seeing giftedness in terms of multidimensionality.

Multidimensionality and Giftedness

Other major theorists in the field have viewed giftedness in terms of multidimensionality and talent development (Gardner, 1983; Sternberg, 1988; Feldhusen, 1992, 1997; Renzulli, 1994; Treffinger & Feldhusen, 1996). Feldhusen (1997) described ten domains of talent that should be nurtured in schools: academic, artistic, athletic/physical, cognition, creative, communication, games, language, personal/social, and technical. He makes a case for assisting students so that they can become aware of and realize their potential in their areas of special strength; they should also have access to classes, courses, mentors, models, and services that allow them to pursue their goals. Morelock (1996) asserts that "Talent development needs to become a foundational concept in general education, with the identification of talent potential and the active fostering of its development a central goal for all children" (p.10).

In his research, Gagné (1997) interviewed forty adolescents identified as multitalented and found that giftedness often appeared in more than one domain but that

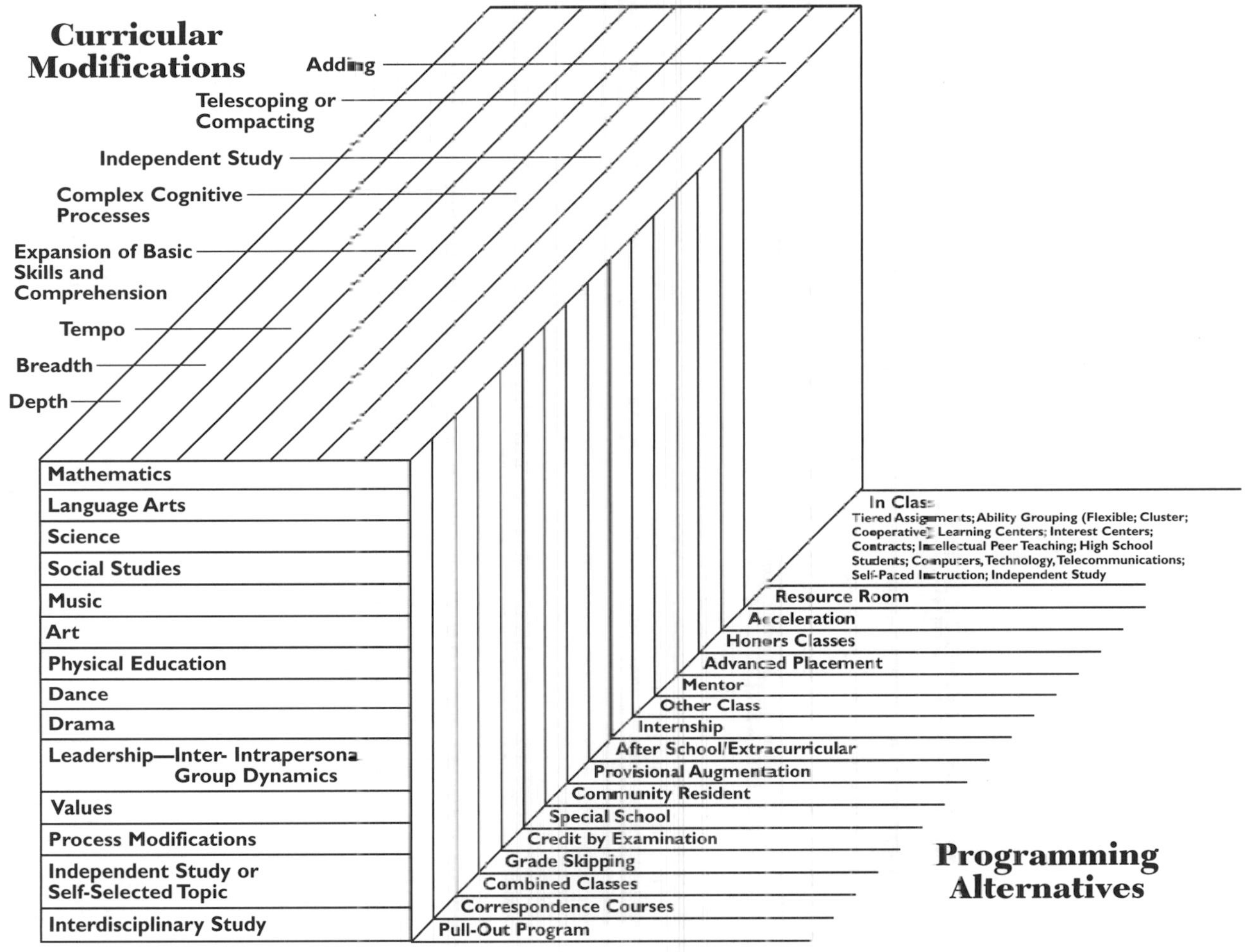

© 1993 Starr Cline, Ed.D.

Curricular Modifications

- Adding
- Telescoping or Compacting
- Independent Study
- Complex Cognitive Processes
- Expansion of Basic Skills and Comprehension
- Tempo
- Breadth
- Depth

Content

- Mathematics
- Language Arts
- Science
- Social Studies
- Music
- Art
- Physical Education
- Dance
- Drama
- Leadership—Inter- Intrapersonal Group Dynamics
- Values
- Process Modifications
- Independent Study or Self-Selected Topic
- Interdisciplinary Study

Programming Alternatives

- In Class: Tiered Assignments; Ability Grouping (Flexible; Cluster; Cooperative); Learning Centers; Interest Centers; Contracts; Intellectual Peer Teaching; High School Students; Computers; Technology; Telecommunications; Self-Paced Instruction; Independent Study
- Resource Room
- Acceleration
- Honors Classes
- Advanced Placement
- Mentor
- Other Class
- Internship
- After School/Extracurricular
- Provisional Augmentation
- Community Resident
- Special School
- Credit by Examination
- Grade Skipping
- Combined Classes
- Correspondence Courses
- Pull-Out Program

Figure 2-2. Cline Model of Curriculum for the Gifted.

profiles varied. Giftedness was described in terms of personal aptitude, creative, soci-affective, cognitive, personal management, sensorimotor and natural talents (arts and communications).

Background

Although giftedness exists in every segment of the population, disabled students and those from culturally diverse populations have previously been overlooked and underserved. Researchers are now seeking ways of validating multiple gifts in terms of alternative assessments (Plucker, Callahan, & Tomchin, 1996), a step which, it is hoped, will go far in remedying past neglect of the full range of gifted individuals.

Integrating Multiple Intelligence Theory into the Cline Model

The Cline Model does not negate those developed by others, nor does it disre-gard information provided by IQ tests. Both Tannenbaum's (1983) matrix and Renzulli's (1977) three-ring conception of giftedness have contributed to its develop-ment. Gardner's (1983) theory is viewed as key in the identification of multiple intelli-gences in the classroom. His philosophy has provided a broader lens through which giftedness can be viewed and developed. Originally, Gardner (1983) had proposed seven broad categories of intelligence; recently, he expanded the theory to include two more: the naturalist and the spiritualist (see Gardner, 1997). The Cline Model uses Gardner's original seven areas (i.e., verbal/linguistic, logical/mathematical, spatial, bod-ily/kinesthetic, musical, and inter- and intrapersonal intelligences) as a guide for teach-ers in recognizing the diverse talents students may bring to classrooms. Each of the intelligences serves as an umbrella for many others, for example, in the mathematical realm, a student may excel in geometry but not in algebra. A student who is spatially gifted may be artistic and not possess navigational skills. A student with verbal linguis-tic gifts may be a gifted poet but not a gifted orator. Support for the theory has been found in neuropsychological research. In his research with brain-damaged adults, Gardner (1975) found that specific faculties could be lost while others remained intact. However, even though each individual faculty is independent, they work in con-cert with one another in different domains. Thus, profiles vary and individuals may possess strengths and deficits in each.

According to multiple intelligence theorists, each of the intelligences is a relative-ly autonomous potential and can function independently of the others. Each has its own developmental trajectory.

In one's school and professional careers, one type of intelligence may dominate even as other intelligences are integrated in actual performance. For example, verbal/linguistic intelligence predominates for the writer and lecturer and combines with the logical/mathematical for the lawyer. Logical/mathematical intelligence pre-dominates for the mathematician and physicist but cuts across all domains. Spatial intelligence evidences itself in the work of the artist, navigator, and chess player and works in concert with logical/mathematical intelligence for the architect. Bodily/kinesthetic intelligence is demonstrated by the athlete and the mime and combines with musical intelligence for the dancer. Musical intelligence will manifest itself in the singer, composer, lyricist, or performer as each works in concert with verbal and/or mathematical/logical skills. Intra- and interpersonal intelligence is dominant among religious leaders, politicians, therapists, and salespeople. Even though personal intelligences have been relatively ignored in schools, their importance cannot be underestimated (Goleman, 1995; Hacker, 1995; Hyatt & Gottlieb, 1987). Empathic understanding of others needs to be acknowledged and encouraged as students of all abilities and disabilities are included in the same classroom.

Verbal/linguistic and logical/mathematical skills have traditionally been the two most valued areas in school settings and the two that intelligence tests or "g" tap into, although a single score does not indicate that individuals perform equally in both areas (Benbow & Stanley, 1982; Benbow & Minor, 1986). Although one of the criticisms levelled against Gardner's theory is that some of his domains, for example, musical, spatial, or bodily/kinesthetic, are talents rather than gifts, one can argue that it is much more democratic because it raises all of the intelligences to the same level. Each of the intelligences has the potential to blossom depending on the culture in which individuals are reared. According to Gardner (1983), notions of giftedness are culturally bound. Thus, to some degree, giftedness is the ability to fashion products and solve problems in a domain(s) that is of value in a particular cultural setting.

The Cline Model has been divided into three sections—content, curricular modifications (strategies that can be used to differentiate the curriculum), and programming alternatives (in-class and administrative options). It integrates current theories of intelligence into classroom practice and is intended as a tool to assist teachers in the identification of talents and abilities in the classroom. The evaluative component of the model is also designed to eliminate some of the concerns and controversies concerning using IQ tests as a primary assessment tool. Use of the model enables teachers to provide opportunities for the expression of potential in each of Gardner's areas of intelligence. Developmental levels in each area are delineated so that potential giftedness can be observed. Once observed, guidelines help teachers to connect curricular strategies with the identified potential(s). Suggestions are included on programming options and on ways in which teachers can extend the classroom walls.

The model has been designed to provide objectives for short- and long-term planning so that education for gifted children can be woven into the fabric of the school. Teachers and/or administrators can use the model to assess present accomplishments and plan for the future at the classroom, school, and district levels.

In this model, the curriculum becomes the tool with which gifts and talents are identified and nurtured. Identification of potential is ongoing. It does not negate the potential of the student who scores high on an IQ test, but it goes beyond IQ score in the identification of giftedness. The model is also designed to serve students who have been underrepresented in programs for the gifted, such as those with disabilities or from culturally diverse backgrounds. Students from all backgrounds may exhibit gifts in one or more areas. Providing optimal matches between ability, curriculum, and instruction prevents boredom and underachievement and allows potential to be reached. Viewing students in terms of strengths rather than deficits in all domains enhances self-esteem (Callahan, 1997).

Administrators and teachers can use the model to guide them in integrating programs for gifted students in their schools. By assessing which parts of the model are already in place, they can build on present programs.

Sections of the Cline Model

The model has three dimensions or sections: content, curricular modifications, and programming alternatives.

Content. This section describes domains of knowledge that all children should be exposed to so that potential giftedness can be allowed to surface.

Curricular Modifications. This section describes strategies, or ways that the curriculum can be differentiated, so that a level of challenge is maintained for able students. It describes how the curriculum should be modified when gifts in specific domains are noted.

Programming Alternatives. Especially for gifted children, the classroom walls need to be eliminated as technology and the Internet become their encyclopedia. This section describes who might be involved in delivering services, in and out of the classroom, depending on school and community resources.

As students are exposed to content, potential giftedness is noted. Area of giftedness is then matched to curricular modifications that provide a level of differentiation for the student. Depending on the extent to which the student is gifted, appropriate programming options need to be implemented. A basic assumption of the Cline Model is that geniuses are not just born, they can and must also be made. And teachers are an important part of the process.

Foundations for Designing Differentiated Curricula

According to Passow (1986), basic to the provision of appropriate educational services for the gifted is an assessment of the following:

> Who are the learners?
> What do they need to know?
> What settings should be established?

Passow (1982a) and VanTassel-Baska (1988) outlined principles that can guide the development of differentiated curricula for the gifted and talented and that have been integrated into the Cline Model:

- All learners should be provided curriculum opportunities that allow them to attain optimum levels of learning.

- Curricula must be adapted or designed to accommodate the learning needs of gifted learners, which are different from those of typical learners.

- The needs of gifted learners cut across cognitive, affective, social, and esthetic areas of curriculum experiences.

It is recommended that the content of curricula for the gifted/talented should:

- Include more elaborate, complex, and in-depth study of major ideas, problems, and themes—those that integrate knowledge with and across systems of thought.
- Allow for the development and application of productive thinking skills that enable students to reconceptualize existing knowledge and/or generate new knowledge.
- Enable students to explore constantly changing knowledge and information and to develop the attitude that knowledge is worth pursuing in an open world.
- Encourage exposure to, selection of, and use of appropriate and specialized resources.
- Promote self-initiated and self-directed learning and growth.
- Provide for the development of self-understanding and the understanding of one's relationships to other persons, societal institutions, nature, and culture.
- Evaluate students on their ability to perform at a level of excellence that demonstrates creativity and higher-level thinking skills.

The curriculum for the gifted should be qualitatively different and its content, process, product and the learning environment should be adjusted to accommodate the special characteristics of gifted students. When students are actively engaged in endeavors that indicate innate proclivities, ability can also be noted through their working style (Ramos-Ford & Gardner, 1997). Working style refers to the level of engagement shown in particular activities. Are the students fully engrossed, focused, and persistent? Do they enjoy the involvement and bring a creative slant to the work?

A Curriculum for the Gifted

Identifying gifted students and planning and implementing an appropriate curriculum involve the following steps:

Step I—Expand on existing lessons or design new ones so as to expose children to the basic skills involved in each and every one of the many talent areas.

Step II—Incorporate higher cognitive processes into lessons.

Step III—Record markers and/or establish portfolios for all students to note areas of strength.

Step IV—Once areas of possible giftedness are noted, outline an instructional plan which denotes areas where curriculum should be differentiated. Depending on domain noted, use appropriate strategies.

Step V—Determine appropriate programming.

Step VI—Communicate with parents, informing them of potential gifts and enlisting their support.

Identifying and planning for the needs of a diverse population will not happen overnight but can be implemented successfully over a period of time. Once "markers" of giftedness are noted and profiles established, a differentiated curriculum can be implemented. "Markers" may indicate that students are gifted in one or more areas and that some students are capable of learning at a faster pace. Schools can arrange for programming alternatives that accommodate special needs to ensure that students are challenged and are not languishing in their classroom, being subjected to work they already know.

Planning Curricula—
Teachers as Designers of Differentiated Curricula

Teachers can be empowered to modify and design appropriate curricula for the gifted. The steps involved include:

- Designing lessons/units and/or tests to include multiple intelligences and cognitive levels and creative thinking activities (see Chapter 5).

- Noting special strengths. A matrix that can assist teachers in doing so appears in Appendix C. Suggestions that can guide in the development of portfolios appear in Chapter 5.

- Choosing appropriate strategies that will differentiate the curriculum for students based on the abilities noted. Strategies are explained in greater detail later on in this chapter.

- Assessing the availability of current human and material resources. Teachers working with administrators can begin to utilize existing resources as they build new connections. Parents and community can be included to enhance existing possibilities.

- Building on ideas, materials, and available staff. Staff can be surveyed to assess expertise that can be utilized.

- Establishing ongoing evaluation procedures using observations, portfolios, and formal tests.

- Recognizing, nurturing, and celebrating students' strengths. This includes finding appropriate audiences for students.

Designing appropriate curricula can be facilitated by teachers working together so that they can become resources for each other. As teachers work collegially and share materials, curriculum differentiation will take place more efficiently. Many of the materials in place may already "fit the bill"; others will have to be adapted or created. Units of study can be delivered in a variety of ways (i.e., tiered assignment, contracts, independent study units, computer software, etc.) as materials are developed. Children should be grouped and regrouped for instruction within the classroom, depending on level of ability, as well as across classes or grades when necessary.

The Cline Model of Curriculum for the Gifted: Defining Content, Curricular Modifications, and Programming Alternatives

Content

The content areas of the Cline Model include topics that are presently included in the common core in schools as well as those suggested by the current research on multiple intelligences. The table presented below identifies key content areas of the Cline Model.

Classroom observations of student interactions with prescribed curricula will help

---

Table 2-1. Core and Expanded Curricula

Core Subjects—Traditionally Part of the Core Curriculum	Extending the Core— The Performing Arts
Mathematics	Dance
Language Arts	Drama
Science	
Social Studies	**Leadership as a Dimension of Giftedness**
Music	
Art	Leadership—Personal Skill Development—
Physical Education	Group Dynamics
	Values

Complex Cognitive Processes/Process Modification

Process modifications include higher-level thinking and reasoning skills as well as strategies that promote creative thinking. Some students are academically precocious, but their gifts may not fall into a particular category. As process modifications become integrated into content, they can identify such students who learn rapidly and may need to have their curriculum differentiated.

Independent Study or Self-Selected Topic—Both an identifier of gifts and a curricular modification.

Interdisciplinary Study—As students are involved in interdisciplinary units, gifts may surface in specific areas.

---

to indicate who the gifted are. Once markers of potential giftedness are noted, curriculum can be differentiated and programming options explored.

Linking Multiple Intelligence Theory to Classroom Curriculum

The Cline Model uses Gardner's (1983) theory of multiple intelligences as an umbrella for identifying different types of gifts in the classroom. As students are introduced to prescribed content areas, their facility and precocity will be noted. The assessment of advanced development in each domain of intelligence is described in the chapters that follow. Gardner's theory allows teachers to view students positively in a variety of ways, an approach that Callahan (1997) found increased student self-esteem.

Language Arts—Ability in the language arts, a core subject in schools, is described by Gardner as verbal/linguistic intelligence: giftedness in the production of language as well as a facility with foreign languages. This intelligence can be seen in poets, playwrights, novelists, public speakers, storytellers, linguists, and other similar professionals.

Mathematics—Precocity in mathematics, a core subject, is described by Gardner as mathematical/logical intelligence and can emerge as students are given the opportunity to work with mathematical problems or situations using logic. This intelligence is also associated with scientific thinking and reasoning. It involves the capacity to recognize patterns, see relationships, and work with abstract symbols. It is evidenced in the work done by such professionals as scientists, computer programmers, accountants, lawyers, mathematicians, among others. This intelligence can be seen as children pursue mathematical, scientific, and historical endeavors.

Science—Science, a core subject, is not always covered in any depth on the elementary level. Scientific precocity is included in what Gardner views as mathematical/logical intelligence. Scientific giftedness can be seen in a student's ability to use higher-order cognitive processes. Opportunities for scientific inquiry allow gifted thinkers to surface.

Social Studies—Social Studies, a part of the core curriculum, requires a combination of verbal/linguistic and logical thinking skills, as for example, among historians. Interpersonal skills would also be needed in other branches of social studies having to do with community and politics. Spatial skills are involved in geography.

In most school districts, physical education, art, and music are part of the prescribed curriculum. Where this is not the case, out-of-school opportunities need to be provided.

Physical Education—Opportunities to demonstrate physical prowess are provided in schools in the form of athletics, one aspect of Gardner's definition of bodily/kinesthetic intelligence. This intelligence involves the ability to use the body to express emotion or participate in sports and is evident particularly among actors, athletes, professional dancers, and mimes, among others.

Art—Artistic ability is included in Gardner's view of visual/spatial intelligence. It plays a part in painting, drawing, architecture, and navigation and can be found, for example, in graphic artists, cartographers, painters, and sculptors. Industrial arts and the fine arts tap into this intelligence. Artistic endeavors depend on the opportunities afforded students in each school.

Music—Opportunities to demonstrate musical ability vary from school district to school district. It is one of Gardner's seven intelligences and involves the capacity to recognize and use rhythmic and tonal patterns. It can be seen in such professionals as musicians, composers, and music teachers. Music classes and/or musical activities assist this gift in surfacing.

Subjects not always considered core but which can assist in the identification of specific intelligences include dance and drama. Opportunities to exhibit these talents can be provided in a variety of ways. Classroom teachers can work with specialists on their school staff or professionals from the community. Students may be given the opportunity to present their work in artistic forms.

Dance—Dance is considered to be a part of bodily/kinesthetic intelligence as defined by Gardner, an intelligence not usually evident in the school curriculum.

Drama—Opportunities for students to perform are sometimes provided in schools and by classroom teachers. The performing arts requires a combination of intelligences: verbal/linguistic, visual/spatial, and bodily/kinesthetic intelligence.

Leadership as a Dimension of Giftedness

The following two intelligences can be observed in cooperative learning groups or in extracurricular activities. As students work together, leadership skills may evidence. Extracurricular activities are potential identifiers of gifts. Students' passions may surface as they participate in school clubs.

Interpersonal intelligence—Ability to notice and respond to contrasts in moods, temperaments, and motivations. Ability to communicate and understand verbal and non-verbal communication among individuals. Visible in counselors, politicians, religious leaders, teachers, and others.

Intrapersonal intelligence—Internal knowledge of the self includes cognitive processes and feelings. Can be seen in philosophers, psychiatrists, and spiritual counselors, among others.

In this work inter- and intrapersonal intelligences are linked. One can be used to inform the other. Self-knowledge and knowledge of others enhance one's development. These intelligences surface as children work cooperatively. As they learn about themselves, they can learn about others. These skills can evidence themselves in the classroom and in extracurricular activities. Indeed, extracurricular activities are potential identifiers of gifts in all areas of intelligence.

The curriculum must provide for the exposure to and development of leadership abilities that involve not only inter- and intrapersonal skills but also the critical areas of values and moral education (Lindsay, 1988; Hegeman, 1997). Leadership and values education have not traditionally been considered a part of the core curriculum for the gifted. The need to include leadership as a concept in the gifted education has been stressed by Gallagher et al. (1982). They define leadership as "the exercise of power or influence in social collectivities, such as groups, organizations, communities or nations, to meet the needs of the group" (p. 8). Leadership skills, personal skill development, and values education are closely intertwined. "Effective leadership in today's world includes the characteristics of self-understanding, self-expression, and openness to personal growth" (Sisk & Shallcross, 1986, p. 16).

Gardner and others have highlighted the importance of personal skill development. Sternberg (1988a, 1988b) has acknowledged the importance of different kinds of "smarts." In their book, *When Smart People Fail*, Hyatt and Gottlieb (1987) have attributed the failure of some smart individuals to their lack of social skills. In his book, *Money*, Andrew Hacker (1995) analyzes income levels in America and concludes that what individuals formally learn in institutions of higher education is not as important in determining success as is the modelling they are exposed to in universities on how to interact with others and appear successful. The issue of the personal intelligences has attracted great interest with the appearance of Daniel Goleman's (1995) book, *Emotional Intelligence*. It is covered in detail in Chapter 3.

Personal knowledge is intertwined with one's ethics and morals (Phenix, 1964). An individual is what he does. One knows himself by his decisions. According to Lindsay (1988), it is imperative that we begin to recognize the need to put moral education at the core of the curriculum, especially for those children who are gifted in leadership:

> If we are to regain our national conscience, our sense of propriety, our hunger for excellence in every endeavor, we must begin with the design of a curriculum in moral education that will provide our future leaders with the appropriate models and methodologies for reestablishing these values at the center of our consciousness. (p. 9)

Lindsay warns us not to confuse moral education with indoctrination. Krathwohl, Bloom, and Masia (1956) outline a classification taxonomy for the affective domain. Their scheme describes the steps involved in establishing a value system. Raths, Harmin, and Simon (1966), Simon, Howe, and Kirschenbaum (1972), and Gailbraith and Jones (1976) suggest that this be accomplished by including value clarification exercises in the classroom curriculum. The suggested approach is not intended to instill any particular set of values. Rather, it is meant to help students examine their own belief systems. According to Raths, Harmin, and Simon (1966, p. 30) "we see values as based on three processes: choosing, prizing and acting."

Choosing:	(1) freely
	(2) from alternatives
	(3) after thoughtful consideration of the consequences of each alternative
Prizing:	(4) cherishing, being happy with the choice
	(5) willing to affirm the choice publicly
Acting:	(6) doing something with the choice
	(7) repeatedly, in some pattern of life

When value clarification exercises are incorporated into classroom activities, activities stress thoughtful examination of decisions that affect others. Is this a decision you are proud of and would stand up for? Would you tell others? How do you let others know how you feel? Students can discuss current events in light of their value system or write down their own moral dilemmas and open them up for discussion. Is it ever right to steal? Are there times when one's actions might appear to betray a friendship? What if you were the mayor of a town and had to decide whether to allow a company to begin operations that would pollute your waters even as it would provide unemployed members of your community with jobs? Values and moral education involves teaching students how to think about their decisions rather than what to think.

Complex Cognitive Processes. Complex cognitive processes include critical and creative thinking skills that are essential to the development and identification of giftedness and should be introduced to all students. Gifted students may possess a higher level of understanding in particular domains at the outset; their "zone of proximal development" (Vygotsky, 1978) can be more advanced with appropriate mediation. Vygotsky recommends that a mediator (teacher, mentor, parent or tutor) help students stretch beyond their comfort level. The mediator provides the "scaffolding" or support necessary in the form of feedback, assistance, and monitoring as needed. Feuerstein (1980) provides evidence that mediated learning can improve intelligence. Developing thinking skills and strategies that enhance metacognition is critical to providing the appropriate environment, especially for gifted students who come from culturally deprived environments.

Self-Selected Topic or Independent Study. These activities allow students to demonstrate task orientation and help identify precocity in its early stages. They are a viable curricular option for students who work quickly and need additional challenges rather than additional workbook pages. Independent study can be an earlier indicator of specific intelligences.

Interdisciplinary Study. This provides teachers with opportunities to view students working in a variety of domains, observe gifted behaviors, and note specific strengths.

Curricular Modifications or Differentiation

Content, Process, Product

In their research with 871 academically gifted students, Gallagher, Herradine, and Coleman (1997) report the need for greater differentiation in schools.

The students generally agreed that special Academically Gifted and Mathematics classes challenged them, but only about half of the students reported a similar satisfaction with their Science, Language Arts, and Social Studies classes. Consistent themes stated by the students about the curriculum's lack of challenge included a slow pace, too much repetition of already mastered information, inability to move on after mastering the regular curriculum, few opportunities to study topics of personal interest, and an emphasis on the mastery of facts rather than the use of thinking skills. (p. 132)

Students learn at different speeds and differ widely in their ability to think abstractly or understand complex ideas. A variety of strategies can be used to differentiate the curriculum for students in the regular classroom. A plan for differentiation should be based on the areas of ability that have been identified. Each content area can be matched to appropriate curricular strategies. There is an optimal match when content meets the level of instruction that provides a level of challenge. In a mixed ability classroom, it is important to provide a variety of alternatives that allow students to move to appropriate levels, to be grouped according to need at a particular time, or to launch ahead on their own. A differentiated assignment requires including activities that involve higher-order thinking skills rather than more of the same. Curricular differentiation needs to be viewed in terms of content, process, and product.

Defining Content. Content refers to the body of knowledge to be learned. Chall and Conrad (1991) stress the importance of the match between a learner's abilities and the difficulty of the instructional task. In the optimal match the task difficulty should be slightly above the learner's understanding of the content. When necessary, it should be extended so that a level of challenge and complexity is sustained. The nature of a discipline, as well as the scope and sequence involved, often dictates the nature of the differentiation that should take place. For example, acceleration is appropriate for mathematics (Stanley, 1977); enrichment or relating material to broad-based themes, problems, or concepts is appropriate for social studies (VanTassel-Baska, 1988); and the methodology of the professional is appropriate for science, history, or writing (Tannenbaum, 1983).

Defining Process. Process involves how students make sense of information and ideas. Processes that involve higher-level, complex thought processes are also important in curriculum differentiation and identification. Gifted students should be involved in investigations that include higher-level thinking skills, skills of inquiry, higher levels of cognitive operations, creative thinking, and problem solving. They should be encouraged to be independent so that their problem finding and problem solving evolve as a result of their own research.

Defining Product. Students demonstrate their learning through their products. Levels of abstraction and complexity of thought will be evidenced. Products can also demonstrate the student's ability to define and solve problems. Students can be exposed to problem-solving strategies that assist them in addressing the issues involved. When students are given choices, they can present their work in whatever forms they deem appropriate, such as projects, papers, presentations, or audio-visual programs, allowing a variety of talents and abilities to surface. When allowed to choose the way they express themselves, a spatially-gifted student might present an artistic work, a verbal/linguistic child might present a play, a logical/mathematical student might choose flow charts or graphs.

Students should be provided with guidelines for evaluating their work. An example of how students might evaluate an independent study project is provided in Appendix B.

Elements of Curricular Modifications and Differentiation

Curricular modifications refer to ways in which the content needs to be differentiated once areas of ability are noted. The domain noted dictates the strategy that is most appropriate. Curricular modifications or differentiation can take place in one or more domains, depending on the areas of ability noted in the classroom. The key elements of curricular modifications are presented in Table 2-2.

Table 2-2. Key Elements of Curricular Modifications and Differentiation.

Depth

Breadth

Tempo

Expansion of Basic Skills and Comprehension

Complex Cognitive Processes

Independent Study or Self-Selected Content

Telescoping or Compacting

Adding on

Depth. Depth refers to researching a topic to allow for greater detail and understanding. A student involved in learning about a subject may wish to select one aspect for in-depth investigation; for example, a student learning about the Civil War became interested in learning more about the causes of the war.

Breadth. When students are introduced to a topic that stimulates their interest, extending the topic and covering it with greater breadth might be appropriate. One student who was reading about a Native American child wanted to find out about Native American children today. The child was connected via the Internet to a tribe and began doing research.

Tempo. Gifted students have often been observed to learn at a faster rate and should be allowed to proceed at their own pace. Teachers can accommodate these students by compacting the curriculum and/or providing them with self-pacing materials in the form of contracts, independent study, or computer-assisted instruction. (A detailed description of compacting is covered later in this chapter.) One fifth-grade student who had a particular affinity for mathematics was permitted to proceed through the curriculum on his own for the year. Work was monitored by the teacher and arrangements were made for him to work with a middle school teacher to continue with a more advanced mathematics curriculum.

Expansion of Basic Skills and Comprehension. If students are to be prepared to become producers of information in our society (Tannenbaum, 1983), when areas of precocity are noted, they need to be introduced to the ways in which professionals work in a particular domain. A budding writer needs to be introduced to professional writers and learn about the writing process. A scientist should learn how scientists hypothesize and experiment. A student interested in history should learn early on about primary, secondary, and tertiary resources. Mentors and professionals can assist teachers as they introduce students to the life and work of the professional.

Complex Cognitive Processes. One of the common identifiers of giftedness is the child's ability to reason well and use complex thought processes. Process modifications include critical and creative thinking skills; they are both content and strategy. They are key in identifying gifted children by their ability to use higher-level thought processes and in nurturing giftedness in children. They affect the curriculum in each of the domains. Some gifted students become bored when not presented with challenges. One young man started becoming an observer in school rather than a participant. He found school to be boring and irrelevant and had considered dropping out of high school. When he attended Columbia University and was introduced to the Socratic method of teaching, he did a complete "about face" and became an interested, and interesting, student. Incorporation of process modifications, such as Bloom's Taxonomy, Taba's Thinking Strategies, and/or other inquiry models into classroom practice, is explained in greater detail in Chapter 3.

Independent Study or Self-Selected Content. Independent study has been included both in content and in curricular strategies. As content, it allows students to select topics that might be indicators of domains of giftedness. One young woman chose creative writing as a topic of study in fifth grade. She had a very high IQ and to her parents a high IQ signified a bright medical career. She enrolled as a pre-med student at university. However, after two years she announced to her parents that she was not going to live their dream, but she was going to follow her own. She is now pursuing a doctorate in journalism. As a curricular strategy, it is important to allow students who are rapid learners to master a topic independently. This can also be an option for students who exhibit precocity or have developed a passion in a domain and who wish to explore a topic in greater depth and wish to pursue it independently. A description of how to implement independent study as a strategy is covered later on in this section.

Telescoping or Compacting. This strategy recognizes that some students have a large reservoir of knowledge, and, for them, it eliminates boredom and unnecessary drill. It involves pretesting to determine how much students know before a curriculum is presented. For students who have been assessed as already having mastered what is to be covered, decisions need to be made as to how they will be allowed to spend the time that is freed up. Options can include advancement in the content area in which the student excels, allowing the student to accelerate in that domain, or providing the student with the opportunity to select a topic not currently covered. Reis, Burns, and Renzulli (1992, p. 8) describe curriculum compacting as an eight-part process in which the teacher can do the following:

1. Identify the relevant learning objectives in a subject area or grade level.
2. Find or develop a means of pretesting students on one or more of these objectives prior to instruction.
3. Identify students who may benefit from curriculum compacting and should be pretested.
4. Pretest students to determine mastery levels of the chosen objectives.
5. Eliminate practice, drill, or instructional time for students who demonstrate prior mastery of these objectives.
6. Streamline instruction of those objectives students have not yet mastered but are capable of mastering more quickly than their classmates.
7. Offer enrichment or acceleration options for students whose curriculum has been compacted.
8. Keep records of this process and the instructional options available to "compacted" students.

Adding on. This is a curricular option for students who can "test out" of parts of or the entire curriculum or who move quickly. Teacher and student can add topics not covered, allow in-depth research in areas of interest, or allow a study of subjects not covered elsewhere. One very bright fourth grade student was tutored in French by a community resident.

Programming Alternatives

Programming alternatives refers to ways in which school districts may begin to program for the gifted. Some programs may already be in place; others may become possible in time. Administrators and teachers, working together, can remove barriers posed by classroom walls by accessing opportunities in the school and the community. Gifted students need to have the opportunity to interact with students of like ability for at least part of the time. The classroom walls often serve as boundaries to differentiated instruction. Current technology allows the use of on-line resources so that the world can be an encyclopedia for the gifted child.

The programming options suggested in this section are intended to "trigger" possibilities. (See Table 2-3.) As teachers assess their present settings, they can mix and match and creatively design new ways to meet the needs of their gifted students. These suggestions can be viewed in terms of "How Might I Utilize _____?"

Table 2-3. Programming Alternatives.

In Class	Resource Room	Provisional Augmentation
• Tiered Assignments	Revolving Door	Community Resident
• Ability Grouping Flexible Clusters Cooperative	Acceleration	Special School
• Learning Centers	Honors Class	Credit by Examination (Testing Out)
• Interest Centers	Advanced Placement	Grade Skipping
• Contracts	Mentor	Combined Classes
• Intellectual Peer Teaching	Other Class	Correspondence Courses
• High School Students	Internship	Pull-Out Program
• Computers, Technology, and Telecommunications	After School/ Extracurricular	
• Self-paced Instruction		
• Independent Study		

In Class

The classroom teacher is key in determining who the gifted are and in designing curricula for them. The classroom becomes the place for demonstrating potential gifts. Opportunities to do so can vary depending on available resources. Classroom management, which includes providing instruction in a variety of ways, takes time and effort. As gifts are noted, teachers can establish individual student profiles and provide differentiated instruction in the classroom. If this cannot be accomplished in the regular classroom, they can enlist the support of additional personnel in and out of the school. Once a differentiated curriculum has been designed, it can be used through the years. Teachers can share curricula with one another. The following strategies can be implemented in the classroom to help identify the gifted child and to provide opportunities that challenge and prevent boredom.

Tiered Assignments. Assignments should allow students to explore new knowledge, tap into prior knowledge, and allow for continued growth. Incorporating activities that allow students to demonstrate the ability to respond to complexity and higher-level thought processes will allow gifts to surface. Students can choose work that is challenging but not anxiety producing.

When creating tiered assignments, teachers need to:

- Focus the task on a key concept or generalization
- Provide a variety of resource materials at differing levels of complexity

- Include tasks that require the use of advanced materials and complex thought processes
- Pose questions that include problem solving
- Encourage students to broaden their reading and extend the assignment if they wish to do so
- Not specify who should take on the more complex aspects of the assignment. Students may surprise teachers and measure up to challenges if allowed to do so on their own initiative
- Create assignments so that they are open-ended
- Allow for creativity
- Establish rubrics so that students can clearly be informed of the criteria used in judging for quality and success

Ability Grouping. Ability grouping can take a variety of forms. Keeping in mind Vygotsky's (1978) zone of proximal development (level of understanding that goes beyond what has been mastered), students should be grouped together so that they have the opportunity to learn new material and to work with students of like ability. The material to be learned can be mediated by the teacher or by other students.

Groups can be established in all of the content areas:

- Allowing students to move quickly through basic skills
- Ensuring that students who have mastered skills can move on
- Providing for the development of advanced skills

There are three basic types of ability groupings: flexible, cluster, and cooperative grouping:

Flexible grouping allows students to move in and out of the group, working with a group or individually, as needed. Groups should be created to match student need and/or interest and can be formed as students are pretested. Assumptions should not be made as to a student's ability or length of time needed for mastery. It is important that observations and testing remain current so that groups are constantly changing. Groups formed around the skills that need to be taught can be disbanded when complete. Once students have achieved 85 percent mastery of a skill, they should be permitted to move on. Flexible grouping can allow students to accelerate in one or more content areas. Teachers need to make sure that when indicated, gifted students are developing skills beyond the basics and that they are acquiring advanced knowledge in their areas of talent.

Cluster grouping brings students together to meet specific needs. According to Hoover, Sayler, and Feldhusen (1993), gifted students benefit from cluster grouping. Cluster grouping can be facilitated by administrators so that all of the identified gifted children in a grade are assigned to one classroom, rather than being dispersed among two or more classes. Clusters of students can also be formed within the class for short- or long-term instruction. Clusters may be based on interest or need. Forming clusters provides for flexible teaching. They can be formed or disbanded as teachers assess needs.

Cooperative grouping can facilitate classroom management in a variety of ways. They can be formed with children of similar ability who may work together and provide stimulation and challenges for one another. A word of caution: gifted students can become easily bored when grouped with students of mixed ability.

Cooperative groups may provide teachers with the opportunity to observe students for qualities other than academics. Leadership abilities may become apparent and social sensitivities may surface. Such grouping can be especially helpful for the gifted child with a disability. It is critical that these students be placed in intellectually stimulating settings. Ascertaining that there are other students in the group who can take on the roles in which the disabled child may have a deficit is essential to the group's success. A child with a learning disability that inhibited writing ability could be placed in a group in which another student would take on that task. Cooperative groups can assist in assessing the development of interpersonal relationships. Teachers can observe and note students who are successful at:

- Analyzing situations
- Participating as a member of a team
- Being helpful to others
- Communicating thoughts, feelings, and ideas to justify a position
- Encouraging, persuading, or convincing others
- Motivating group members
- Negotiating and working toward consensus

Learning Centers. Learning centers can house a collection of materials related to the units of instruction. When children have completed their regular assignments, learning centers are places they can go to extend their learning, especially if they are allowed to move quickly through the materials and skills to be mastered. For the gifted, learning centers can include suggestions for exploring topics in greater depth or breath. Advanced reading material should be provided. Questions that identify real problems should be included.

Whenever possible, a learning center should include:

- Materials necessary for learning the topic on a level that allows students to gain in-depth knowledge
- Written and audiovisual materials on the topic so that students can select those that accommodate their individual learning style preferences.
- CD-ROMs for computers
- Puzzles and games to assess which learning strategies appeal to students

Learning centers can also contain packets that provide opportunities to stimulate different intelligences (e.g., questions that address mathematical/logical inquiry, and opportunities for gifted writers or artists to evidence special capabilities). When they have completed these packets, students should have options for presenting what they have learned in various forms—in a logically written form (for the logical/mathematically gifted child), as a creative piece (for the verbal/linguistically gifted child), in diagrams (for the visual/spatially gifted child), or as plays that might include music or bodily/kinesthetic performances.

For example, a science learning center should include:

- Rules and supervision, when necessary, if safety is an issue, e.g., chemistry experiments.
- All of the background information for a unit
- Materials that can be used for experimentation
- Guidelines for students to write up their experiences in scientific laboratory reports

A teacher covering a unit on Native Americans might include materials on how to access information on Native Americans today. Personal interviews might be arranged with local tribes or can be conducted over the Internet. Questions might include:

- What are some of the difficulties and challenges they face?
- Are all tribes faced with the same dilemmas?
- How might some of these challenges be addressed?

Interest Centers. Interest centers differ from learning centers. Learning centers address core curriculum, whereas interest centers expose students to areas not covered in the curriculum and are places that children can go to when other work is complete. As such, they can serve as valuable tools. Commercial or teacher-made interest centers can be used if they:

- Provide opportunities for students to explore new areas of interest
- Enrich students who demonstrate mastery of required work
- Incorporate opportunities to become involved at all levels of thinking
- Allow for in-depth study

An interest center, also known as an Interest Development Center (Burns, 1985), should include newspapers, magazines, books, videos, CD-ROMs, Internet addresses, manipulatives if needed, names and addresses of resources, etc. A center might be constructed around a famous person (for example, John F. Kennedy or Mother Teresa) or around an extracurricular topic, such as lasers.

Questions investigating the life of a famous person might include analyzing the aspects of a person's life and determining what it was that made them "famous." Was the fame deserved? What constitutes fame?

A center for lasers might include investigations of current uses of lasers. What possible ways might they be used in the future? Visit or interview a physician who uses lasers in his or her practice. How has the laser changed our world? Are changes always positive?

Both learning and interest centers can be of an interdisciplinary nature and allow for student choices. They provide excellent opportunities to express varied areas of intelligence. As students become involved, observations of their performance can provide additional markers of giftedness.

Once learning and interest centers are designed, they can be shared by teachers. They can be designed by individual teachers or teachers may work collaboratively.

Contracts. Contracts provide the opportunity for students to work at their own pace, completing assigned work according to certain specifications. Students who like to work independently will thrive on learning contracts. They allow the student to make decisions, encouraging and recognizing the ability to work independently. Students establish the appropriate pace at which to work. Contracts can blend skills and content. They can encourage extended learning and include questions that foster research and critical thinking. They can provide opportunities for creativity to surface. With some students involved in independent contract work, time is freed up for the teacher to work with other individuals or small groups. Guidelines for success need to be provided.

According to Winebrenner (1992), a learning contract should include:

- Clear instructions outlining the material to be covered
- Suggested resources
- Opportunities to go beyond the content required by the prescribed curriculum
- Material that focuses on concepts, themes, and problems

Assignments to be covered should have a master contract and provide check-off points as concepts are covered. Enrichment and/or alternative activities should be provided as students work through the materials. Each section should include a pre- and post-test and assess an 80 to 85 percent level of mastery. Students should be shown how to keep track of their work, and teachers should periodically provide time to discuss material covered. Work should be evaluated by students and teachers jointly.

Winebrenner (1992, p. 22) suggests that contracts should specify working conditions, such as:

1. No talking to the teacher while he or she is teaching.
2. When you need help and the teacher is busy, ask someone else.
3. If no one can help you right way, keep trying or go on to something else.
4. If you must go in and out of the room, do it quietly.
5. Don't bother anyone else.
6. Don't call attention to yourself.

Students who work quickly can cover required material easily, making room for in-depth research or independent study.

Intellectual Peer Teaching. Teachers may allow peers who are at the same intellectual or academic level to work together on new learnings, accelerated learnings, or reviewing learnings. They may be at the same grade level or well above.

High School Students. High school students can be enlisted to work with younger students as mentors, tutors, or mini-course teachers in any of the domains. High school staff can provide information as to which students can serve. For example, when classroom teachers deem acceleration to be appropriate in areas where they do not have the expertise, such as higher mathematics, high school mentors can be very effective. High school mentors can also be used to teach "mini-courses" to groups of students in which they are exposed to topics such as biology or chemistry. Mentors can:

- Work with students on topics related to student interest
- Introduce students to the mentor's area of expertise
- Work with a small group of students teaching a mini-course

Computers, Technology, and Telecommunications. Computers have opened up a whole world of instruction for students. As new software becomes available, these programs can give students a great deal of independence in rate and quantity of instruction, allowing them to move through content at a rapid rate. Telecommunications can make instruction available in any of the content areas for advanced students. Often, school districts discontinue or do not offer courses which are unusual or at advanced levels because there is not enough participation to support paying a teacher. Telecommunications makes it possible for a teacher at one location to teach students at any other location. Current technology allows students with special needs, for example, the visually or hearing impaired, to participate with intellectual peers when they are provided with the appropriate devices, such as opticons or auditrons.

Computers allow classrooms and students to connect to the Internet. Instruction can be provided by accessing different Web sites. Students and teachers can use directories and search engines to access information. WWW search engines and directories include:

- AltaVista—http://www.altavista.digital.com
- Dogpile—http://www.dogpile.com
- Excite—http://www.excite.com
- Lycos—http://www.lycos.com
- Webcrawler—http://www.WebCrawler.com
- Yahoo!—a searchable directory—http://www.yahoo.com
- Magellan—http://www.mckinley.com
- Snap Online—http://home.snap.com

A variety of others can be seen at: http://cuiwww.unige.ch/meta-index.html or http://infopeople.berkeley.edu:8000/src/srctools.html

Surfing the net is a skill that requires students to select and weed out irrelevant information. It can be very time consuming. Teachers can provide parents with a list of Web sites that can be explored at home, in local libraries, or other places that provide access to the Internet. Learning to surf and distinguish relevant from irrelevant information is an important skill in the new information age.

A valuable publication that can assist teachers and students as they make their way through cyberspace is Classroom Connect (Address: 1866 Colonial Village Lane, PO Box 10488, Lancaster, Pennsylvania 17605-9981. Telephone: 888-252-7776). Issues provide information on how to connect to other classrooms, about educational sites, how to teach with the Net, etc.

Students and teachers can access sites that are domain specific. For example, Reis and Gavin (1997) have recommended several on-line resources for promising mathematics students:

- Don Cohen "The MathMan"— http://www.shoutnet-mathman
- ERIC—http://ericir.syr.edu or askeric@ericir.syr.edu
- MathMagic Project—Project ahodson@tenet.edu
- National Council of Teachers of Mathematics—http://www.nctm.org
- National Science Teachers Association—http://www.nsta.org
- National Science Foundation Mathematics Forum— http://forum.swarthmore.edu

Self-paced Instruction. Computers are not the only way of providing students with self-paced instruction. Contracts, commercial kits, or other teacher-designed materials can move students along as required. Teachers can begin by asking themselves the following questions: Are materials available that can be used for self-paced instruction? Are parts of the curriculum organized so that students may move through quickly with appropriate check points?

Independent Study or Self/Selected Topic. Independent study can take a variety of forms, within and beyond the classroom walls. According to Renzulli and Gable (1979), independent study is a preferred learning strategy for the gifted. It can be used if content in other domains is compacted. Independent study is a strategy that demonstrates task orientation and can be used to accommodate learners who have completed other tasks. It is also useful when teachers observe that certain parts of the curriculum that "turned a student on"; that topic can then be explored in greater depth or breadth. It is a viable option for students who are rapid learners and can cover specified curriculum independently or can explore topics of interest that are not a part of the school curriculum. It can also identify potential areas of giftedness. For the classroom teacher, Cline (1986, pp. 10–11) recommends the following steps:

1. Student selects the topic to be studied.
2. Teacher guides the student as the student designs the study and formulates key questions.
3. Student learns the appropriate research skills and/or basic skills and expanded basic skills relevant to the topic.
4. Teacher reviews the student's basic outline for the study and makes

suggestions so that educational ideas that differentiate the curriculum are included.

5. Student and teacher locate appropriate resources for the study.

6. Student conducts necessary research.

7. Student is responsible for broadening or narrowing topic. Teacher assists when necessary.

8. Student is allowed as much time as is deemed necessary to conduct the research.

9. If the student becomes aware of problems associated with the study, problem-solving strategies are taught which assist in seeking solutions.

10. Student is responsible for designing how to communicate what has been learned. Various kinds of media are used. The student chooses the way in which material will be presented (e.g., writes a book, produces a slide-sound program or video show, makes a film strip, presents a chalk talk, etc.)

11. Student evaluates what has been accomplished in terms of individual capabilities and assesses independent study as an appropriate learning strategy, helping students to become educational connoisseurs.

12. Teacher assists in seeking appropriate audiences for completed projects (e.g., classmates, peers, parents, professional publications, contests, etc.).

Resource Room. Depending on the school, the term "resource room" may have a variety of connotations. It can be a place where children who require remediation are provided with additional instruction or where gifted students work with a teacher in small groups or individually. If a resource room exists, does it presently accommodate gifted learners? If not, how can it be changed to do so? Are personnel acquainted with the nature and needs of the gifted? If not, is someone available to guide them? Are the necessary materials available? Teachers and administrators can work together in its development.

Revolving Door. In some school districts, students who are identified as gifted in the regular classroom, "revolve" or spend time in a gifted program when they have topics they wish to pursue (see Renzulli & Smith, 1978). In some districts, a specially-trained individual may be assigned the task of assisting gifted students in designing appropriate curricula when they revolve in the program. For instance, a librarian in a school may be assigned the task.

Acceleration. Acceleration refers to the speed at which a student may cover curriculum. It can take place within or outside of the classroom. Some school districts have classes in specific subjects that move through the curriculum more rapidly and may cover two years' work in one year. In some schools, acceleration might involve "skipping" a year of content, moving to the next grade. For highly-gifted children, this might be a viable option. Domains of giftedness and level of ability should be the determining factors. Social and emotional issues come into play. Parents, the child, and counselors need to evaluate each individual situation. Acceleration should not be limited to one year or to one subject. Acceleration in one domain can make room for other classes or additional advanced course work. When acceleration takes place in the classroom, teachers have the responsibility of making sure that when students move into the next grade, they will not have to repeat material already covered.

Honors Class. Some school districts group students homogeneously when they reach middle or high school. Honors classes offer students of like ability in particular domains the opportunity to learn an enriched curriculum together. The curriculum covers what has been prescribed for the "regular" class, but teachers have the opportunity to accelerate, enrich, and incorporate materials from other disciplines. Honors classes are sometimes precursors to AP or Advanced Placement classes.

Advanced Placement. Some school districts provide opportunities for students to take advanced placement courses. When students demonstrate the ability to move quickly and with great understanding, these classes allow students to take college-level courses while still in high school. Not only does it allow students to maintain a level of challenge, but when college credit is given, it can save time and money later on.

Mentor. A mentor is a special person who has expertise in a particular area and works with a student within or outside of the classroom. A mentor may meet with a student on a regular basis or may meet on an "as needed" basis. This process allows learning to be extended beyond the classroom, making learning a partnership. Mentors allow teachers to provide for student need, interest, and strength. Mentorships can focus on the design and execution of advanced projects or exploration of particular work settings. Mentorships are one of the most effective ways of influencing gifted students (Zorman, 1993). Mentors can be parents, other faculty from either within the school or the district, college/university faculty, or members of the community at large.

Goals of the mentorship need to be clearly stated for mentor, student, and teacher. Teachers should provide information about the student to the mentor and monitor progress from the point of view of the mentor and the student.

Other Class. When special abilities are noted, it behooves the classroom teacher to provide opportunities for students to continue to work at a level of challenge. Groups may be formed with students across the same grade, with like ability with one teacher in the grade, or among different grades. Students can be moved up in any of the domains. A student who is mathematically precocious may move to a higher grade for mathematics. Groups of students who are reading above grade level can be taken from a number of classrooms to form a cluster.

Internship. The community should be viewed as a resource and companies canvassed to ascertain if internships are available. Internships might provide opportunities for gifted children to "shadow" or accompany professionals as they work.

After School/Extracurricular. If students take it upon themselves to study topics that are not a part of the curriculum (e.g., language or culture), or to cover required content through courses at other institutions after school, or in the summer, credit should be given.

Provisional Augmentation. Provisional augmentation (Tannenbaum, 1983) refers to the opportunities that a particular teacher is already providing or might provide that are not presently a part of the school curriculum. Provisional augmentation can spark students' interest or provide for additional instruction in areas of interest. It can also include topics that can be integrated into the existing curriculum (e.g., values or leadership education lend themselves well to provisional augmentation). Or, for example, a teacher might expose students to a unit that involves hatching chicks in the classroom.

Community Resident. Community residents can come to schools to speak on a variety of careers that can spark interest in students or serve as mentors for students on a one-time or regular basis. They might offer to teach a mini-course to students. Certain professions, often those in the medical field, have a day during the week when they might wish to volunteer their services. They may be senior citizens or individuals of any age who have expertise in particular topics. They can work with a student on a one-on-one basis or work with a group of students. It might be a topic they have expertise in, or they might work with students to free up the teacher so that individual attention can be paid to one child.

Special School. Special schools might meet the needs of some gifted students. Special schools can include schools that specialize in particular domains, such as math, science, music, or art. This option depends on the community, available resources, and financial constraints.

Credit by Examination—Testing Out. If students wish to cover curriculum areas on their own and pass the required tests, they should be permitted to do so. Some states, such as West Virginia, have developed formal policies for the procedure (see AEGIS, 1998). Their Policy 2510 Testing Out for Credit provides students with the opportunity to earn credit for a course by demonstrating mastery of the content. It provides that the test be developed at the school or district level by the teacher(s) credentialed and assigned to teach the course. The test is comprehensive and provides students with an opportunity to demonstrate mastery of the entire course. Standards used to evaluate student performance would be the same as for those following the traditional course of study. Students may elect to test out of a course only once per semester.

Grade Skipping. Grade skipping is a form of acceleration. A child actually "skips" a year rather than moving through content at a faster pace. In some cases, grade skipping may be a viable option. Depending on the district, the child, and the family, grade skipping can be considered. Issues that should be considered are: the student's level of maturity, physical and emotional factors, how advanced the individual is, and other options that could be made available.

Combined Classes. Are there opportunities for teachers to work together and form groups so that each teacher can work with students in areas where gifts have surfaced and teachers are inclined to provide guidance?

Correspondence Courses. When courses are available and students succeed in meeting prescribed requirements, they should be given credit for such courses.

Examples include:

- High school and university math programs available on CD and by mail from Stanford University. Contact Ted Alper, Mathematics Instruction Coordinator, EPGY, Ventura Hall, Stanford, California 94305-4115—e-mail: alper@epgy.stanford.edu
- High level high school mathematics correspondence course—I. M. Gelfand, Rutgers University. Contact Harriet Schweitzer, Assoc. Dir., Rutgers University Center for Math, Science and Computer Education, SERC Building, Room 239 Busch Campus, Piscataway, New Jersey 08855-1179—e-mail: harriets@gandalf.rutgers.edu

Pull-out Program. In some schools, students who have been identified as gifted are taken out of the classroom to work with a teacher. The amount of time varies from a few hours per week, to a whole day, or cycles, where students will be placed in a program for a few weeks or months.

Combining Opportunities. One currently available program that combines opportunities is the mathematics program developed at Stanford University and available through Johns Hopkins. The EPGY program allows students to receive math instruction at home using CD-ROMs that track student progress. Students are provided with challenging material as they achieve mastery of content. A tutor is assigned to the student and can communicate with the student through the Internet and by telephone. How might teachers combine opportunities for students that might include books, computers, and/or mentors?

Teachers can develop a data base for the class, or a schoolwide data base can be developed to allow easy access to programming resources. The questionnaire in Appendix A has been designed to assist teachers and schools in this task. When gifts are noted in areas not specifically provided for in the curriculum, such as art, drama, or dance, specialists should be called and parents notified. If the school does not have a way of cultivating a particular talent, parents might wish to go outside of the school or seek special schools.

Finding Appropriate Audiences. Teachers can also seek appropriate audiences for students' work so that students are recognized and applauded for their efforts. Some forums for doing so are presented below:

Writing contests—Some examples include:

- Publish a Book Contest for grades 2–3 and 4–5, sponsored by the Raintree/Steck-Vaughn Publishing Company, P.O. Box 26015, Austin, Texas 78755
- Written and Illustrated By, sponsored by Landmark Editions, Inc., P. O. Box 4469, Kansas City, Missouri 64127
- *Merlyn's Pen*—A magazine that publishes student writing in an attempt to broaden and reward young authors' interest in writing

and strengthen self-confidence of beginning writers. *Merlyn's Pen*, P. O. Box 1058, East Greenwich, Rhode Island 02818

- *Young Author's Guide to Publishers* introduces students to the writing and publishing process and lists possible sources for publication. Distributed by Rasberry Publications, Inc., P. O. Box 925, Westerville, Ohio 43086-6925. See also *Market Guide for Young Writers: Where and How to Sell What You Write* by K. Henderson (1993), Cincinnati, Ohio: Writer's Digest Books.
- Math fairs
- Science competitions. For example, Westinghouse Awards are presented to students in both mathematical and science categories. Students enter the competition in high school and winners receive monetary awards.
- Art exhibits
- Musical, dance, or dramatic performances
- Local schools and communities often sponsor such events.

If our children are to achieve in the particular domains in which they are gifted, they have to be introduced to those domains, learn the basic skills involved, be exposed to advanced basic skills, be introduced to professionals in those fields, and learn about their world of work. In this way, the gifted can be provided with an education that allows them to become producers of information in our society (Tannenbaum, 1983).

Summary

As teachers work with students in classrooms, it will become apparent that student profiles vary greatly. Some students will require minor modifications to the curriculum that can be accommodated in the classroom. For others, meeting their needs might present greater challenges and might not be accomplished all at once. Exceptionally gifted students should surface as challenging materials are presented. Individual intelligence tests may provide clues about such children. Accommodations need to be made in and out of the classroom and may require more than one option or more than one opportunity for acceleration.

If we are to help the gifted reach their potential, we need to weave appropriate curricula for the gifted into the fabric of the school. To do so, we have to develop a variety of services that provide able students with challenging educational opportunities in all content areas. This task cannot be accomplished without including the classroom teacher in the process of identifying problems and finding solutions. Furthermore, research indicates that many veteran teachers lack the skill and/or the will to design educational settings that can accommodate gifted learners (Archambault,

Westberg, Brown, Hallmark, Zhang, & Emmons, 1993; Tomlinson, 1995; Westberg, Archambault, Dobyns, & Slavin, 1993). All teachers—veterans, newcomers, and those studying to enter the profession—need to be introduced to the many faces of giftedness, to learn how to identify the gifted, plan for them, and provide optimal matches between students and curriculum. Research supports the effectiveness of trained teachers in gifted education (Karnes & Whorton, 1996). Teachers cannot meet the needs of all of the children in the classroom—unless they are provided with the appropriate educational background and administrative support!

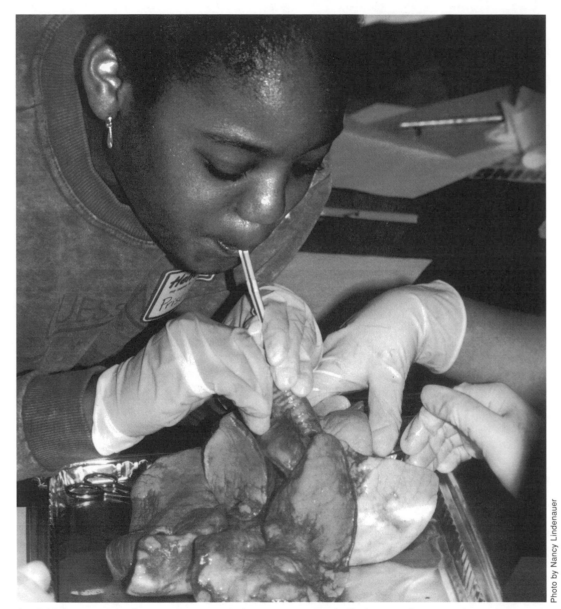

As children are exposed to content in curriculum areas, potential giftedness surfaces.

Photo by Nancy Lindenauer

Chapter 3
Multiple Intelligences

Typical questions a classroom teacher might ask:

- What are multiple intelligences?
- How might I provide activities to identify each of the intelligences?
- How might I identify gifts in each of the domains?
- How do I assess giftedness in each domain?

To address these questions, this chapter includes:

- An expanded view of multiple intelligences, and related attributes based on Gardner's (1983) work.
- Using the curriculum to identify gifts, thus replacing the IQ test which has posed "gates" or barriers.
- Strategies that differentiate the curriculum when gifts have been identified.
- Activities that can introduce students to each domain.
- Developmental levels related to giftedness.
- A system for recording "markers" of giftedness.

The Multiple Intelligence Inventory

The author designed this inventory so that teachers might become aware of their own strengths and weaknesses. Individual profiles vary. One might have skills that predominate in one area or more. As we gain insight into our own areas of dominance, we can reflect on how we would respond to tasks that required use of the domain that is least dominant. We then need to look at our students in terms of what "they can do" and provide opportunities for them to perform in ways in which they are most comfortable.

During a workshop that included interpretive dance, one of the participants looked at me and informed me that she "could not do that" nor could she be made to do it. Then she was asked to think about the students in her room. When was she demanding something of them that they "could not" or "would not" do?

The inventory is not a "test" but an instrument to pinpoint possible patterns of strength or weakness.

Draw a grid with eight columns and eight rows as shown in Figure 3-1. As you answer each of the following questions rate yourself on a scale of 1 to 5, with 5 being the highest. Begin in column 1 and work your way across the chart, completing each row before coming back to the first column.

Figure 3-1. The Cline Multiple Intelligence Inventory grid						
1	2	3	4	5	6	7
Total						

When you have responded to each of the 42 items, you should have a score in each box of the grid. Add the scores for each column to provide you with seven total scores. Since each column represents one of the intelligences, the total scores will reveal an individual profile of strengths and weaknesses.

1. I am a good tennis player
2. I have a good sense of rhythm
3. I sculpt well with clay
4. I am a good chess player
5. I perform well when speaking before groups
6. I am always counted on to plan social get-togethers for friends
7. I like trying new things
8. I know how to move my body to music
9. When listening to music, I can tell if a note is off key.
10. I draw well
11. I am good with numbers
12. I enjoy debating
13. I enjoy teaching others
14. I like taking tests which tell me about myself
15. I am a good athlete
16. If I hear a musical selection once or twice, I can sing it back accurately.

17. I have great skill at creating mobiles
18. I always look for patterns and sequences in things.
19. I am good at performing in plays
20. Others always come to me for advice
21. I like subjects that deal with philosophy
22. I exercise to relieve stress
23. I exhibit talent when playing musical instruments
24. I can take apart and put together appliances
25. I was always good at math
26. I have a talent for writing poetry
27. I am very sensitive to others
28. I like trying new things to see what I like
29. I am good at playing charades
30. I carry a tune well
31. I was always better in geometry than math
32. I am good at solving logic puzzles
33. I write well to express myself
34. I am counted on to organize events
35. I like telling people about myself
36. I enjoy watching sports events to improve my game
37. I am always tapping out melodies
38. I have an excellent sense of space
39. I can figure numerical problems in my head
40. I always do well with word games
41. I appreciate the "helping" professions
42. I don't like anyone making decisions for me

The seven columns represent the seven intelligences as follows:

- The total in column 1—Bodily/Kinesthetic Intelligence
- The total in column 2—Musical Intelligence
- The total in column 3—Visual/Spatial Intelligence
- The total in column 4—Logical/Mathematical Intelligence
- The total in column 5—Verbal/Linguistic Intelligence
- The total in column 6—Interpersonal Intelligence
- The total in column 7—Intrapersonal Intelligence

Each of the intelligences serves as an umbrella for many others. Individuals may have an affinity for one of the domains without having a talent for it. For example, a strong passion for music may not translate into a musical skill. However, combined with verbal/linguistic and logical/mathematical gifts, it could, eventually form the basis for a career as a music critic. Thus, exposure to experiences in all of the intelligence domains is important. Gaining insight into one's strengths can not only dictate the direction of one's life but can help in the development of self-esteem. As a society, we wish not only to nurture scientists and mathematicians but also to cultivate the innate gifts of artists, musicians, moral leaders, social activists, and mechanics. As teachers design lessons, they may note further strengths. The emphasis is on building positive profiles. Hyatt and Gottlieb (1987) point out, in their book *When Smart People Fail*, that one of the causes of failure may be a mismatch between peoples' innate abilities and their chosen field. Proper matches between innate proclivities as they relate to a chosen fields can help the gifted achieve eminence and live more personally and professionally rewarding lives.

In the following sections, each of the multiple intelligences is discussed at length. Profiles of famous individuals introduce each section. These descriptions draw upon profiles provided by Gardner (1993) and have been included to demonstrate how profiles differ and how one intelligence comes to the fore in creative acts.

To assist teachers in recognizing precocity, development in the domain is outlined. Giftedness in the domain is defined as advanced development.

Logical/Mathematical Intelligence

The Adult in the World

> I spoke late and slowly and I was never a verbal child. I was always interested in the world of objects. I loved algebra and geometry and enjoyed hands-on and theoretical science. I had a disdain for rote learning and performed poorly. I was both defiant and arrogant. The first time I tried to gain admission into the Zurich Polytechnic Institute I failed the entrance examination, but I was admitted a year later. I valued my gift of fantasy more than my talent for absorbing knowledge. I was able to integrate spatial imagery and mathematical formulas.

An examination of Albert Einstein's biography would reveal strengths in logical and spatial domains and weaknesses in personal skills.

The "Kid" in the Classroom

CB's mom would talk about how CB loved money. He didn't love money for what it could buy, but was fascinated by its "numberness." He loved counting. Where other little boys and girls would take teddy bears to bed, CB would take his calculator to bed so that he could figure out problems. When he was three, he loved to play with blocks that had numbers on them so that he could add. When he was five, he would ask for the check when his parents went to a restaurant because he loved to figure out how much it cost and how much change they would receive. When he entered first grade, he intimidated his teacher and classmates when he discussed square roots.

CB did not qualify for the gifted program in his early elementary school years

Logical/mathematical intelligence surfaces as children are exposed to mathematical and logical activities that include computer programming.

because his group IQ score was not high enough. However, because his classroom teacher was so insistent, he was permitted to participate in the gifted program on a trial basis. In fourth grade, he studied the Pythagorean Theorem, Boolean algebra, and was fascinated with perfect numbers. In fifth grade, he studied money and financial planning.

CB is a case history of a young boy who was mathematically precocious but who may not have been a good "test taker." An alert and persistent teacher did not allow an IQ test score to be the "gate" or barrier it can so easily become.

Logical/Mathematical Talent

Krutetskii's (1976) work has contributed greatly to the understanding of the structure of mathematical abilities. Figure 3-2 presents his conception of how mathematical information is obtained, processed, and retained.

Wieczerkowski and Prado (1993) report that aspects of mathematical talent include general traits, such as task commitment, memory for symbols, numbers, principles, mathematical structures and patterns, flexibility in mathematical abilities, and visualizations of problems and relations. According to them,

> Acquisition, application and extension of mathematical knowledge
> vary on a time continuum not only quantitatively, in regard to
> more rapid insight or the mastery of a math problem, but also

---

Figure 3-2. Structure of Mathematical Abilities

Obtaining mathematical information

- The ability for formalized perception of mathematical material, for grasping the formal structure of a problem

Processing mathematical information

- The ability for logical thought in the sphere of quantitative and spatial relationships, number and letter symbols; the ability to think with mathematical symbols

- The ability for rapid and broad generalizations of mathematical objects, relations and operations

- The ability to curtail the process of mathematical reasoning and the system of corresponding operations; the ability to think in curtailed structures

- Flexibility of mental processes in mathematical activity

- Striving for clarity, simplicity, economy, and rationality of solutions

- The ability for rapid and free reconstruction of the direction of a mental process, switching from a reverse train of thought (reversibility of the mental process in mathematical reasoning)

Retention of mathematical information

- Mathematical memory (generalized memory for mathematical relationships, type characteristics, schemes of arguments and proofs, methods of problem solving, and principles of approach)

(Kruteskii, 1976, p. 350)

---

qualitatively, in regard to a broader and increasingly discriminant spectrum of knowledge, and proficiency far in advance of curricular requirements. (p. 444)

Miserandino, Subotnik, and Ou (1995) address the importance of cultivating mathematics talent in students. Their research revealed that the attrition of students leading to quantitative careers begins in the seventh grade. They stress the need to implement strong mathematics programs for mathematically-talented secondary students that include highly committed and trained teachers, parental and peer support, emphasis on enrichment rather than remediation, strong mathematics preparation, and high expectations on the part of all. They also recommend homogeneous grouping to help prevent boredom.

How to Identify the Logical/Mathematically Talented Child in Your Room

Miller (1990) describes characteristics and behavior that may yield clues to identify mathematical precocity in students. He cites an unusual awareness and curiosity about numeric information; quickness in learning, understanding, and applying mathematical concepts; an exceptional ability for abstract thinking; ability to see mathematical patterns and relationships; creative and flexible thinking with math problems; ability to transfer learning to new mathematical situations.

Teachers can identify mathematically precocious students as they interact with mathematics in the classroom. Sheffield (1994) highlights the variety of ways in which mathematical ability can be demonstrated. The characteristics attributed to mathematically able students include:

- Early and keen awareness, curiosity, and understanding about quantitative information.
- Ability to perceive, visualize, and generalize patterns and relationships.
- Ability to reason analytically, deductively, and inductively.
- Ability to reverse reasoning processes and to switch methods easily but not impulsively.
- Ability to work with mathematical concepts in fluent, flexible, and creative ways.
- Energy and persistence in solving difficult problems.
- Ability to transfer learning to novel situations.
- Tendency to formulate mathematical questions not just to answer them.
- Ability to organize and work with data in a variety of ways and to disregard irrelevant data.

Sheffield states that not all students with mathematical talent will have all of the abilities listed. Some may exhibit some of the characteristics spontaneously whereas others will only perform when presented with interesting problems. The ability to compute rapidly and accurately is not necessarily indicative of mathematical talent.

Sheffield points out that mathematically talented students may:

- Be able to recognize patterns and work with abstract symbols.
- Exhibit the ability to discern relationships and/or see connections between separate distinct pieces of information.
- Show a curiosity about numbers, shapes, and patterns.
- Demonstrate an interest in math stories and numbers.
- Exhibit an interest in mathematics, computer programming, or chess.
- Become a master chess player, a scientist, computer programmer, an accountant, a lawyer, a private investigator, a mathematician, or a banker.

Miller (1990) suggests that IQ tests can yield valuable information but should not be used alone. Mathematics achievement tests and mathematics aptitude tests should be used along with out-of-level mathematics aptitude tests.

How to Plan Learning Activities for the Logical/Mathematically Talented Child

According to Sheffield, the mathematics curricula should be challenging and include opportunities to use logical, inductive, and deductive reasoning. Students should be:

- Encouraged to question and make generalizations that go beyond the material presented.
- Exposed to an integrated curriculum which includes geometry, algebra, statistics, and probability.
- Given the opportunity to discuss mathematical concepts with others at the same developmental level.
- Allowed to work independently and in homogeneous groups.
- Encouraged to work on assignments that allow for deeper investigation.
- Introduced to numbers.
- Learn about the different branches of mathematics as they relate to fields of work, such as engineering and astronomy.

Mathematical intelligence, which is necessary for "scientific thinking," deals with inductive and deductive thinking, reasoning, numbers, and the recognition of patterns. Children should be:

- Introduced to the history and methodology of mathematics.
- Introduced to activities which require sequencing.
- Involved in classifying and categorizing objects and information.
- Introduced to activities which use inductive and deductive reasoning.
- Shown how analogies are drawn.
- Introduced to the skills of estimating, "guesstimating," and measuring.
- Helped to look for patterns.
- Instructed in the use of timelines.
- Engaged in mathematical problem-solving activities.

According to Lenchner (1983), in the mathematics curriculum, students should be introduced to problem-solving strategies such as:

- Drawing a picture to solve a problem
- Looking for a pattern
- Making an organized list
- Solving a simpler problem
- Using trial and error
- Experimenting
- Acting out the problem
- Working backwards
- Writing an equation
- Changing points of view

Lenchner (1983) has compiled 280 mathematical problems for use in elementary and middle schools. Broadwin, Lenchner, and Rudolph (1998) have written a solutions book for AP (advanced placement) calculus.

Tangrams and geoboards are manipulatives that allow students to explore relationships. Commercial materials are available that allow children to explore mathematical concepts, encouraging them to develop logical thinking skills. These materials can be incorporated into lessons, or made available to students when classroom work is completed. For example, Dandy Lion Publications publishes paperbacks, such as *One-Hour Mysteries*, *Primarily Logic*, *The Chocolate Caper*, *Logic Countdown* and *No Problem! Taking the Problem out of Mathematical Problem Solving*.

How to Assess Logical/Mathematical Ability

Sheffield (1994) suggests that achievement should be measured in multiple ways, for example, observations, interviews, exhibitions, demonstrations, portfolios, open-ended questions, and performance. Ability should be noted as the mathematics curriculum is presented. Students should be pretested to ascertain if they have already mastered the concepts to be presented. If they succeed with 85 percent of the material, instruction can proceed at a challenging level. Mathematical markers should be noted in children's profiles if they consistently have the ability to move ahead.

The mathematics program should provide for flexible pacing through continuous progress so that students can move at their own pace, compacting the coursework; advancing the level of instruction; grade skipping; early entrance to school; dual enrollment allowing an elementary school child to take classes at the middle or high school; credit by examination.

When planning interdisciplinary lessons which integrate mathematical/logical skills, teachers should note which skills are primary and which ones secondary. Some activities might include:

- Introducing students to robotic-type computer toys which use flow charting and allow students to use their logical skills.
- Listing the steps involved in activities that they usually perform, (e.g., making a peanut butter and jelly sandwich) to see if they are aware of all of the steps involved.
- Establishing collections of items (e.g., buttons, blocks, pictures from magazines), having children categorize and classify them in as many ways as possible, and using the buttons or blocks, have them establish a pattern.
- Seeing if the child can imitate a pattern produced by another child.
- Presenting word problems using mathematical concepts.
- Taking students on a detective investigation—allow students to enter a room and use inductive and deductive reasoning skills to ascertain what happened in that room.

Many activities contain logical/mathematical components. Pose the following scenario for students to ponder and write about: Historical events can provide grist for the mill. Analyze and document a sequence of events. Establish a time-line. Describe how one event led to another. What might have happened if one of the events had been different? Rewrite the events and discuss the impact of your changes on the results. This assignment requires students to think logically, and it also reveals verbal/linguistic and intrapersonal skills. A drawing component can be added for the student who has artistic tendencies, demonstrating spatial skills.

Waxman, Robinson, and Mukhopadhayay (1996) at the Halbert Robinson Center for the Study of Capable Youth, University of Washington, Box 351630, Seattle, WA 98195-1630, have developed a manual, *Teachers Nurturing Math-Talented Young Children*, which addresses how students can be identified as well as alternatives for programming and curriculum.

By observing children in each of a series of logical/mathematical encounters, teachers will have enough information to "mark" logical/mathematical intelligence in their profiles if warranted.

How Teachers Can Locate Competitions and Special Opportunities for Gifted Students

Teachers can arrange for students with potential to attend presentations of other students who are competing in math and science fair competitions. Provide information to students and parents who are in intermediate or high school grades about summer programs that cultivate mathematical skills. For example: Johns Hopkins University, Duke University, and Northwestern University at Denver sponsor a talent search. The talent search process at Duke University (TIP) and at Johns Hopkins (CTY) acknowledges seventh grade students who score in the top 3% on a nationally normed class achievement test.

Ohio State University sponsors a summer program called Ross Young Scholars Program for pre-college students.

Boston University offers PROMYS (Program in Mathematics for Young Scientists) a summer program for high school students to work with faculty members and experienced undergraduates who are embarking on their own mathematical careers.

According to Jarwan and Feldhusen (1993), state-supported residential schools offer very high-quality programs to academically-talented mathematicians.

Wieczerkowski and Prado (1993) and Pyryt, Masharov, and Feng (1993) describe mathematical programs for the gifted in the *International Handbook of Research and Development of Giftedness and Talent*. In the same volume, Goldstein and Wagner describe after-school programs, competitions, school olympics, and summer programs that assist in the development of gifts.

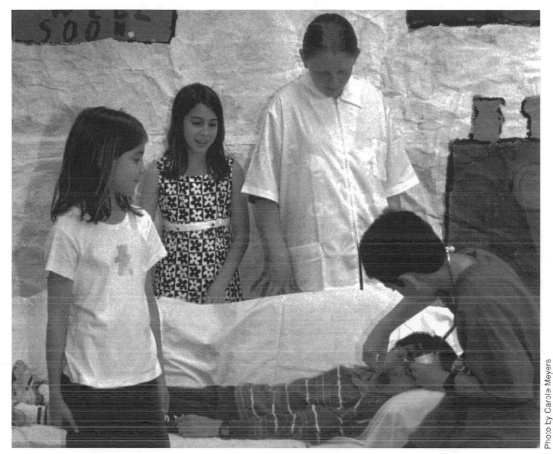

As children become involved in writing scripts and performing, verbal/linguistic abilities surface.

Photo by Carole Meyers

Verbal/Linguistic Intelligence

The Adult in the World

My sister observed that as I was learning to talk I would produce the rhythm of sentences without shaping words. I was entranced by sensory impressions, smells, noises, and sights. I was drawn to effigies, candles and incense. My linguistic memory was remarkable. I performed well in school and enjoyed reading widely in English, Latin, Greek and French. I did not do well in physics and had no interest or ability in science. I went to Harvard where I received a doctorate in philosophy. I studied Sanskrit, Hindu, and the Buddhist texts. My writings revealed my sensitivities to my own emotional life.

T. S. Eliot's biography demonstrates gifts in linguistic and scholastic areas and weaknesses in scientific endeavors.

The "Kid" in the Classroom

AI began speaking before he reached his first birthday. He was an early and voracious reader. When he entered school, his teachers hesitated to call on him. He responded in paragraphs rather than sentences. His love of language spread into the area of writing. In the beginning of third grade, he was afforded the opportunity of reading and writing about a country of his choice. The following excerpts are from a tale AI wrote when he was eight years old:

> The Tale of Two Echidnas
>
> Jack Sprout, an eight-year-old boy, and his father, 58, are taking a trip to Australia. They're planning to go to a zoo to see an exhibit, a special exhibit: "The Echidnas" two to be exact. When they got there, they noticed how monumental the building was. But when they saw the mammoth majority of people in the building, they were astonished. Jack had to urge his father on till finally they got to the Echidna House....
>
> "W-w'what are you doing here?" stammered the bandicoot. With no spines and claws not half as sharp nor long as the much larger echidna's, the bandicoot was quivering in terror. "If this is your part of the country, you might be able to help us," replied Joey courteously. "Could you direct us to the next billabong?" "Well, maybe, but you have to help me first by scaring away the dingo who has been bothering me by taking my tucker and trying to be mean to me. Is it a deal?" "Sure is," agreed Joe, remembering that long ago the dingo made him leave the zoo....

At the end of his story, he included this section:

> Echidnas: Inside Story
>
> An echidna is a one-and-a-half-foot monotreme that can get as old as fifty and can lay one to three eggs at a time. It can be found in Tasmania, New Guinea, and Northern Territory. The echidna naturally eats termites and ants, but in captivity it will eat minced meat. It has yellow spines and coarse hair in between. On its heel, it has a little poisonous hook. It has a snout with a tongue twice the size of the snout. The tongue is exactly like cellophane tape and the echidna will stick out its tongue to capture its food. It also has a pouch, like all other monotreme, through which milk oozes because the echidna has no teats. But this pouch disappears as soon as the baby is old enough to leave it. When it does leave, the mother hides it in a crevice in the rocks. The echidna weighs twenty pounds. If an echidna is trapped on rocky ground, it will curl up into a ball and hold the ground so that the attacker will get a mouthful of spines. The dingo is the only animal in Australia that can dig up an echidna.

AI's interests spread into many other domains. He became bored with school and by fifth grade became very argumentative. He attended a gifted program for two hours per week for purposes of independent study, but this was not sufficient. It became obvious that even in the gifted program he needed a more differentiated curriculum than other students.

Verbal/Linguistic Talent

Tangherlini and Durden (1993) divide verbal talent into the following five categories, each of which may overlap but which can exist independently of each other in the same individual: oral expression, reading, foreign language, creative writing, and general verbal reasoning. Verbal/linguistic abilities may take a variety of forms. The child may:

- Excel at writing—either poetry or prose, or both.
- Be capable of learning many languages
- Have oral talents that denote a future orator. Be a good humorist or story teller.
- Exhibit talents in reading, speaking, and/or writing, or all three.

How to Identify the Verbal/Linguistically Gifted Child

VanTassel-Baska (1993) describes the characteristics of the able language arts student and asserts that the curriculum should be designed to reflect these characteristics. The child usually exhibits:

- Advanced reading ability
- Advanced vocabulary
- Abstract reasoning skills
- The ability to make connections
- Power of concentration and a concern for moral and ethical issues
- Emotional sensitivity and the ability to generate original ideas.

How to Identify the Orator and/or Advanced Reader. Budding orators and/or precocious readers should easily identify themselves. Standardized tests of reading achievement can provide a fairly accurate assessment of students' abilities. Verbally precocious gifted children will probably surface without provocation. In fact, classroom teachers sometimes complain that such children have a tendency to take over and "show off." They may respond to questions in paragraphs rather than in a word or in a sentence.

How to Identify the Student with Foreign Language Ability. Tangherlini and Durden (1993) describe how to identify students with a talent for foreign languages. These individuals "can readily imitate dialects in their native language or who have learned to speak Ediging-lidigish or similar transformational argots" (p. 429). The Modern Language Aptitude Test can provide a means of predicting which students may have an affinity for learning languages.

How to Identify the Child with Creative Writing Ability. Analytical writing requires examining a piece of literature to make patterns out of the details, connecting parts of the piece, and understanding the interactions of the parts in a sophisticated way. In regard to writing fiction, the student early on begins to:

- Write longer sentences, using sophisticated vocabulary and selecting the correct word with a beauty and freshness of expression.
- Effectively manipulate the grammar of the language and use it, not as a trick, but as technique.
- Exhibit a sensitivity to the use of language, choosing words that may not always be advanced but might be surprising.
- Evidence an understanding of how words are spoken.

Both in poetry and fiction, students may:

- Show an ability to see detail.
- Express emotional and physical details.
- Understand that all can be said and be selective in communicating what is important.

Poets are even more sensitive to the nuances of words and their meanings. They:

- Are aware of the impact of sound and rhythm.
- Understand the emotional content of words.
- See similarities between events and things that others would not consider.
- See parallels in life that reveal unusual insights.

The Johns Hopkins Talent Search Model (Stanley, 1991) provides useful information about individuals who possess exceptional verbal reasoning skills.

How to Plan Learning Activities for the Verbal/Linguistically Gifted Child

All activities in this domain should emphasize vocabulary development and a high reasoning level whether in discussions of literature, writing assignments, or oral presentations. Presented below are some learning activities that will enable both the emergence and the development of verbal/linguistic skills in the gifted child.

- Oral expression can be encouraged by providing the opportunity to listen to video/audio taped speeches of fine orators. Students can initially work on their oral expressiveness by memorizing speeches or poems and slowly work their way up to the practice of speaking extemporaneously. Debates, speaking contests, and acting will also provide valuable opportunities for oral expression.

- The widely-used whole language approach, which uses as its starting point the students' particular interests, allows them to work at their own level in areas of special interest to them both in the reading materials they use as well as in expressive writing, transactional writing, and poetic writing (Collins & Parkhurst, 1996). Robinson (1986) reports that:

  > Interest has been found to affect the reading comprehension of gifted elementary students (Stevens, 1980) and is related to their attitudes toward reading (Martin, 1984). Self-selection of reading materials is a form of study-interest-based curriculum and, hence, is inherently differentiated if supported and extended by the teacher. In other words, the gifted reader is likely to select material of appropriate difficulty and move through it at a faster pace if provided with freedom of choice rather than confined to grade-level materials. Secondly, time for individualized reading is necessary if gifted elementary students are to engage in investigative study and independent projects. (p. 179)

- The emergence and development of verbal/linguistic skills can be triggered by exposure to fine pieces of writing. Reading and listening to the finest poetry and prose available may open doors for the budding writer. Listening to recordings of famous works is an important element. The materials available should provide a rich and complex literature base. Students should be introduced to the many different genres of writing: biography, general nonfiction, fiction, drama, poetry, memoirs, etc. Students should have the opportunity to meet with authors and attend both prose and poetry readings. For some students, a good starting point may be familiar fairy tales.

- A publishing center and a classroom library in the classroom for student's own creations will allow student authors and their peers to read each others' stories.

- Writing, at whatever level, should be encouraged. It is important to keep in mind that young children go through different stages of writing, beginning with the drawing of pictures. They go on to scribbles, begin approximating letters, start using inventive spelling, and then move on to adult writing.

- Keeping a basket of "empty books" encourages writing. These may simply be blank pages fastened together to form a "book" with some of the pages in shapes to stimulate thinking (e.g., animals, people, objects).

- Children who are not able to write in recognizable ways, whether because of their young age, poor coordination, or a disability, can be asked to tell you about their writing. These can be taped or dictated to the teacher. Setting up a corner of the room with a tape recorder will help them. Allow them to make up stories and speak into the tape recorder.

- Word games can be used to encourage students to start creating stories. Some examples include:
  What goes _____ when you _____?
  This is the answer, what is the question?
  How many words can you use to describe _____?

- An acting corner in the room, with puppets and costumes, will allow children the opportunity to act out favorite stories or original tales. Apart from contributing to verbal/linguistic development, acting also provides a forum for bodily/kinesthetic intelligence. And if students engage in a discussion of the play being acted out, for example, what would happen if certain events had not taken place, logical/mathematical intelligence comes into play.

- Another writing/oral expression activity involves placing a group of pictures in front of students and asking them, for instance:
  How would you group them?
  Which belong together?
  Write or tell a story around them.
  Students can be encouraged to keep journals.

- Small group discussions with the teacher in which students are encouraged to address topics of interest from a variety of ways of perspectives and in which they feel comfortable about expressing their opinions without reproach provide a suitable climate for expressive activity.

- Students should be exposed to reference materials of all kinds: dictionary, encyclopedia, thesaurus, electronic library, audiovisual material, among others.

It is especially important for teachers to understand that verbally/linguistically gifted children have a need to be seen, heard, and appreciated. Teachers should be aware of their own inclination to avoid calling on such students because of the likelihood of being subjected to a mini-thesis on a topic.

The National Javits Language Arts Curriculum Project has produced many viable curriculum units for verbally-talented students, K-9, that can be ordered from the WSWHE BOCES, Henning Road, Resource Center, Saratoga Springs, New York 12866, attn: Javits Units.

The College of William and Mary School of Education, Center for Gifted Education, 232 Jamestown Road, Williamsburg, Virginia 23185, has produced a series of materials, *Language Arts Curriculum for High Ability Learners—Exemplary Teaching Units* for students in grades 2 through 9.

Judith W. Halsted (1994) has published *Some of My Best Friends Are Books—Guiding Gifted Readers from Pre-School to High School*, Dayton, Ohio: Ohio Psychology.

How to Assess Verbal/Linguistic Abilities

Children's responses to verbal/linguistic activities are a good starting place for assessing their abilities. Does a child:

- Have a flair for writing?
- Use language to express ideas and feelings in ways that communicate with special feeling?
- Have a natural instinct when it comes to rhyme?

Portfolios that use standard samples—a written assignment given to all students—can assist teachers in identifying the gifted writer. Once accomplishments are noted, teachers can be instrumental in helping students getting their due recognition. Entering students in competitions and providing information as to where their work can be published are helpful. Davis and Johns (1989) offer suggestions on how to write and publish. Henderson's (1993) *Market Guide for Young Writers—Where and How to Sell What You Write*, and Whitfield's (1994) *Getting Kids Published* can be used as resources by teachers, students, and their parents.

Musical Intelligence

The Adult in the World

> I was not a good student and I performed at below average in school. When I began taking piano lessons at the age of nine I progressed very rapidly. I became interested in painting and theater but to please my father I went to law school. My interest in music, theater and art helped me as I chose my career. My work reveals my visual and bodily/kinesthetic intelligence.

Igor Stravinsky's profile demonstrates strengths in musical and other artistic domains.

The "Kid" in the Classroom

In discussions with professional musicians, JK was brought to my attention for her superior musical ability. JK also possesses superior talents in other domains as a poet and an artist. Her mother, a singer, reports that as early as four months, JK could imitate sounds, rhythm, and pitch changes. She was sensitive to and changed the intervals sung by her mother. They enjoyed musical experiences together, and her mother

Exposure and training help to identify musical precocity.

continued singing with her, teaching her to harmonize. Early on, her mother took her to concerts.

When JK was six, her family inherited a piano. JK asked questions about the notes on the keyboard and within two hours she became familiar with them. When she asked her father to teach her, he bought her a book which was an introduction to note reading. Reading the book, she taught herself the notes. She was always interested in the mechanics of music. When JK was seven years old, her mother took her to a Montessori school to meet with a prospective piano teacher, who spent 45 minutes with her and was amazed with her understanding of composition and theory. She began lessons by the time she was eight, and at nine years of age she wrote and performed a piano piece at the Long Island Composers Alliance; at eleven she wrote a choral work for four voices. She has continued singing and began viola lessons at twelve. She also composed songs for guitar, piano, and voice at twelve. She sang at Lincoln Center at the premiere of "Mass for the Twenty First Century." She has also appeared in concerts at St. John the Divine.

Her interest at this time appears to be music composition. In a period of three weeks, she composed a string quartet that was performed at Hofstra University at the Long Island Composers Alliance. Her mother reported that what she observes about JK now is her desire to go to her piano and compose.

Musicality

Hargreaves (1996) describes music development in four specific music domains, i.e., singing, musical representation, melodic perception, and composition. Marek-Schroer and Schroer (1993) address the importance of identifying and providing for the musically gifted child, for themselves, for society, and for posterity. "The core ability of the musically gifted child is a sensitivity to the structure of music: tonality, key, harmony, and rhythm. This sensitivity allows the child to remember music and to play it back with ease, either in song or an instrument. The sensitivity to structure allows the gifted child to transpose a theme to a new key, to improvise on a given theme and to invent melodies." (Winner and Martino, 1993, p. 267). One of the earliest signs of musical giftedness is the ability to sing accurately songs they have heard, often after only one exposure. Perfect pitch (the ability to name notes heard, and the ability to sing notes named) is not consistently associated with musical giftedness. There is a distinction between performing and composing. The ability to compose in early childhood is much rarer than the ability to interpret at that age (Winner & Martino, 1993). The development of musical giftedness requires strong discipline and formal training. Children who go on to become adult musicians generally connect to music emotionally when they reach adolescence.

Shuter (1968, pp. 237–238) cites Teplov on three basic musical aptitudes:

- A sense of tonality which enables us to sense the tonal relationships of the notes of a melody and the emotions expressed by melodic movement. This is closely connected with pitch discrimination.

- The ability which enables us to reproduce a tune by singing, to play by ear, and to develop an "inner ear" for music.

- A sense of rhythm by which we are able to feel the rhythmic movement of the music and to reproduce it.

In *The Classification of Educational Objectives, Psychomotor Domain* (1966, pp. 103–104), Elizabeth Simpson outlines the five elements of a complex motor act, presented below in Table 3-1.

Shuter (1968) addresses the development of melodic skills. At eight months, a child was able to repeat intervals, such as the notes of a cuckoo clock. The appearance of various melodic skills in young children was reported as early as nine months, as was reproducing a note correctly. At one year, three months, a child could sing several songs correctly. Memory for general melodic shape was witnessed at one year, four months.

Gesell and Ilg (1943) record the following developmental stages in melodic skills (Shuter, p. 69):

2 years	Sings phrases of song, generally not on pitch.
2½ years	All of parts of several songs sung spontaneously at home or school.
3 years	Whole songs reproduced though generally not on pitch;

> **Table 3-1. The Classification of Educational Objectives, Psychomotor Domain**
>
> **1.0 Perception:** the process of becoming aware of objects, qualities, or relations by use of the sense organs.
> **1.1 Sensory stimulation:** impingement of a stimulus upon one or more of the sense organs.
> **1.2 Cue selection:** deciding what cues to respond to in meeting the requirements of a task (ability to distinguish among sensory stimuli).
> **1.3 Translation:** determining the meaning of the cues for action.
>
> **2.0 Set:** preparatory adjustment or readiness for a particular kind of action or experience.
> **2.1 Mental set:** readiness to perform a motor act (knowledge of).
> **2.2 Physical set:** having made the anatomical adjustments necessary for a motor act.
> **2.3 Emotional set:** readiness in terms of favorable attitude.
>
> **3.0 Guided response:** overt behavioral action under the guidance of an instructor.
> **3.1 Imitation:** execution of an act in response to another person performing the act.
> **3.2 Trial and error:** trying various responses until an appropriate response is achieved.
>
> **4.0 Mechanism:** the learned response has become habitual
>
> **5.0 Complex overt response:** smooth and efficient performance of a complex motor act.
> **5.1 Resolution of uncertainty:** knowledge of the sequence; proceeding with confidence.
> **5.2 Automatic performance:** ability to perform a finely coordinated motor skill with much ease and muscle control.

	can recognize several melodies; is beginning to match simple tunes.
4 years	A few can sing entire songs correctly.

How to Identify the Musically Talented Child

Gordon (1998) offers a critique of many of the musical achievements available. He speaks to the importance of music aptitude.

> Important as music aptitude is, however, other factors are also significant indicators of success in musical endeavors, and an understanding of the research in the psychology of music would be incomplete without thorough knowledge of these factors. For example, one may have the aptitude to achieve high standards in music but may lack corresponding music achievement. Thus, one would be hampered to some degree from enjoying and participating in music to the fullest extent possible. Obviously, just as we need to diagnose students' musical potential in terms of their musical strengths and weaknesses, we need to understand whether students' actual musical achievement reflects their capabilities. It is for that reason that music achievement tests serve a need in music education (p. 157).

Musically talented children are sensitive to rhythm and tonal patterns and to sounds from the environment, the human voice, and musical instruments. As adults, they may become professional musicians, singers, composers, conductors, or music teachers. Commercial musical programs on the market can help classroom teachers identify potential talent. One such test is the Seashore Test of Musical Talents, which can be administered and interpreted by the classroom teacher. The Edwin Gordon Musical Aptitude Profile can be administered by the classroom teacher but must be interpreted by a professional. Teachers may consult with music teachers in their school concerning other tests that measure musical aptitude. Some of them include:

> *The Mainwaring Tests of Musical Ability*
> *Madison Music Tests, Seashore Measures of Musical Talents*
> *Kwalwasser-Dyema Music Tests*
> *The Drake Musical Aptitude Tests*
> *Indiana Oregon Music Test*
> *Wing Standardized Tests of Musical Intelligence*
> *Gaston Test of Musicality*
> *Whistler and Thorpe Musical Aptitude Test*
> *Bentley Measures of Musical Ability*
> *Thackray Tests of Rhythmic Aptitude*
> *Aliferis Music Achievement Test.*

IQ and musical giftedness are not necessarily linked. According to Shuter-Dyson (1982), once an IQ of about 90 is attained, intelligence that is measured by an IQ test is not predictive of musical ability. Students at the Yehudi Menuhin school of music generally had IQs averaging 130. However, the student with the lowest IQ, who was quite deficient in both mathematics and reading, was given an award for musicianship.

Musically gifted children should be given the opportunity to demonstrate their sensitivity to the structure of music: tonality, key, harmony, and rhythm and to demonstrate these skills. Winner and Martino (1993) report that the earliest clue that children are musically gifted is the way they express strong interest and delight in musical sounds. Musical memory and the ability to imitate a song after only one exposure is another early sign of musical giftedness. Musical children may have perfect pitch, the ability to name notes, and sing notes heard. Although Blakeslee (1995) suggests that perfect pitch may be of genetic origin, Walters, Krechevsky, and Gardner (1985) argue that it is a function of training. Among children who had begun instruction before age four, 95% had perfect pitch. Ability to sight read is helpful but not consistently associated with musical giftedness.

Musically gifted children enjoy music as a performing art. They are able to recognize tunes and distinguish among musical styles or instruments. They can differentiate patterns and sounds, may integrate musical activities into projects, and may enjoy creating and/or designing musical compositions or instruments.

How to Plan Activities for the Musical Child

Introducing students to classical works, to recordings and radio stations that play fine works, and taking them to concerts can spark the interest necessary for talent development. Music lessons will also help to identify musicality in children. Learning activities can include:

- Introducing children to music as a listening activity.
- Teaching them about beat and rhythm.
- Listening for patterns in the music and asking, for example:
    What is the tempo of the music?
    What are the different kinds of music?
- Acquainting them with opera, jazz, rock, classical, and country music.
- Identifying different textures.
- Drumming the beat.
- Looking for the patterns.
- Feeling the movement.
- Introducing them to a musical vocabulary and discussing what is pitch, tone, timbre, and rhythm.
- Singing with them and having them sing alone.
- Allowing them to express themselves and improvise.

It is not up to classroom teachers to develop the student's abilities, but if these abilities become apparent, teachers should notify the music specialists and parents.

How to Assess Musicality

As children perform, note their musicality in their responses as they:

- Listen to a song and clap out the rhythm.
- Mimic a popular song after listening to it.
- Mimic or change the words after listening to musical commercials.
- Express themselves musically at the completion of a project or a unit.
- Write a song.
- Create a pattern for a dance.
- Become energized and involved in musical activities.

Other sample activities which can be used to assist in assessing musical ability might include:

- Having children choose from a list of vocabulary words and locate songs that best typify the feeling.
- Using makeshift instruments and having children create sounds that match the feeling:

Happy	Mad	Sad	Glad
Excited	Comfortable	Angry	At Ease

- Playing different musical scores and having children listen to the texture of the music.
- Having the children sing familiar songs.
- Playing the musical score with the story from "Peter and the Wolf," having the children create their own sounds for each of the animals.
- Listening to sounds in the classroom and asking children how they would duplicate them using an instrument.
- Playing different musical selections for the students:
  Classical   Jazz   Pop   Rock and roll
- Having students respond to the music.

After observing students, teachers will become aware that some have a natural ability to listen to the beat of music, move to it, and/or perform. Once accomplishments are noted, teachers can be instrumental in helping students to be recognized for their special abilities. Specialists, administrators, and parents should be alerted so that opportunities can be made available to students in and/or outside of school.

Bodily/Kinesthetic Intelligence

The Adult in the World

I grew up in a small town near Pittsburgh. My father was a physician who loved music and would sing and play music for me and my sisters. My mother was a descendant of Miles Standish. I was not an easy child. Because I was always getting into trouble and telling lies, my mother encouraged me to set up a small theater at home so that I could pretend. We moved to California when I was a teenager where I did well in high school, becoming editor of the literary magazine and acting in the school's productions.

When I was seventeen my father took me to the Los Angeles Opera House to see Ruth St. Denis. I was so taken with the performance that I couldn't wait to learn to dance as she did. My family was not pleased with the idea of my becoming a dancer. When I was twenty, my father died and I decided to chart my own course. At twenty-two, I enrolled in a dancing school founded by Ruth St. Denis and her husband, Ted Shawn. St. Denis was not impressed with my ability and had her husband instruct me. I proved my talents to be in the bodily kinesthetic sphere.

Photo by Carole Meyers

Bodily/kinesthetic intelligence surfaces in activities involving dance and/or athletic activities.

Martha Graham's profile demonstrates strong gifts and talents in the bodily/kinesthetic and linguistic domains.

The "Kid" in the Classroom

Shawn missed the first two weeks of dance class. In the third week, he took off his shoes and socks and joined his classmates. The dance instructor silently demonstrated a combination of movements and all of the children tried them. Each time, across the floor, she made them more difficult. Finally, only Shawn could replicate them: a complex pattern of steps, turns, backward and forward runs. The classroom teacher watched in amazement, nodding, his hand over his open mouth. Shawn accurately repeated the pattern for the class, full of confidence and joy in moving. "I can't believe he even took his shoes off," his teacher whispered. "He has no skills. He doesn't read at all. He spent first grade in the closet at the back of the classroom and most of second grade with his turtleneck pulled up over his face. How can he do this?"

Bodily/Kinesthetic Talent

Bodily/kinesthetic intelligence can be seen in the athlete, the mime, and the dancer—all of whom use the body to express emotion or play a game. Athletic abilities are often recognized and developed as part of physical education programs in schools. Potential athletes will:

- Demonstrate fine and gross motor coordination.
- Participate enthusiastically with playground equipment.
- Talk about, attend, and participate in sports.
- Select a sport when given the opportunity to select a topic for independent study.

As children participate in a variety of sports, abilities should be noted that evidence gifts. As athletic abilities are noted, discussions with physical education personnel can confirm observations.

Abilities in dance might not be recognized and might require the assistance of outside professionals if they are to be nurtured. Depending on the type of dance a child is interested in pursuing, body structure may play an important part. A body structure that is well suited for ballet training is made up of:

- Good feet—definite arches and insteps
- Long legs
- A long neck
- Slenderness

Professionals also refer to the importance of having a "balletic" mind and the ability to look at a dance and remember it. It is difficult to detect who has the potential to become a ballet dancer early on inasmuch as the first three years require training of a mechanical nature. Once the mechanics are mastered, students can be observed to see if they add their own personal dimension to the art. Characteristics necessary for all types of dancing would be "musicality," denoting someone who moved well to the music, and demonstrated flexibility of body.

How to Identify the Future Dancer

Potential dancers who display this intelligence:

- Enjoy moving their body to music.
- Demonstrate a sense of rhythm in movements.
- Demonstrate a sense of space.
- Enjoy observing and participating in activities that require movement.
- Enjoy games using mime such as charades.

If professionals are not available in the school to assist in the identification of gifted dancers, they can be called in from outside to train the staff. Professionals at the Arts Connection (Baum, Owen, & Oreck, 1996) have developed criteria that can be used in schools to expose students to the styles and techniques inherent in jazz, ballet, African, Afro-Caribbean, and modern dance. They have delineated key words and definitions to assist in the identification of gifted dancers, as presented in Table 3-2 (see Baum et al., 1996, p. 95).

How to Plan Activities for the Bodily/Kinesthetically Talented Child

Body movement is the key to bodily/kinesthetic intelligence. Opportunities to observe artists in action in a variety of styles (i.e., ballet, modern, tap, etc.) can provide inspiration for young children and help them develop an appreciation for the essentials of fine dance. Having students meet with dancers provides wonderful exposure. With any kind of dance, rhythm and musicality are essential. Sample activities might include:

- Designing lessons that combine music and movement.
- Providing activities that help students to develop a sensory awareness.
- Involving students in marches.
- Allowing students to create dances.
- Encouraging students to move like an animal or a butterfly or a bird.
- Including activities that use mime.

Arts Connection artists (Baum et al., 1996) have developed a multi-session process which focuses on different aspects of student abilities during different sessions to expose and assist in the identification of gifted dancers (see Table 3-3).

How to Assess Bodily/Kinesthetic Intelligence

Baum et al. (1996) suggest establishing a matrix for each student using the criteria established in the curriculum outlined in Table 3-3. A talent profile is developed as students are given from one to four checks in each of the areas. To assist in the identification of gifted dancers, Winter (1987) suggests some of the following activities:

- Ask children to create a dance using their imagination, after they have listened to a piece of music.
- Play a fast song, a waltz, fast and then only moderately fast music and have them move to it.
- Demonstrate three dance-step patterns and ask children to dance to each as music is played.
- Begin a dance with children and then ask each child to finish the dance alone.

Table 3-2. Key Words and Definitions for Identification of Talent in Dance*

SKILLS

1. Physical Control
knows by feeling; can make adjustments, can balance on one leg; has strength in legs, arms, torso, can maintain corrections

2. Coordination and Agility
can combine movements, executes complex locomotor patterns, can isolate body parts from one another, moves freely through space, moves quickly

3. Spatial Awareness
Is aware of other people, adjusts to other dancers and space, evens up the circle or line, is accurate in time and space

4. Memory and Recall
remembers information, can perform without following, can see and replicate movements accurately, can build sequences

5. Rhythm
puts the beat in the body, repeats rhythmic patterns accurately, anticipates, waits for proper moment to begin, can find the underlying pulse or beat

MOTIVATION

6. Ability to Focus
directs attention, makes full commitment to the movement, is interested and involved in class

7. Perseverance
doesn't give up easily, practices, improves over time, takes time to think, tries hard to get it right

CREATIVITY

8. Expressiveness
shows pleasure in movement, performs with energy and intensity, is fully involved, communicates feelings

9. Movement qualities
displays a range of dynamics; has facility moving in levels, directions, styles; communicates subtlety; moves fully; connects body parts

10. Improvisation
responds spontaneously, uses focus to create reality, shows the details, gives surprising or unusual answers

Reprinted with permission of the National Association for Gifted Children, Gifted Child Quarterly, 1996, Vol. 38, No. 2.

- After placing five large hoops on the floor, ask children to step into and out of the hoops in time with the music.

In my 1996 interview with Lotte Goslar, Director and Producer of the dance company "Pantomime Circus," and Lance Westgard, dancer in the company, as well as choreographer and instructor at Hofstra University and Sarah Lawrence College, they highlighted attributes they believed to be important in the identification of gifted dancers:

Table 3-3. Curriculum for Music and Dance Identification*

Week 1—Rhythm
   following and leading rhythmic patterns, improvising in time, across-the-floor patterns
Week 2—Coordination and Agility
   mirroring, opposites, clapping and signing
Week 3—Recall and Combine
   review of previous material and new combinations
Week 4—Physical Control and Use of the Torso
   improvisations and spatial explorations involving energy in the torso
Week 5—Spatial Awareness
   combinations, changing facing, creative explorations, across-the-floor, moving with others
Week 6—Movement Qualities
   contrasting movement qualities, improvisation, and composition
Week 7—Focus (Silent Class)
   review of previous material, exploration of movement and isolation through imagery,
   observation, and directed focus

Reprinted with permission of the National Association for Gifted Children, Gifted Child Quarterly, 1996, Vol. 38, No. 2.

- Rhythm
- Sense of Space
- Originality
- Inventiveness
- Expressiveness

Gifted dancers have a compulsion to dance. They respond to and get lost in the quality of the music. They cannot be a carbon copy of someone else but must express their own uniqueness through dance. Goslar and Westgard believe that in the early years children should be exposed to and be allowed to explore space and rhythm and express themselves through dance. Formal instruction should not begin before approximately nine years of age.

Dance for the theater requires other kinds of talents. For Broadway performers, the ability to perform and project becomes important. Once on the stage, a transformation takes place. A glow can be observed as individuals lend their own personal creativity to the performance.

For athletes, physical education personnel can determine who has superior athletic ability. Once again, as with musical talents, it is not up to classroom teachers alone to identify and develop innate bodily/kinesthetic ability in students. In both cases, parents should be informed when talent is identified. Specialists should be part of the team, parents should be notified so that opportunities outside of the school can be arranged.

As children are exposed to a variety of materials involving spatial skills, gifts emerge.

Visual/Spatial Intelligence

The Adult in the World

> It is reported that I began to draw by the time I spoke my first word. As a young child, I always drew and became quite good early on. I had a remarkable memory for noticing visual details and I was fascinated by the world and human beings. My work revealed my visual-spatial, bodily-kinesthetic and interpersonal intelligences. Many of my works portrayed the dire circumstances of beggars and poor families. I hated school so I tried to avoid attending. When I did attend, I did not do well because I had problems learning to read and write and my difficulties were even worse when it came to numbers. My inability to perform scholastically and inability to think abstractly kept me away from the world of the intellectual.

Pablo Picasso's strengths were evidenced in his spatial, personal, and bodily intelligences. His weakness appeared in his scholastic endeavors.

Spatial abilities are important in understanding spatial relations in certain branches of mathematics, in science, and in art.

The "Kid" in the Classroom

TM was recommended to me when he was in fourth grade as being the most gifted artist in a K-5 elementary school. The art teacher informed me that TM was also a gifted musician. Conversations with his mother revealed that his interest in drawing appeared before he started kindergarten at four years of age. He loved to draw, would become very focussed, and appeared to attend to details. The school district did have a gifted program, but TM did not meet the criteria for admittance, a score of 128 on a group IQ test. According to Winner and Martino (1993), giftedness in the visual arts appears to be independent of intelligence, as measured by an IQ test, but is correlated with high imagery skills, no right handedness, and with verbal deficits.

Visual/Spatial Talent

Spatial abilities have been reported as an important factor in scientific discoveries. Dixon (1983) chronicles the work of individuals who have achieved eminence in their fields and who possessed extraordinary spatial abilities but had difficulties in school, especially with formal language (e.g., Auguste Rodin, Pablo Picasso, Isaac Newton, Leonardo da Vinci, and Harvey Cushing). Children whose spatial control center in the brain is dominant for all thinking can be competent in spatial ability but deficient in language ability. The language functions subserve the spatial functions. The sub-tests of IQ tests can reveal irregularities in individual profiles and, if utilized, can be helpful in determining spatial strengths.

According to Dixon (1983):

> Spatial understanding depends on grasping the consistency in relationships between things when these relationships occur in the context of fluid, changing patterns. The fluidity presents infinite possibilities like a face seen from different angles. But the grasp of the relationships holds this infinity together to accomplish two things. First, grasp of the relationships allows people to recognize that they are seeing different instances of the same thing within the fluid, infinite possibilities of the pattern because the relationships remain consistent. Second, grasp of the relationships allows a person to anticipate instances in the infinite flow of possibilities, even though the person may never actually have observed that given instance before. (p. 27)

Spatial understanding evolves from three groups of related skills:

- Topological relationships—proximity separation, order, enclosure, and continuity
- Projective relationships—observation of two things that occur near each other

- Euclidean relationships—observation that two things are separate, even if they occur near each other

Topological Space. Dixon (1983) reports on Piaget's developmental levels of spatial abilities. He placed a screen in front of children. They could put their hand under the screen and feel objects. Children were asked to either name the object, choose the object they were handling behind the screen from a set of drawings, or draw the object. His findings were as follows:

- Before the age of two and one-half years—children rejected handling objects they couldn't see.
- Between two and one-half and three and one-half—children were willing to handle objects and could recognize familiar objects but could not recognize other shapes being handled.
- Between three and one-half and four—children could distinguish objects on the basis of gross topological features.
- Around five—children noticed angles and corners. They began to explore the two directions created from corners and angles. Drawings began to take on angular features.
- Age six—children explored more actively but with some hesitation as they related features to each other. They were able to draw simple shapes.
- Age seven—children began to exhibit operational behavior. Children used reference points to integrate an object as a whole and reverse their actions.

Projective Space. Piaget asked children to imagine that matchsticks were telephone poles. They were then asked to place them in a plasticine base to form a straight line.

- Under four—children could recognize a straight line and pick one out from pictures. They were unable to construct a straight line.
- Between four and seven—children were capable of constructing a fairly straight line if a guiding edge was straight. If the base was not straight, the children attempted to straighten it.
- Age seven—children developed concrete operational strategy. They used their own line of sight to assist them in constructing a straight line.

Coordination of Perspectives. Piaget created a pasteboard model of three mountains, one with a small house on it, one capped with snow, and one with another small house on it. Large pictures of the model seen from different directions were used. A small doll could be placed in different positions. Children were asked to rearrange separate mountains to reconstruct the way a model would be seen from other positions. Another procedure involved having a child pick the picture that depicted how the mountains would look from a different position.

- Under four—children demonstrated no indication of understanding.
- Between five and seven—children could place the separate mountains in positions that represent the model but were unable to imagine how it would look from another position.
- Age seven or eight—children began to represent the doll's point of view.
- Age eight or nine—children could accurately shift to the doll's point of view. Children could understand right-left relationships and foreground and background.

Euclidean Space. Piaget showed children a pair of "lazy tongs" with handles far apart. Children were asked to notice the diamond or rhombus-shaped holes and determine how the shapes would change as the tongs were opened and closed.

- Under age four—children were unable to draw anything resembling a diamond.
- Around five—children could draw a credible diamond when following a model that was front of them but could not reproduce what they could not see.
- Around six—children could anticipate in gross ways the direction of the shape of the holes as the tongs change position. Children still could not grasp real transformations.
- Age seven or eight—children could construct a series of diamonds and show parallelism. Once operational thinking was established, children could work with geometric figures.

Dixon (1983) reports research indicating that spatial abilities are not correlated with intelligence. In fact, as spatial abilities increase, verbal abilities may decrease. The better students performed on spatial tests, the worse was their performance in foreign language. If individual IQ tests are administered, large discrepancies between verbal and performance scores should be noted and subtests examined. Teachers should be sensitive to children who appear to have visual/spatial gifts. These children are often overlooked because of their poor performance on verbal tasks.

Visual/Spatial Abilities and the Arts

"The 'core' indicator of giftedness in drawing is the ability to draw recognizable shapes at least one year in advance of the normal time of emergence of this skill" (Winner and Martino, 1993).

Visual/spatial abilities can surface in a variety of artistic endeavors. D'Amico

(1942), Lowenfeld (1957) and Porath (1993) describe the stages that children go through in the development of artistic ability:

Ages Two to Four: The Scribbling Stage. In its early stages scribbling is disordered; later lines become controlled, longitudinal and circular lines are repeated. Children begin to name their scribbles.

Ages Four to Seven: The Pre-schematic Stage. Children begin to abstract a line from previous scribbling. A circle now becomes a head and longitudinal scribbling becomes parts of the body, but there are no spatial correlations. Proportions are drawn according to their significance for the children. From four to six years of age, children

beginning kindergarten

middle of kindergarten

third grade

third grade

are born painters and a brush is more natural than a pencil. They are relaxed and free as they are allowed to explore. When working with paint, they begin with mere daubs, often without response to color. A pattern period comes next. They make various designs which include stripes, dots, or swirls. They then proceed to abstract painting.

Ages Seven to Eleven: The Schematic Stage. Symbols appear flat and static and indicate that children have become aware of the real world in their art. Children begin representing and communicating their ideas. During this period, children enter the schematic state in which they develop a definite order in spatial relationships. In about fifth and sixth grade, children become conscious designers and become aware of line, mass, and color. Between nine and eleven years, they attempt to represent reality as a visual concept as they are becoming conscious of the significance of their environment.

Ages Eleven to Thirteen: Pseudorealistic Stage. According to Lowenfeld (1957), children are capable of noting changing optical effects in the human figure in regard to light, space, and atmospheric conditions. They add optical changes to their work as they represent wrinkles, shadows, and changes in body position, and with time, they include more detailed observations. Lowenfeld provides evaluative charts to observe differences in growth.

In working with clay, the children's development is characterized by three stages:

- The manipulative stage, where they play and squeeze and pull apart the clay and begin describing their clay, naming it.

- The exploration stage, where they begin to make strips, coils, balls, and forms that may appear meaningless to the adult.

- The expressive stage, where they begin to form objects.

How to Identify the Visual/Spatially Talented Child

Clark and Zimmerman (1992) caution against the use of standardized tests to identify artistic ability because it is not necessarily correlated with a high IQ and creativity tests are only nominally related to artistic talent. They suggest using the following instead:

- Non-structured nominations that simply ask nominators to recommend prospective students.

- Structured nominations that outline required information that can be compared from student to student.

- Group IQ, achievement tests, and academic records that might be a component in selecting students who qualify for advanced art classes.

- Informal art instruments, which can be a valuable part of a larger set of identification procedures.

- Portfolio and performance review, with students being told about all requirements and judgment criteria in advance.

- Interviewing procedures, valuable in helping to identify students for specific types of programs.
- Observation procedures using trained observers, which can be very accurate in identifying artistically gifted and talented students working in classrooms.
- Age/grade procedures, which should include multiple criteria systems that are hierarchically arranged.

Kay (1982) suggests that portfolio evaluation of artistic works should include:

- Technical Ability—composition, line quality and control, etc.
- Communication of Ideas—ability to make a strong statement
- Inventiveness—imaginative ability

How to Plan Learning Activities for the Visual/Spatial Gifted Child

Suggested activities include:

- Allowing children to develop concepts of above, below, between, beneath, beside, inside, outside, off, on, down, and entwined.
- Introducing children to such concepts as texture, design, color, composition, and brilliance.
- Allowing children to express themselves in a variety of media.
- Designing with paint, clay, or collage.
- Using play-doh, popsicle sticks, and cookie cutters to design, manipulate, and create.
- Building with tinker toys and tangrams.
- Examining ways that space may be used, introducing students to architectural concepts.
- Designing mobiles.

Teachers should note whether students pass through the developmental stages described more rapidly and demonstrate maturity in their work. Gifted children go through all of the stages involved in the development of artistic talent but begin at a younger than average age to draw in a more differentiated, realistic, non-schematic style. Even though an early ability to draw realistically may be the most typical characteristic of the gifted artist, skills in design, form, color, and composition should not be overlooked (Winner & Martino, 1993). Art teachers also report that gifted artists appear to "lose" themselves in their work.

How to Assess Visual/Spatial Abilities

Children's abilities will be evidenced through drawing, painting, sculpting, and map-making. Visual/spatial intelligence lies in children's keen sense of sight and the ability to form mental images and pictures in their mind. They may become architects, graphic design artists, cartographers, industrial design draftspeople, painters, or sculptors. Winter (1987) suggests that the following criteria should be considered when uncovering the gifted artist:

- Students should be given opportunities to combine real and imagined forms in an original way.
- Compositions should be viewed in terms of the balance, rhythm, color, line, and texture.
- Their work should be observed to ascertain if they communicate a personal response and if the students have paid attention to detail.

Sample activities might include:

- Free and open-ended activities in art.
- Problem solving using materials provided.
- Art projects may be given as a way of culminating research.
- Construction of murals or dioramas to accompany written work for units of study.

Professionals in the school and community can work with the classroom teacher in the assessment and nurturance of visual/spatial ability. Parents should be notified if talent is observed so that school personnel and parents can provide enrichment for gifted children. In order for artists to excel, exposure to painters and fine works of painting is important. Trips to museums with teachers or family members can help children to develop an appreciation for the world of art. Either guided tours or audiotapes provided to accompany individuals through exhibits are valuable. Computer programs now offer CD-ROMs that provide an introduction to the masters. Inviting artists to the classroom or visiting artists in their studios can be extremely beneficial.

Personal Intelligences:
Inter- and Intrapersonal Intelligence

The following profiles present individuals who have demonstrated gifts in the inter- and intrapersonal domains. The first is Mahatma Gandhi, whose intelligences surfaced in the personal and linguistic domains.

Knowledge of self increases awareness of others.

The Adult in the World

As a child, I was puny and reluctant to engage in athletic activities. I did not like school and was not a good student. I always had a sense of right and wrong and would not participate in a false scheme to protect my teacher from public embarrassment. My marriage was arranged at the age of thirteen. I left my wife and first surviving son to attend school in England to become a barrister against the wishes of my community.

When I returned home I met Raychandbai, who became my mentor. He convinced me to remain a Hindu and pursue a life of good works in my profession. I left to go to South Africa and was successful in my legal encounters. I became involved in many political struggles and proceeded through peaceful and legal means, writing petitions, holding meetings, launching organizations, arguing cases and looking for legal loopholes. I constantly sought to improve my performance through self-study and self-observation. In 1897, I was almost beaten to death. I felt sorry for the ignorant mob who attacked me and did not press charges. In 1908 I was sent to jail for the first time. Although I was not always loved, I was respected for the calm way in which I pursued my goals. (Mahatma Gandhi)

The second profile is that of Sigmund Freud who also showed evidence of strong linguistic and personal intelligence.

The Adult in the World

> I did not excel in mathematics or the physical sciences and my sensitivity to music was limited. I was highly articulate and always interested in the world of other human beings.
>
> I decided to study medicine and pursued research in neuroanatomy although I was not interested in the daily practice of clinical medicine, and was not sufficiently stimulated by the laboratory work of neuroanatomy. I became fascinated with the world of nervous disorders.

The "Kid" in the Classroom

In second grade, BD was noticed because of her self-knowledge and empathy for others. Brought to the attention of her teacher by her parents, she missed the IQ requirement specified for entrance into a special Saturday program for gifted students by two points. The classroom teacher reported that this child had exceptional inter- and intrapersonal skills and performed at a higher level in many areas than her high IQ classmates. Her mathematical abilities allowed her to see relationships and patterns in the mathematics lesson. When her teacher used strategies to teach mathematics that allowed the children to construct knowledge, BD became fascinated with mathematical patterns.

In BD's interaction with her classmates and the teacher she always demonstrated a great deal of empathy. Her metacognitive skills allowed her to see mistakes being made by her classmates. She would correct them but always preface her statements with, "I understand why you think that, but I disagree because. . ." or "I don't mean to make you feel bad, but I may be able to help. . . ." One of the students in the classroom had recently come from a South American country. The teacher reported that many of the children assisted him, but they did so with an eye to showing off their own abilities. BD went home one weekend and the following week presented him with a homemade Spanish-English dictionary with pictures.

Following are some of examples of letters she wrote in second grade that her teacher shared with me to demonstrate her intra- and interpersonal skills.

Personal Intelligences

Inter- and intrapersonal intelligences are included together in the section on personal intelligences. Even though, at times, each one may be separate, learning about each can inform the other. Goleman (1995) suggests that interventional programs be implemented when deficits in emotional intelligence are noted. Elias et al. (1997) address promoting social and emotional learning in schools. Individuals who are gifted in the

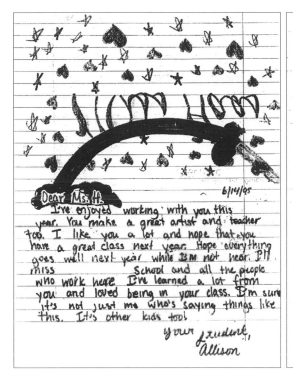

Dear Ms. H.,
I've enjoyed working with you this year. You make a great artist and teacher too. I like you a lot and hope that you have a great class next year. Hope everything goes well next year while I'm not hear. I'll miss School and all the people who work here. I've learned a lot from you and loved being in your class. I'm sure it's not just me who's saying things like this. It's other kids too!
                    your student,
                         Allison

6/14/95

Dear Miss H.,
   You are a great teacher and as much as I love this school, I also love my new house. I love the song that you are walking down the aisle to! It is very pretty. Today when I gave my questions to Mrs. M., she said, "Allison, who wrote these? Ms. H.?" I told her that I wrote them, And she said "Allison, you have wonderful handwriting!" That made me feel so good. You have wonderful writing too Ms. H.!

            Love, Allison

You're special.

area of personal intelligences may become future politicians, therapists, philosophers, or spiritual leaders. These individuals have knowledge of themselves, their feelings, their emotional responses, and their thinking processes. They are capable of self-reflection, are intuitive, and have the capacity to discern higher states of consciousness.

Identifying and developing personal skills are also important ways of helping individuals who may be gifted in other areas but deficient in personal intelligence. Often, such individuals are unable to achieve success unless they remedy their personal intelligence deficits. Hyatt and Gottlieb (1987) highlight areas responsible for the fact that smart people fail. One is a lack of intrapersonal knowledge, which leads individuals to choose professions for which they are not suited, causing a mismatch. Another is a lack of social skills. Goleman (1995) has claimed that emotional intelligence is an important factor in becoming successful in any field of endeavor. Deficits in this area can be noted early on and students can be helped to improve their skills. Goleman suggests that personal skills should be cultivated in all students and suggests programs that can be effective. He addresses ways of identifying students who are both gifted and deficient in the personal intelligences. Unlike the other areas, with personal intelligences, it is just as important to work on the deficit as it is to acknowledge the strength.

Hyatt and Gottlieb (1987) and Goleman (1995) have provided insights into the kind of intelligence that "makes for success." In *When Smart People Fail*, Hyatt and Gottlieb attribute some failures to the lack of social skills. Goleman asserts that emotional intelligence can matter more than IQ. He presents research that points to the success of individuals with modest IQs while those with high IQs flounder.

How to Identify Children with Personal Intelligences

According to Goleman (1995), emotional intelligence includes self-awareness, impulse control, persistence, zeal and self-motivation, empathy, and social deftness.
Children with interpersonal intelligence:

- Demonstrate an interest in others and are able to discern moods, feelings, and intentions
- Communicate needs verbally
- Participate in group activities and discussions
- Volunteer to help others in need
- Can be assertive in appropriate situations
- Understand and accept constructive feedback
- Organize and influence others
- Exhibit leadership
- Enable others

Children with intrapersonal intelligence:

- Are aware of their feelings and abilities
- Recognize that different feelings exist and can identify them
- Can recognize their own strengths and weaknesses
- Know when to ask for help
- Are able to reflect on feelings
- Are willing to take risks and try to accomplish tasks in areas of deficit
- Accept responsibility for their own actions
- Can align themselves with others who are strong in an area in which they are weak

These children work well with others in a group. They can communicate verbally and non-verbally with other people, notice distinctions among others and the environment, and understand moods, temperaments, motivations, and intentions. They are capable of genuine empathy for another's feelings, fears, anticipations, and beliefs.

Elias et al. (1997) echo Goleman's ideas and advocate promoting social and emotional learning in the classroom. They provide a curriculum, covering pre-school, elementary/intermediate, middle, and high school, that addresses:

emotion—becoming aware and expressing emotion

cognition—becoming reflective, focussing on strengths of self and others, and anticipating consequences

behavior—learning self-management and respect for others

integration—integrating feeling with thinking and language, differentiating emotions, and resisting inappropriate behaviors

key concepts—understanding of honesty, justice, fairness, goals, promises, and empathy

Observing Personal Intelligence. Children can be observed in a variety of settings: in the classroom, on the playground, in the lunchroom, on a class trip, or in special classes, such as physical education or art. Teachers can consult with specialists in the building who may provide insights into the students' social skills.

How to Use Sociograms to Identify Personal Intelligences. A sociogram is an instrument that can be easily designed and used in a variety of ways to assist in identifying children who are socially gifted. When planning a trip, teachers can ask students to write down in private whom they would like to sit next to on the bus. Teachers should then diagram the results to determine who has been chosen most often as well as who has not been chosen. Teachers can also ask students to name two students with whom they would like to work on a project.

When the results are diagrammed, three types of groups and isolated individuals will appear (see Figure 3-2, reprinted from Davies, 1981, p. 294):

- Star leaders—Students who have been selected by an unusually high number of other students.

- Islands or cliques—Small groups of children who have chosen each other but who have not been chosen by anyone else.

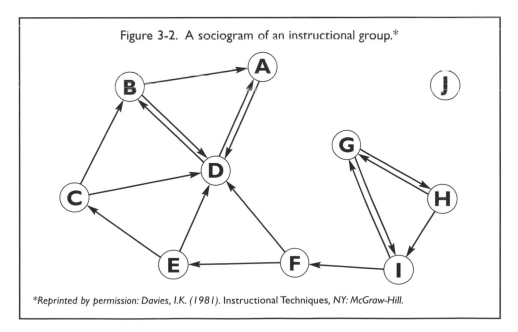

Figure 3-2. A sociogram of an instructional group.*

*Reprinted by permission: Davies, I.K. (1981). Instructional Techniques, NY: McGraw-Hill.

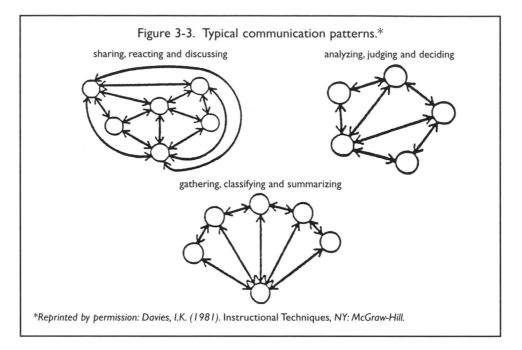

Figure 3-3. Typical communication patterns.*

sharing, reacting and discussing

analyzing, judging and deciding

gathering, classifying and summarizing

*Reprinted by permission: Davies, I.K. (1981). Instructional Techniques, NY: McGraw-Hill.

- Mutual pairs—Children who have selected each other and may or may not have been chosen by others.
- Isolates—Children who have not been chosen by anyone in the class.

Teachers might observe different results in different settings. Although a child may be a social isolate, when students select partners for projects, if the child is gifted or has expertise in a content area, that child might become a star.

How to Use Class Discussions to Observe Personal Intelligences. Observations of discussions can reveal how many students participate in a discussion, those who take leadership roles, and those who are left out. Teachers should present a topic for discussion that all students have a background or stake in, for example, "How might we set up the room to ensure freedom and control?" (see Figure 3-3, reprinted from Davies, 1981, p. 315).

How to Use Peer Nominations to Assess Personal Intelligences. Asking students to answer the following questions will provide insight into how students view one another:

- Whom do you go to when you need help in (name content area)?
- Whom would you ask to take charge if the teacher had to leave the room?
- Who knows the most about topics before we study them?
- Who would you choose to work on a project with?
- Who would you choose to have lunch with?

• Who would you invite to play at home after school?

Teachers can observe and accumulate data to assess the personal intelligence of their students. As they analyze data, they can identify "popular" children in the class as well as those who lack social skills. Some students may be popular because they are socially adept and others because of their "knowledge." Teachers can design activities that enhance personal skill development in a way that can be useful for all children as they concentrate on assisting those with a deficit in this area to improve.

How to Plan Learning Activities to Foster Development of Personal Intelligence

Some activities emphasize self-knowledge; others emphasize interactions with others. As students become aware of their own strengths and weaknesses and likes and dislikes, their awareness of others is enhanced. Activities might include:

- Providing children opportunities to evaluate themselves.
  What are their likes and dislikes?
  How are they the same as and different from other children?
  Who are their heroes and why?
  What are their talents?
  What makes them angry?
  How do they like to spend their leisure time?
- Providing cooperative learning experiences and cooperation games.
- Discussing characters in works in literature:
  What are their qualities?
  How are they feeling at particular moments in their lives?
- Studying famous leaders to determine qualities involved in leadership.
- Allowing students to design a "Tower of Me."
- Keeping a journal.
- Having students record their favorite things.
- Asking students to write about their heroes.
- Having students create an "I wish" list.
- Allowing student choices in presenting completed work.
- Allowing students to select an independent study.
- Inviting politicians or social workers to speak with students to help teachers discuss the special qualities involved in the helping professions.
- Assessing children's learning styles and sharing the information with them.

Information on learning style inventories that can aid in self-knowledge has been provided at the end of the chapter.

How to Play the Mirror Game. To help students understand that their body language communicates a certain image and, in turn, elicits responses from those around them, have students play the mirror game. Select two students. Give one student a card with a description of an event or an emotion that elicits a particular feeling, such as:

Happy	Sad	Disgruntled	Confident
Elated	Angry	Unhappy	Tentative
Depressed	Mad	Disinterested	Unsure

Have a student role play with another student. As one individual acts out the emotion, the other student mirrors back the exact body language. After each student has had a chance to role play, have the students reflect on their feelings as the principal role player and as the mirror. Questions to be discussed during a debriefing would include:

- How did you feel as the person who was experiencing the feeling?
- How did you feel as the emotion was mirrored back?
- How did you feel about the individual who was providing the actions that you mirrored?
- How did the students in the room feel about the scenario?
- What kind of person would you be more apt to approach?
- What kinds of behaviors cause you to avoid others?

How to Use Bibliotherapy as a Tool to Increase Personal Intelligence. Teachers should work with the librarian in the school to develop a collection of books to draw upon. These books should depict individuals in a variety of situations that mimic situations that occur in the room. A source that can be used is *The Bookfinder, A Guide to Children's Literature About the Needs and Problems of Youth Aged 2 and Up*, published by the American Guidance Service, Circle Pines, Minnesota. After reading a selection, teachers should discuss the events and feelings demonstrated in the story and have children analyze the cause-and-effect relationships that occurred in terms of behaviors and feelings.

- Which behaviors were positive?
- Which were negative?
- How might characters change their behaviors to elicit a positive response?

How to Use Drama and Puppets in Personal Intelligence Activities. Teachers can provide creative materials, such as puppets or scripts, so that students can act out specific scenarios. These can be tailored to incidents found in books or they can be written to address specific problem behaviors in the classroom, playground, or home. Students can be involved in writing the scripts.

How to Use Boundary Breaking as an Activity to Increase Personal Intelligences. Boundary-breaking activities include a series of questions designed to develop intuitive expression and listening skills. Most important, they help students relate to others and assist in the development of self-awareness. The procedure for using boundary breaking as a technique is simple. It requires no equipment, only a circular arrangement of individuals either in chairs or on the floor. The leader states the question and then begins by asking which students would like to respond. Individuals respond as they wish. It is important that the leader is a group member and responds as well. Now and then an individual cannot respond either because they block the question or need more time to reflect. This can be indicated by saying "pass." The leader may return to that person when and if he or she is ready. Passes are accepted as positively as any other response. Psychological safety and acceptance are critical to the success of boundary breaking.

The leader must model keen interest. If there are side comments, the leader waits patiently and gently moves on to the next person. After several sessions, the side comments which are often prompted by nervousness dwindle to a minimum as the group members begin to enjoy talking to one another—"I didn't know he felt that way—I do, too" or "and I thought he was such a cold fish" are just a few of the thoughts that might well go through the minds of gifted students as they listen to one another's responses and correct their perceptions of themselves and others.

Boundary breakers can be used at the beginning of a lesson to encourage transition from other classes and to spark interest in an upcoming topic or at the end of a lesson to tone down enthusiasm and to rebuild a feeling of "groupness."

As each question is posed, respondents are asked to elaborate and tell why. Examples of boundary-breaking questions

- If you were to take an animal trait, what trait would you choose?
- If you were to star in a television show, what show would you choose?
- If you were a famous person, who would you be?
- What is your favorite time of day?
- If you were making a record of happiness, what sound would that be?
- If you were a product in a dairy bar, what would you be?
- If you were an animal, which one would you be?
- If you were a musical instrument, which one would you be?

Students gain insights into themselves and others. In one session with a group of students, the question was posed as to what famous person they would choose to be. One young lady replied that she wished to become the first female president. Another responded that she did not wish to become famous because famous people get killed.

How to Incorporate Learning Style as a Component of Personal Intelligence. Awareness of style can aid in the development of personal intelligence as it relates to oneself and to others. Armstrong (1994) suggests a link between one's multiple intelligence profile and the way one learns best, for example, the child who has a strong verbal/linguistic profile might enjoy lectures and discussions and prefer to read and to write. The logical/mathematically talented child might enjoy critical thinking exercises, performing experiments, using math manipulatives and number games. The visual/spatially gifted child might prefer visual presentations, graphs, maps, visualization activities, and mind mapping. The child who displays bodily/kinesthetic attributes might enjoy hands-on learning, which includes drama, dance, manipulatives, and tactile activities. The musical child might choose tape recorders, musical instruments, and songs that teach. The child who has interpersonal skills might prefer learning with a peer, tutoring, and collaborating. The intrapersonally gifted child might prefer individualized instruction, independent study, and self-checking materials.

Griggs and Dunn (1984) report increasing support for the positive relationship between improvement in student academic achievement, attitudes, and behavior and accommodation of the student's learning style preferences in the classroom. Gifted learners as a group seem to show evidence of preferring certain learning styles. Gifted elementary and junior high school children show high tactile and kinesthetic and low auditory preferences. The gifted prefer less structure, more independence, and flexibility in learning; they are highly persistent and self-motivated; they resist conformity. Researchers comparing the learning styles of gifted and nongifted learners (Price, Dunn, Dunn, & Griggs, 1981) indicate that elementary and secondary gifted learners prefer (1) less supervision in the learning setting; (2) manipulative and active, real-life experiences to lectures, discussions, and tapes; and (3) more small group, individual, and self-designed instructional opportunities. Renzulli and Smith (1978) designed an inventory to determine preferences for teachers and students which includes lecture, discussion, programmed instruction, drill and recitation, projects, independent study and simulation and games. Gifted students prefer independent study and simulation.

Some of the researchers in the field who have proposed their own theories concerning learning styles include: Gregorc (1982) designed an inventory to determine the characteristics of the learner as defined by concrete sequential, abstract sequential, abstract random, or concrete random. Myers & McCaulley (1985) define learning style as differentiating between introverts and extroverts, sensors and intuitors, thinkers and feelers, and judgers and perceivers. Torrance (1988) has designed an instrument to determine hemispheric preference which is associated with creativity. Finding out and helping students become aware of their preferences, either by formal inventories or observations, increases a student's ability to work at optimum levels. Awareness of learning style preferences can also assist in the identification of multi-cultural and African-American populations.

Commercial materials available which can assist in developing the personal intelligences include paperbacks such as:

- *Roundtable: Discussion Questions for Independent Growth*
  (Draze, 1991)

- *I Want to Be Like* (McAlpine, Weincek, Jeweler, & Finkbinder, 1994)
- *Winners' Circle: A Guide for Achievement* (Draze, 1987)
- Halsted's (1994) anthology of works that can be used as bibliotherapy in the classroom, which includes descriptions of books that will assist in discussing inter- and intrapersonal relationships with students.
- *Bananas and Fifty-Four Other Varieties* (Grenough, Marshall, McGuire, Orourke, & Spector, 1980), is a program of theater techniques with a series of games going from simple to complex structure.

How to Assess Personal Intelligences

After activities are conducted in the classroom, profiles of children will emerge revealing a continuum of strengths and deficits. Some students will appear to have a great deal of confidence and self-esteem in all that they do. Others will surface as isolates. Some may shine in some settings and not in others. Students may fall into categories. Students who are self-confident in all settings and are viewed as leaders by other students are often elected to offices in the classroom and in the school. Some students are recognized by others for a special gift. These gifts may include academic excellence, exceptional ability in art or music, or outstanding athletic performance.

Social and emotional learning or personal intelligence is important in all walks of life. Assessment of social skills allows teachers to identify those students who are socially adept as well as those that are not. This provides teachers with an opportunity to acknowledge and reward those who show empathy for others and assist those who lack these skills.

Introducing personal skill development into classroom curriculum allows leadership to be recognized and developed. Self-understanding and empathy are skills that enhance all individuals. Students who exhibit superior skill development can be used as models for others.

Multiple Intelligence Education for Every Child

The work world demands a variety of skills, abilities, and talents. Giftedness in one area can lead to many diverse career paths. Thus, spatial abilities are necessary not only for the artist, but the architect, surgeon, dentist, mechanic, etc. Logical/mathematical abilities are important for the scientist, computer programmer, and police investigator. Verbal/linguistic abilities and inter-/intrapersonal skills are necessary for the politician and indeed, for everyone who works with other people. A true education should prepare students for the variety of professions available to them. It should also enhance the quality of their lives on multiple dimensions. For instance, the development of artistic, musical and bodily/kinesthetic awareness is important to those entering professions in the arts and also assists in the development of aesthetic sensibilities.

Benita was a fourth-grade student in an independent study program for the gifted. She chose art as a topic to explore. It became evident that Benita did not have artistic ability but did have an unusual aesthetic appreciation of works of art. She articulated her feelings as she viewed fine works. She spoke of how she became one with the work and responded emotionally to what was presented to her. The same was true of Sam and his love of music. He had a modicum of musical talent but also described how doors opened in his mind as he listened to classical pieces.

Teachers need not be experts in every area. They can discuss the different disciplines with specialists in and out of the school and include other individuals in identifying and nurturing special gifts and talents. As teachers design lessons, they might discuss with specialists what makes a great musical piece, a fine piece of writing, a work of art, etc. Administrators need to support teachers as well. Workshops, conferences, and in-service training should be a part of the overall plan.

The following publications that can be used to introduce multiple intelligence theory and practice into the classroom include:

- *Multiple Intelligences in the Classroom* by Armstrong (1994)
- *Multiple Assessments for Multiple Intelligences* by Bellanca, Chapman, and Swartz (1994)
- *Multiple Intelligence Approaches to Assessment: Solving the Assessment Conundrum* by Lazear (1994)
- *If The Shoe Fits: How to Develop Multiple Intelligences in the Classroom* by Chapman (1993)
- *Celebrating Multiple Intelligence: Teaching for Success: A Practical Guide Created by the Faculty of the New City School Faculty of the New City School* (1994)
- *Seven Ways of Knowing: Teaching for Multiple Intelligences* by Lazear (1991)
- *Creating Minds: An Anatomy of Creativity Seen Through the Lives of Freud, Einstein, Picasso, Stravinsky, Eliot, Graham, and Gandhi* by Gardner (1993)
- *To Open Minds: Chinese Clues to the Dilemma of Contemporary Education* by Gardner (1989)

Summary

As teachers begin to view students in their room from a multiple intelligence perspective, student strengths can be noted that build positive profiles. Children may exhibit potential in only one intelligence or domain or may be multitalented. What becomes important is that as potential gifts are noted, strategies for curriculum differentiation, as described in Chapter 2, are implemented so that a level of challenge is maintained. As teachers, administrators, staff, and community begin to work together to design settings where potential giftedness in all domains can be expressed, identified, and nurtured, the education of potentially gifted students will be integrated into the fabric of the school. The quality, depth, and breath of education will be enhanced for all children and for our society.

Additional Resources for Leadership Education

Publications

Cox, J., Daniel, N., and Boston, B. (1985). *Educating Able Learners*. Austin: University of Texas Press.

Feldhusen, J. F. (1994). "Leadership Curriculum." In J. VanTassel-Baska (Ed.), *Comprehensive Curriculum for Gifted Learners* (pp. 347–398). Boston: Allyn & Bacon.

Heller, K., Mönks, F., & Passow, A. H. (Eds.). (1993). *International Handbook of Research and Development of Giftedness and Talent*. Oxford: Pergamon Press. A sampling of some of the most effective out-of-school provisions for highly able young people.

Karnes, F. A., & Chauvin, J. C. (1985). *Leadership Skills Inventory*. NY: DOK.

Karnes, F. A., & McGinnis, J. C. (1995, January/February). "Looking for Leadership. Students' Perceptions of Leaders for the Next Millennium." *Gifted Child Today Magazine*, 18 (1), 30–35.

Parnes, S. J. (1985). *A Facilitating Style of Leadership*. NY: Bearly Limited.

Sisk, D. (1993). "Leadership Education for the Gifted." In K. Heller, F. Mönks & A. H. Passow (Eds.), *International Handbook of Research and Development of Giftedness and Talent* (pp. 491–506). Oxford: Pergamon Press.

Sisk, D. A., & Shallcross, D. J. (1986). *Leadership—Making Things Happen*. New York: Bearly Limited.

Special Programs for Gifted Students

The Advanced Academy of Georgia, West Georgia College, Carrolton, Georgia 30118
For highly able juniors and seniors who wish to accelerate their educational program, opportunities are available. For example, students have the opportunity to live and learn with other academically-talented students, are enrolled in regularly-scheduled college classes, and receive the same credit as regular college students.

After School Programs and Summer Programs
College Gifted Programs, 120 Littleton Road, Suite 201, Parsippany, New Jersey 07054
A summer institute for the gifted is a three-week residential co-educational summer program for academically-talented students. The campuses of a number of colleges in New York, New Jersey, Pennsylvania, and Ohio are used.

Curriculum for High Ability Learners, grades K–12
Science, Mathematics and Language Arts, Center for Gifted Education, The College of William and Mary, P.O. Box 8795, Williamsburg, Virginia 23187-8795, 757-221-2362

Program for Exceptionally Gifted, Mary Baldwin College, Staunton, Virginia 24401
PEG is for exceptionally gifted young women who have completed 8th grade or beyond.

Simons Rock College of Bard, 84 Alford Road, Great Barrington, Massachusetts 01230-9702
The College for Younger Scholars is for high school students who are capable of early entrance to college. It is an accredited four-year residential college.

The Texas Academy for Leadership in the Humanities, Lamar University, P.O. Box 10034, Beaumont, Texas 77710
The Texas Academy of Leadership in the Humanities is a two-year residential early admissions program for gifted high school students who are interested in outstanding achievement and advancement in the humanities. Gifted Texas students can complete their last two years of high school and first two years of college concurrently in residence on the Lamar University Campus in Beaumont.

Texas Academy of Math and Science
University of North Texas, Denton, Texas 76203
Available to Texas high school juniors and seniors so that they can simultaneously complete their last two years of high school and first two years of college in an accelerated math and science program.

The University of Washington Transition School and Early Entrance Program, Halbert Robinson Center for the Study of Capable Youth. University of Washington, Box 351630, Seattle, WA 98195-1630. The university offers summer programs for gifted students in Grades 5 through 8. In addition, students with exceptional academic capability who are in junior high or middle school are granted early entrance to the university and have the opportunity for full-time study.

Giftedness combines above-average intelligence, task orientation, motivation, knowledge, and background experience.

Photo by Carole Meyers

Chapter 4
The Identification and Development of Giftedness

Typical questions a classroom teacher might ask:

- How might I provide the background to ensure the development of cognitive processes?
- How might I provide a background that encourages creativity?
- What is the role of background experience in the identification and development of giftedness?
- How might I provide opportunities that allow gifts to flourish?

To answer these questions, this chapter includes:

- The foundations of the Cline Model, including definitions of:
  Intelligence
  Creativity
  Task orientation, motivation
  Knowledge, background, experience
  External environment, opportunity
- The role of cognitive development
- How cognitive development might be stimulated.
- How creativity may be enhanced.
- The role of background experience in children's development
- The role of the environment and of opportunity in students' development

Renzulli (1977) described giftedness in terms of a Venn diagram consisting of "three rings" (above-average ability, creativity, and task commitment) model. In the development of the Model of Human Potential, Cline (1989) elaborated on Renzulli's definition, using current research on key factors in giftedness: multiple intelligences, creativity (internal and external states), task orientation and motivation, knowledge and/or background of experience, and the external environment. Each of these factors is discussed in detail in the following sections.

Intelligence

In this book, intelligence is seen as being dependent upon genetic predisposition and environmental factors. It involves the capacity to think rationally and act purposefully in any given situation. It includes the ability to analyze information previously acquired and to transfer concepts and ideas to new situations. The ability to apply critical and creative thinking skills to all domains is essential to the reasoning process.

Students suffering from lack of intellectual stimulation may not have been fed the appropriate "food for the brain." Diamond (1988) examined the possible impact on brain growth in mice when they were provided with stimulation. Kuhl (Blakeslee, 1997) studied human brain development from infancy as the result of human interaction. After birth, environmental factors predominated. Children who had the greatest exposure to the spoken language scored highest on standardized tests. Proponents of "culture-fair" IQ tests understand that children from ghetto environments or other cultures may not be able to work up to their potential.

Teachers cannot assume that students entering their classrooms have had the opportunity to develop their thinking skills. Some may never have had the benefit of metacognitive stimulation. Students need to be taught critical and creative thinking skills and must be exposed to skills involved in each of Gardner's (1983) domains of intelligence, so that gifts can surface in one or more domains. For some students, specific proclivities may not be as evident in any particular area, but their giftedness may become apparent in the quality of their responses, for example, the use of complex thought processes and speed in learning.

Teaching Cognitive Skills

Thinking processes are tied to cognitive development. Piaget (Pulaski, 1980) and Fischer (1985) have described stages of cognitive development. In his hundreds of observations of infant development, Piaget formulated his genetic theory of knowledge. He postulated that stages of development evolve in a broad continuous sequence, each one arising from the one that has come before. The behaviors observed provide milestones in cognitive development. From birth to 18 months Piaget describes the child in terms of the sensory-motor period of development. The thinking of the preschool child is egocentric and limited to experience. He works his way toward ideas that Piaget calls semi-logical. The period between two and a half and six or seven is referred to as preoperational; operations implies logical necessity— information that is logical and self-evident to the knower. During his sixth and seventh year the child is able to formulate true operations. He can operate using concrete examples. The period from seven to eleven or twelve is called concrete operations. Each level lays a foundation for the next. The last period is known as formal operations. The child can now think about ideas as well as concrete things. The form of reasoning can be followed while ignoring content.

Intelligence Can Be Taught. Costa (1981, 1984a, 1984b, 1985), Feuerstein,

(1979,1980), Feuerstein, Hoffman, Egozi, and Schachar-Segeu (1994), and Vygotsky (1978) are some of the key proponents of the importance of providing appropriate mediating interactions with students in the classroom to assess levels of ability and to improve thinking. According to Costa (1984b), gifted students are often overlooked because they do poorly under testing conditions. Many teachers are unimpressed with standardized tests (Harootunian & Yarger, 1981; Lazer-Morrison et al., 1980). Test performance is influenced by the degree to which the students have been introduced to the subject matter. Scores do not yield any information on how the student arrived at the answer (metacognition) or the emotional state of the student at the time the test was being taken. Many students are deemed gifted simply because they are "test wise."

Fischer (1988) has delineated six stages of cognitive development, from infancy to adulthood (see Table 4-1). One way to assess potential giftedness is to identify students who are functioning at more advanced stages at a younger age.

As teachers observe the way students interact with curriculum that requires higher levels of cognitive development, they can identify "gifted thinkers"—those children who are performing at advanced levels early on. In order to recognize precocious thinkers, they may need to be introduced to concepts that require high-level thought processes.

The Role of the Zone of Proximal Development and Mediated Learning. The works of Vygotsky (1978), Cole, John-Steiner, Scribner, & Souberman (1978) and Feuerstein (1979) have also helped to refine existing definitions of intelligence. These theorists provide insight into how children learn and the need to match and "mediate" learning experiences. In his theory of mediated learning and the Zone of Proximal Development, Vygotsky (1978) was scornful of "pedology" (problems of education or educational psychology) that emphasized tests of intellectual ability patterned after the IQ tests that were gaining prominence in the United States and Western Europe. It was his ambition to reform pedology. He believed that in order to study developmental processes, opportunities had to be provided for subjects to be engaged in a variety of activities that could be observed, not rigidly controlled. Vygotsky sought to reconstruct the series of changes that occur in intellectual development. He sought to discover the rudimentary beginnings of new skills. He proposed that higher mental processes were the result of mediated activity. He saw historical and cultural differences as integral to the socialization and enculturation processes that affect intelligence (John-Steiner, 1985). He outlined three classes of mediators: material tools, psychological tools, and other human beings.

Vygotsky takes issue with Piaget and his theories about the relationship between learning and development and the specific features of this relationship when children reach school age. He believed that learning should be in advance of the child's developmental level. Two developmental levels must be established. The first level is called the actual developmental level. This is the level of development that has been established as a result of already completed developmental cycles. Mental age is typically established through testing the extent of mental development on the basis of the difficulty of problems children can solve alone. If, however, leading questions are offered

Table 4-1. Fischer's (1988) Stages of Cognitive Development*		
Level	**Age of Emergence**	**Examples of Skills**
R1:	18–24 months	Coordination of action systems produce concrete representations of actions, objects, or agents: Pretending that a doll is walking. Saying, "Mommy eat toast."
R2:	3,5–4,5 years	Relations of concrete representations: Pretending that two dolls are Mommy and Daddy interacting. Understanding that self knows a secret and Daddy does not know it.
R3: Representational Systems (also called Concrete Operations)	6–7 years	Complex relations of subsets of concrete representations: Pretending that two dolls are both Mommy and Daddy as well as a doctor and a teacher simultaneously. Understanding that when water is poured from one glass to another, the amount of water stays the same.
R4/A1: Single Abstractions (also called Formal Operations)	10–12 years	Coordination of concrete representational systems to produce general intangible concepts: Concept of operation of addition. Evaluating how one's parents' behavior demonstrates conformity. Concept of honesty as a general quality of an interaction.
A2: Abstract Mappings	14–16 years	Relations of intangible concepts: Understanding that operations of addition and subtraction are opposites. Integrating two concepts, such as honesty and kindness, in the idea of a social lie.
A3: Abstract Systems	18–20 years	Complex relations of subsets of intangible concepts: Understanding the operations of addition and division are related through how numbers are grouped and how they are combined. Integrating several types of honesty and kindness in the idea of constructive criticism.
A4: † Principles	25 years?	General principles for integrating systems of intangible concepts: Moral principle of justice. Knowledge principle of reflective judgment. Scientific principle of evolution by natural selection.

* Printed by permission. Fischer, K.W. (1988, May-June). Cognitive development in real children: Levels and variations: Teaching Thinking and Problem Solving. (10)3, 1–4.

† This level is hypothesized, but to date there are too few data to test its existence unequivocally.

Note: Ages given are modal ages at which a level first appears based on research with middle-class American or European children. They may differ across cultures and other social groups.

on how the problem can be solved and the child solves it, the solution is not regarded as indicative of that child's mental development. The notion that children can solve even higher levels of problems with some help and that this might be, in some sense, even more indicative of their mental potential than what they could do alone, was not previously considered. For example, a child might be assessed as being able to handle problems without any assistance, on an eight-year-old level. However, if the child was exposed to various ways of dealing with a problem (e.g., running through an entire demonstration and asking the child to repeat it, or initiating a solution and asking the child to complete it, or offering leading questions), the child might be able to solve problems at the level of a twelve-year-old. The difference between twelve and eight is what Vygotsky referred to as the zone of proximal development. "It is the distance between the actual development level as determined by independent problem solving and the level of potential development as determined through problem solving under adult guidance or in collaboration with more capable peers" (Cole et al., 1978, p. 86). The zone of proximal development defines functions that have not yet matured but are in the process of maturation. The actual developmental level characterizes mental development that has already occurred, while the zone of proximal development characterizes prospective development. Children can imitate a variety of actions that go well beyond the limits of their capabilities. Learning that is oriented toward developmental levels already reached is ineffective from the viewpoint of a child's overall development. Establishing a zone of proximal development provides for learning that is in advance of the current stage of development. An essential feature of learning is that it creates the zone of proximal development. It awakens a variety of internal developmental processes that are able to operate only when children are interacting with people in their environment and in cooperation with their peers. Once internalized, they become part of the individual's independent developmental achievement. Properly organized, learning results in mental development. It can set in motion a variety of developmental processes that would be impossible apart from learning. Learning is a necessary element in the development of psychological functions. Developmental processes do not coincide with learning processes but lag behind the learning process. When a child masters an operation, such as addition, developmental processes are not completed; in fact, they have just begun. The former learning provides the basis for the subsequent development of a variety of complex internal processes in thinking. Even though learning is directly related to the course of development, the two are never accomplished in equal measure. Each school subject has its own specific relationship to the course of child development that varies as children move from one stage to another.

Simply put, as a teacher introduces concepts unknown to the child, the teacher can determine which tasks can be performed with assistance. This is the level of potential development. To promote cognitive development, teachers should present classroom tasks and assignments that can be performed successfully with assistance so as to establish a student's potential.

Mediated Learning—Instrumental Enrichment Can Increase Intelligence. Reuben Feuerstein, an eminent cognitive psychologist, studied in Geneva under the direction of Andre Rey and Jean Piaget. He was greatly influenced by Piaget and expanded on Vygotsky's concepts to develop his approach to the mediated learning experience (Presseisen & Kozulin, 1994).

> The approach of mediated learning suggests a new paradigm for education, one in which intelligence itself is redefined and conceived. What is intelligence, asks Feuerstein? The ability to learn and change. Intelligence is now much more broadly understood than a narrow, static I.Q. test presumes. In fact, according to current researchers (Detterman & Sternberg, 1982; Diamond, 1988), reflective, intelligent

behavior can actually be enhanced. Understanding the work of Vygotsky and Feuerstein is to begin to discover what the new educational paradigm is all about. (Presseisen & Kozulin, 1994, p. 57)

Feuerstein's (1979) theory of instrumental enrichment has three components:

1. Structural Cognitive Modifiability
   Human beings can "change or modify the structure of their cognitive functioning in order to adapt to changing demands of life situations" (p. 11). They can be considered cognitive structural changes when they are self-perpetuating and autonomous. Human beings are open systems and can continue to change throughout their lives.
2. Mediated Learning Experiences
   Structural changes in human cognition can occur through the mediated learning experience. Mediated learning experiences can assist learners in mediating behavior and in building competence.
3. Learning Potential
   Feuerstein assesses human potential in terms of how much a person has the potential to learn rather than how much a person knows.

According to Feuerstein, mediated learning is defined by experiences that influence the individual's ability to learn. The central aspect of his theory is that change qualitatively affects learners and enables them to develop the prerequisite skills to learn on their own. Different learners have different capacities to learn from the mediated experience. Feuerstein conducted extensive research on cognitive mediation and practice (see Feuerstein, Hoffman, Egozi, & Shachar-Segev, 1994). Through his work with culturally deprived, retarded, and autistic children, he established the principle that all children's intelligence can be increased. He developed a classroom curriculum designed to build the cognitive functions of students diagnosed by others as incapable of learning. His program, Instrumental Enrichment, provides students with the concepts, skills, strategies, operations, and techniques necessary to become independent thinkers (Feuerstein, 1979).

> The formulation of "insufficient mediated learning experience" postulates that cognitive impairments emerge not necessarily nor directly because of poor genetic endowment or organic deficiencies. They result instead from the absence, paucity, or ineffectiveness of the adult-child interactions that produce in the child an enhanced capacity to become modified, that is to learn. (Feuerstein, 1979, p. 70)

Mediated learning does not rely on chance encounters between the individual and environmental stimulation. In mediated learning, adults plan for a successful mediation of the experience using techniques such as orienting, framing, summation, repetition, comparison, selection, and labeling. As examiners, they take an active role in assuring the success of the examinees. They discuss, summarize, and alert students to possible pitfalls. They create an atmosphere in which the examinees can feel challenged but are capable of completing the task. Feuerstein (1979) defines intelligence "as the capacity of an individual to use previously acquired experiences to adjust to new situations" (p. 76). His model, the Learning Potential Assessment Device (LPAD), provides a model upon which a variety of assessment tools can be constructed. When presented with a problem, the elementary functions that serve as prerequisites for cognitive process are mediated. Once mastery is achieved, more complex operations are presented. Metacognitive strategies become an important part of the program.

Feuerstein's work helps us to understand that not all children come to school with the same background of experience. Mediated learning can mine the ore within each child, revealing potential gifts. Vygotsky provides us with additional insight into gifted potential in terms of children who start out ahead of their peers and who, with assistance, show themselves to be capable of an even higher level of understanding.

How to Teach and Model Thinking in the Classroom

Teaching critical and creative thinking skills in the classroom provides students with a background that prepares them to perform complex mental tasks. As teachers involve students in higher-level complex operations, the gifted child begins to surface. Not all of the strategies or skills will be used at once. Teachers can begin to experiment with and incorporate ideas promoted by different theorists and begin to internalize the strategies into their repertoire.

Defining Thinking Skills and Thinking Strategies. The word skill connotes a specific cognitive operation, such as inferring, comparing, contrasting, analyzing, etc. When processes become complex and require more than one operation, they are often referred to as strategies or heuristics. A thinking skill involves one kind of thinking, whereas a thinking strategy involves using several thinking skills in a particular sequence. Heuristic teaching encourages students to discover answers on their own.

Seiger (1984) discusses the difference between a thinker and a thinking strategist and outlines the thinking strategists' responses to problem-solving situations. Their responses, which should be articulated and discussed as problems are being solved, include:

- Establishing the following in advance:
  The kind of thinking that will be required
  What to focus the thinking on
  The qualities the resultant ideas should have
- Considering alternative ways to do the thinking and choosing the procedure that is most appropriate or efficient for the task at hand
- Using the planned procedure effectively to produce the ideas
- Critiquing the resultant ideas (own and others') by applying the criteria established in advance.

Thinking skills need to be addressed as strategies are developed. As students learn thinking skills, they can combine skills into strategies.

Presented below are Bloom's (1956) and Taba's (1966) conceptualizations of thinking skills, both of which have contributed heavily to the Cline Model.

How to Use Bloom's Taxonomy to Develop Thinking Skills. Benjamin Bloom (1956) developed a hierarchy of thinking levels that can serve as an excellent guide to developing cognitive skills. It raises the level of thinking for students and helps teachers to identify those students who can, and who enjoy, thinking that is challenging. It creates an awareness of skills involved in higher-level thought processes. Teachers may use Bloom's Taxonomy to assist them in designing lessons and tests. The Taxonomy can also be used in evaluating materials currently in use. Teachers can integrate higher-level thinking skills into existing materials when necessary. Bloom has divided thinking into six cognitive levels:

1. Knowledge—This level involves recalling material that has been previously learned. It represents the lowest level of thinking and does not require any interpretation of facts. Words used by teachers in written and verbal assignments at this level would include:

recall	underline	list
recite	tell	recount
say	observe	memorize
select	repeat	

The student might be responsible for answering a question or completing an assignment in a workbook that required underlining, circling, or labeling.

Sample activities: Locate the capitals in each of these states.
Group together all of the words that have four syllables.
List the first five presidents of the United States.

2. Comprehension—Comprehension involves translating material learned into another form so that a level of understanding is communicated. Students are asked to:

define	restate	paraphrase
explain	describe	summarize

Students would be expected to give examples, paraphrase, predict, or communicate an idea in a different form.

Sample activities: Give reasons for the current cutting back of expenditures in health care.
Explain why we have rules that should be followed in our classroom.
Outline the steps necessary before an idea becomes a law.
Interpret the graph that indicates that the price of gasoline has risen.

3. Application—This refers to the ability to use the knowledge learned in new and concrete situations that demonstrate understanding of:

rules	concepts	laws
methods	principles	theories

Application requires a higher level of understanding than comprehension. Questions and statements would include words such as:

relate	exercise	apply
solve	organize	put to use

Students would use knowledge learned and might put the information in a graph form. They would be asked to apply ideas to a new situation or be asked to conduct experiments.

Sample activities: How does the principle of estimation help you in your private life?

Compare and contrast attitudes toward women in the work force today with the attitudes of thirty years ago.

After reading about people who have been accepted into the Hall of Fame, explain why you would nominate a particular individual.

After conducting the experiment outlined in the assignment, design a new one to test the hypothesis once more.

4. Analysis—This refers to the ability to break down information learned into its component parts so that the structure of the materials learned is understood. It may include an analysis of relationships or recognition of organizational structure and requires understanding beyond comprehension and application. Students would be asked to:

distinguish	refute	compare
question	analyze	contrast
interpret	examine	
conclude	scrutinize	

Students would be required to analyze a given situation and interpret it.

Sample activities: Select a number of books and place them in categories according to their genre.

Read the works of one author and decide if there is a theme running through the works.

After reading the news every day for a week, determine what the most pressing issues for legislators are today and explain.

5. Synthesis—Once a level of understanding on the analysis level has been accomplished, synthesis becomes possible. This requires that parts be put together to form a new whole. Synthesis emphasizes creative behaviors and may exhibit itself in a unique type of communication or a new product. Assignments that require synthesis would include words such as:

compose	plan	design
construct	invent	originate
generate	formulate	produce

Students would be asked to design or compose an original work based on prior knowledge.

Sample activities: After studying a particular topic, design a game that includes important content to be learned.

Read a story and communicate it in another way.

Identify a problem area in the room and come up with a solution.

Develop a theme for our class for our year-end production.

6. Evaluation—Evaluation involves judgement. The value of the poem, statement, theorem, research must be evaluated based on clearly-defined criteria. Learning on this level subsumes all of the others. Words that would be included in lessons for evaluation would include:

appraise	rate	persuade
evaluate	decide	judge
justify	criticize	

Students might judge the value of a work of art, a piece of music, or the effectiveness of a former president.

Sample activities: Design a list of criteria that should be used to evaluate someone's independent study.

How would you determine how to judge posters for a poster contest?

What are the qualities you would admire in a principal?

Justify President Truman's decision to use the atomic bomb.

How to Use Taba's Thinking Strategies. Taba (1966) has developed a method of instruction that requires that students process information, develop concepts, and formulate generalizations for themselves. When put to use and integrated into lessons, it provides an opportunity to raise the level of complexity for students. The steps involved in Taba's strategies include concept development, interpretation of data, application of generalizations, and resolution of conflict.

During *concept development*, concepts are formed, clarified, and extended as the teacher asks open-ended questions that encourage students to identify and name relationships among data and to organize and reorganize the data. Taba (1966, p. 39) summarizes concept formation as presented in Table 4-2.

In interpretation of data, students respond to questions that require that they draw inferences that they can support. What are the cause-effect relationships? What conclusion can be drawn so that generalizations can evolve?

Table 4-2. Concept Formation.

Overt Activity	Covert Mental Operation	Eliciting Questions
1. Enumeration, listing	Differentiation	What did you see? Hear? Note?
2. Grouping	Identifying common properties, abstracting	What belongs together? On what criterion?
3. Labeling, categorizing	Determining the hierarchical order of items. Super- and subordination	What would you call these groups? What belongs under what?

Taba's (1966) summary of inferring and generalizing is presented in Table 4-3. The essence of applying generalizations involves having students predict the future as it relates to situations that they are familiar with. Predictions must be supported by data. See Taba's (1966) summary in Table 4-4.

Resolution of conflict emphasizes the complexity of various conflict situations. Attitudes, values, and feelings are interpreted. Alternative solutions are explored.

Taba (1966) found that "Generally speaking, the use of specific teaching strategies designed to foster development of cognitive skills seemed to make a difference in

Table 4-3. Inferring and Generalizing.

Overt Activity	Covert Mental Operation	Eliciting Questions
1. Identifying points	Differentiating; distinguishing relevant information from irrelevant	What did you note? See? Find?
2. Explaining identified items of information	Relating points to each other; establishing cause-and-effect relationships	Why did so-and-so happen? Why is so-and-so true?
3. Making inferences or generalizations	Going beyond what is given; finding implications, extrapolating	What does this mean? What would you conclude? What generalizations can you make?

Table 4-4. Application of Principles

Overt Activity	Covert Mental Operation	Eliciting Questions
1. Predicting consequences, explaining unfamiliar phenomena, hypothesizing	Analyzing the nature and the dimensions and the problem of of condition	What would happen if . . . ?
2. Explaining and supporting the predictions and hypotheses	Determining the causal links leading to a prediction or hypothesis	When do you think this would happen?
3. Verifying the predictions and hypotheses	Using logical reasoning to determine the necessary conditions and the degree of universality of the prediction of hypothesis	What would it take for so-and-so to be true? Would it be true in all cases? At what times? Etc.

the general productivity of thought as well as in the type of cognitive operations in which students engaged" (p. 222).

How to Develop and Use Critical Thinking Skills

Although, we cannot make assumptions that students come to us with a background in thinking skills, having such a background allows them to think critically. According to Ennis (1986), "Critical thinking is not equivalent to the higher order thinking skills, in part because that idea is so vague. However, critical thinking, a practical activity, includes most or all of the directly practical higher-order thinking skills. Furthermore critical thinking includes dispositions, which would not be included in a listing of skills. (p. 10) . . . Critical thinking is reasonable reflective thinking that is focused on deciding what to believe or do" (p. 12). Critical thinking involves:

- Taking the whole problem into account.
- Looking for alternatives and being open minded.
- Being able to focus on a question and analyze an argument.
- Asking questions and judging the credibility of sources.
- Observing and corroborating.
- Using deductive and inductive reasoning as one investigates.
- Making value judgements.
- Planning strategies.
- Identifying assumptions.
- Deciding upon plans of actions

In the following section, some approaches to the teaching of critical thinking are presented and discussed.

How to Bring Socrates into the Classroom. The Socratic method searches for hidden assumptions or hypotheses. Socratic questioning leads to further questions and can be unnerving and upsetting. Goldman (1984) believes that Socratic questioning is inappropriate for classroom use because it teaches children to question adult authority before they have the necessary experience. When students have a background in thinking skills, Socratic questioning can enhance their repertoire.

Paul (1984) disagrees with Goldman. He believes that there are many versions of the Socratic method and suggests using questions such as:

- Why?
- If that is so, what follows?
- Aren't you assuming that____?
- How do you know that?
- Is the point that you are making that____?
- What is your reason for saying that?
- What do you mean when using this word?
- Is it possible that____?

- Are there other ways of looking at it?
- How else could we view this matter? (p. 63)

It is this author's contention that students, especially those deemed gifted, need to be introduced to the Socratic method. When integrated into content and classroom discussions, this technique can be extremely helpful in assisting students to think critically, to examine their thought processes, and to begin to use metacognitive strategies.

How to Use Inquiry Training. Students need to be encouraged to question as they learn to think critically.

> Inquiry Training begins with a puzzling event. Suchman believes that individuals, faced with a puzzling situation, are motivated to pursue meaning in it. They naturally seek to understand what they encounter. In order to understand puzzling situations, they must increase the complexity of their thinking and understand better how to link data into concepts and how to apply those concepts toward the identification of principles of causation. Thus, the underlying assumption of the model is that individuals, when puzzled, need to explore the data surrounding the puzzlement and put these data together in new ways. They inquire and as they inquire, they reorganize their knowledge. (Weil & Joyce, 1976, p. 111)

After the presentation of a puzzling situation, the students proceed to ask questions. The teacher structures the situation so that questions may be answered either "yes" or "no." If questions are asked that cannot be responded to in this manner, the teacher requests that the student rephrase the question. The teacher can make new information available as the inquiry continues. The primary role of the teacher is to keep the inquiry directed toward the process of investigation itself.

How to Use Inductive and Deductive Reasoning. Students need to be introduced to both deductive and inductive reasoning skills. "A deductive argument is one which is necessarily valid given the premises. In contrast, an inductive argument entails an element of novelty within the conclusion and is thus open to varying amounts of uncertainty" (Wagner & Penner, 1984, p. 189). In a deductive argument, the conclusion is contained in the information given. In an inductive argument, the conclusion contains more information than was given in the premises. The inductive argument involves observing and, based on observations of facts or circumstances available at the time, drawing a logical conclusion. The analogy between deductive reasoning and detective work can be drawn. A detective examines all available clues and, based on the evidence, draws a conclusion. An inductive argument involves gathering additional and/or new data to draw a conclusion.

As students master thinking skills, they can add sophistication to their thought processes by combining skills to design a repertoire of strategies. Developing thinking strategies assists in problem solving.

How to Emphasize
Thinking Strategies (Heuristics)

Instruction in the use of thinking strategies and developing a repertoire of such strategies is basic for all students. Scruggs, Mastropieri, Monson, and Jorgensen (1985) found that both gifted and nongifted students benefited from strategy instruction, but the gifted benefited to a greater degree and were able to transfer the strategy successfully to another content area. They concluded that specific strategy instruction is essential to maximize learning for the gifted. When all students have the benefit of such instruction, the gifted can be identified through the curriculum rather than through an isolated "process" of testing. As Perkins (1995, p. 91) states, "We can help people to behave more intelligently, even retarded people, by expanding their strategic repertoires and nurturing their knowledge and attitudes about thinking and learning." Jonathan Baron previously examined the relationship between strategies and intelligence. Retarded children performed almost as well as normal children when strategies were taught. Intelligent behavior is more the result of a strategic repertoire than an IQ score. Nisbet (1993) found that students showed appreciable benefits when reasoning was taught and then tested.

The teaching of heuristics involves the teaching of strategies that can be used to solve problems. Heuristic teaching encourages students to discover the answers for themselves. Many of the skills traditionally taught to students involve following set procedures to arrive at the right answer. Heuristics, on the other hand, involves techniques for the process of problem solving and is not necessarily concerned with arriving at the correct answer. Polya (1945) believed that problem solving involved a grain of discovery in every solution, that could challenge curiosity and "leave an imprint on mind and character for a lifetime" (p. v). He also believed that teachers who taught heuristics and integrated questioning strategies into the curriculum could lead students in the act of discovery which helped to play an important role in mathematical problem solving. Problem solving is a practical skill seen by Polya as being acquired by imitation and practice. The four phases in trying to find a solution to a problem include: understanding the problem, devising a plan, carrying out the plan, and checking.

Once the problem is understood, suggestions for the second phase, devising a plan, include answering the following questions:

- Can you relate it to another problem?
- Can you think of a familiar problem with a similar unknown?
- If you cannot solve it, can you try to solve a related problem?
- Did you use all your data?

The third step is carrying out the plan.

- Check each step.
- Can you prove it is correct?

The fourth step is checking.

- Examine the solution obtained.
- Can you check your argument?
- Can you use the result for another problem?

Lenchner (1983) has generated a list of strategies for students interested in improving their problem-solving ability in mathematics. These strategies are used to help train students for the Math Olympiad, an international problem-solving competition that engages young mathematicians. The training and strategies should be taught to all students because it is only after students are introduced to the skills that giftedness has the opportunity to surface. Lenchner's list of strategies includes:

- Draw a picture or diagram
- Find a pattern
- Make an organized list
- Make a table
- Solve a simpler problem
- Trial and error
- Experiment
- Act out the problem
- Work backwards
- Write an equation
- Use deduction
- Change your point of view

Creativity

Creativity is like murder; both depend on motive, means and opportunity (Johnson-Laird, 1988, p. 208).

The crux of the problem of defining creativity may lie in our seeming inability to separate the individual from the process, and the process from its application; that is, do we define creativity as the "things" one does, or as the ability to do them given the right conditions and circumstances, an ability that cannot be determined until the behavior is exhibited? (Haensly & Reynolds, 1989, p. 117)

Numerous theories about creativity and the creative process have emerged through the years:

- Freud believed that creative energy is sublimated sexual energy.
- Wallas believed that the creative process involved:
  Preparation (information gathering)
  Incubation (unconscious mental work)

Illumination (the solution emerges)
Verification or revision (the solution is tested and evaluated)

- Rogers believed creativity to be the result of self-actualization and was one of the humanistic theorists who recognized mental health as the source of creativity.
- Galton believed creativity had a genetic basis.
- Guilford and Merrifield saw creativity as a composite of personality traits that capitalize on four creative thinking abilities—fluency, flexibility, originality, and elaboration.
- Jung recognized the unconscious as a source of creative thinking.
- Arieti linked creativity to the religious and mystical.
- Gowan proposed a developmental stage theory of creativity.

Others, such as Mozart, believed that ideas flourished when one was in a relaxed state:

> When I am, as it were, completely by myself, entirely alone, and of good cheer—say traveling in carriage, or walking after a good meal, or during the night when I cannot sleep; it is on such occasions that my ideas flow best and most abundantly. Whence and how they come, I know not; nor can I force them. (as cited in Vernon, 1970, p. 55)

Gardner (1993b) proposes that creativity is an interactive process combining three elements:

- Individual talent
- Domain/Discipline
- Field (judges, institutions)

When one assesses a creative product or performance, its value is measured by its uniqueness and its contribution to society. The creative product is the result of the ability to translate one's background of knowledge, synthesizing it in such a way that a creative product is judged to have emerged. It is generally agreed that creative products possess a degree of novelty and are deemed valuable to society at a given time (Amabile, 1983; Gardner, 1983, 1993; Tannenbaum, 1983).

Creativity can be viewed on a continuum that ranges from making individual creative connections in personal thinking, to creative ideas that have an impact on others and then extend to an entire field or society. At any of the points on the continuum, going from personal to societal creativity, multiple factors in the content or domain involved and thinking processes combine as the creative thought or product emerges. We see the product, but the process is not always as obvious or easily understood.

Clark and Zimmerman's (1992) demonstration acknowledges the different traits (such as spontaneous, expressive, able to integrate, self-accepting, and capacity to be puzzled) demonstrated by creative individuals. Mackinnon (1978) found that an unusually high IQ did not necessarily predict creative achievement later on in life. The creative student is not always valued in the classroom. Getzels and Jackson (1962) in their research found that creative students demonstrated superiority in scholastic achievement although they were not in the top of the class in IQ. These students were sometimes labeled "overachievers." Teachers preferred the high IQ students as opposed to the highly creative.

The Need to Stress Creativity in the Classroom

The classroom needs to be a place in which students are provided with opportunities to develop and demonstrate their creative abilities. Research on the creative individual, creative processes, and contexts that promote creative behaviors needs to be translated into classroom practices. According to Tannenbaum (1983, p. 326), "However we define the concept [creativity] one fact seems clear: there is little stress on cultivating it either in or out of school." And Baron and Sternberg (1987, p. 96) state that:

> Creative potential is not identified systematically and nurtured responsibly. This failure begins in the school system in the elementary grades, and it continues right through the undergraduate years in most colleges. Not until graduate school is there any explicit crediting of creativity as an important qualification for admission to training in independent intellectual work and social leadership.

We cannot foresee who will make creative contributions to society, but we can provide the atmosphere and skills that can assist individuals in their creative endeavors.

The Ebb and Flow of Creativity

Torrance (1967) noted that children had an increased tendency to consult with peers in the fourth grade that was accompanied by a creative "slump." According to Torrance (1964), creativity undergoes stages of maturation and growth during childhood, citing evidence that creativity in the United States:

- Reaches one peak at about age four and a half
- Drops at age five when children enter kindergarten
- Grows steadily through the first three grades
- Declines sharply in the fourth grade
- Recovers, particularly among girls, in the fifth and sixth grades
- Drops again at the end of elementary school on into junior high

How Teachers Can Influence the Social-Psychological Conditions Associated with Creativity

Amabile (1983) uncovered the following social-psychological conditions that should be avoided if creativity is to be maintained.

- Restriction of choice, which can undermine creativity
- Reward or coercion, which is often detrimental
- Evaluation by external sources (Poor or inadequate evaluation, even if it is positive, can also lead to decreases.)
- Peer pressure or pressure to conform, which can lead to temporary decreases in creativity
- Surveillance or monitoring by others while engaging in creativity

The motivation to be creative emanates from real interest, enjoyment, satisfaction, challenge, and intrinsic involvement. Factors that positively influence creativity include encouraging children to take risks, to explore and develop intrinsic motivation toward their work. When internal needs are satisfied, creativity is enhanced. A high degree of choice in task engagement is also beneficial to creativity.

Chambers (1973) asked creative psychologists and chemists to describe teachers who influenced creative development. The characteristics of the most facilitative teachers and the most inhibitory teachers are listed below in order of importance:

Teachers Who Encouraged Creativity:
- Encouraged students to be independent
- Served as models
- Spent considerable amount of time with students outside of class
- Indicated that excellence was expected and could be achieved
- Were enthusiastic
- Accepted students as equals
- Directly rewarded students' creative behavior or work
- Were interesting, dynamic lecturers
- Were excellent on a one-to-one basis
- Treated students as individuals

Teachers Who Inhibited Creativity:
- Discouraged students' ideas and creativity
- Were insecure
- Were hypercritical
- Were sarcastic
- Were unenthusiastic
- Emphasized rote learning
- Were dogmatic and rigid
- Did not keep up with the field
- Were generally incompetent
- Had narrow interests

- Made themselves unavailable outside the classroom

The classroom becomes a place where creative behaviors can either be observed and nurtured or stifled. Classroom teachers can further enhance and develop creativity in the classroom by:

- De-emphasizing rote learning
- Exposing students to higher-level thought processes and questioning strategies
- Integrating creative thinking exercises into all aspects of the curriculum
- Helping students to recognize similarities and differences

Using these approaches creates an atmosphere where unorthodox ideas are accepted, norms are questioned, and creative ideas can emerge.

How to Link Creative Instruction to Classroom Curriculum—Divergent Thinking

Time should be spent in the classroom on developing divergent thinking. Students can improve their abilities when trained (Pyryt, 1997). In *The Nature of Human Intelligence*, Guilford (1967) defines divergent thinking as "the generation of information from given information where the emphasis is upon variety and quantity of output from the same source; likely to involve transfer" (p. 213).

Guilford hypothesizes that four thinking abilities associated with creativity involve divergent thinking: fluency, flexibility, originality, and elaboration.

Fluency. Fluency is the ability to produce as many ideas as possible. All divergent production assessment involves fluency.

Ideational fluency (divergent semantic units) denotes the ability to generate quantities of ideas, as seen in brainstorming activities used in problem-solving situations. Sample activity: Provide students with an object that is familiar or not easily identifiable. Ask them to list as many uses for the object as possible, refraining from judgment.

Associational fluency (divergent semantic relations) refers to the ability to produce meaningful associations to a given idea. Sample activity: Write a number on the board, say, 7. Ask students to find as many combinations of numbers that would add up to 7 that they can think of.

Expressional fluency (divergent semantic systems) refers to the skills involved in juxtaposing limited elements to create as many combinations as possible. Sample activity: Write a scrambled sentence on the board and have children unscramble it to make as many sentences as possible.

Flexibility. Flexibility is the ability to change and/or adapt an idea. It is the skill involved in the ability to change the direction of one's thinking.

Spontaneous flexibility (divergent semantic classes) involves changing direction in thinking when not instructed in any particular way about what to do. Sample activity: Have students classify objects present in the room.

Adaptive flexibility (divergent figural transformation) involves a change in thinking with figural content. Sample activity: Present students with a scribble on a piece of paper. Have them create a picture incorporating the scribble.

Originality. Originality (divergent semantic transformations) involves the ability to produce an unusual, one-of-a-kind response, idea, or product. It involves ideation of products that are unusual, offbeat, or unexpected. Sample activity: Ask students to read a news story and create a headline. Invent a different _____. Think of a new way to _____. Create a new _____.

Elaboration. Elaboration (divergent semantic implications) is the ability to improve upon, perfect, or embellish an idea or a product. It requires that one fill in the details to complete outlined activities. How might you expand, predict, pretend, describe or project _____. Sample activity: You are in charge of planning an end-of-year activity for the class. Describe the activity. Include information about where it will take place, whether food will be served, and games will be played. List all the steps you would take to ensure its success.

How to Incorporate Classroom Strategies That Enhance the Creative Process

There are a variety of strategies that can be integrated into classroom use. When assessing whether an approach stimulates creativity, the following might be investigated:

- Does the approach encourage curiosity?
- Does it include divergent aspects of thinking?
- Does it have a component that is open-ended?
- Does it allow students to take safe risks?
- Does it allow students to use their imagination?
- Can complexity of thinking be recognized?

Brainstorming. Alex Osborn, founder of a large advertising agency, coined the term "brainstorming" in his book *Applied Imagination* (1953), in which he describes the rules that govern brainstorming sessions. Pyryt (1997), in his meta-analysis, found that brainstorming increased creative production.

(1) Criticism is ruled out. Adverse judgement of ideas must be withheld until later.
(2) "Free-wheeling" is welcomed. The wilder the idea, the better; it is easier to tame down than to think up.
(3) Quantity is desirable. The greater the number of ideas, the more the likelihood of useful ideas.
(4) Combination and improvement are sought. In addition to contributing ideas of their own, participants should suggest how ideas

of others can be turned into better ideas; or how two more ideas can be joined into still another idea. (p. 156)

Brainstorming can be used in every aspect of curriculum development and classroom management. For students, situations in the classroom can be viewed in terms of: How Might We _____

Determine what rules we need in the room?
Determine what activities we might use to culminate a unit?
Establish ways that students can evaluate their own work?

After students brainstorm possibilities, they learn to converge and select the best ideas.

Eberle (1971) incorporated Osborn's brainstorming devices into a very useful mnemonic device called SCAMPER. After brainstorming sessions, individuals review their list of ideas with SCAMPER in mind.

S	Substitute
C	Combine
A	Adjust
M	Magnify
	Minify
	Modify
P	Put to Other Uses
E	Eliminate
	Elaborate
R	Reverse
	Rearrange

Using such techniques helps to create a nonjudgmental atmosphere for developing and encouraging fluent, flexible, elaborative, and original thinking.

Talents Unlimited. Talents Unlimited is a program based on the work of Taylor (1967) and Guilford (1964). It is designed to assist teachers to identify and nurture youngsters' talents in productive thinking, forecasting, communicating, planning, decision making, and academics. The program emphasizes incorporating the divergent thinking activities presented below into classroom curriculum:

• Productive Thinking
• Forecasting
• Communication
• Planning
• Decision Making

Schlichter (1993) describes how to integrate such skills into all areas of the curriculum. For example:

• To stimulate productive thinking in a mathematics unit, students are asked to think of unusual topics to be used in a survey and a graph.

- As students make decisions about which books to order, they generate a list of alternative criteria.
- As a part of a science unit plan, learners design experiments to answer questions already generated.
- Students conducting a poll are encouraged to forecast and generate predictions about the number of individuals responding to the poll.
- Children studying the American Revolution describe the different emotions they believe would be experienced by the colonists.
- To develop academic concepts, students gather information from a number of resources about a period of art and discuss ideas as they relate to a particular painting.

Creative Problem Solving. Problem-finding and problem-solving abilities are markers of gifted behavior. When students have the opportunity to address challenges in the classroom, problem-solving strategies that can be incorporated into classroom instruction include:

- Fact Finding—Investigating a problem situation to determine what caused the problem, who is involved, where it happened, why it happened, and when it happened.
- Problem Finding—When the facts are accumulated, it usually becomes evident that the problem consists of many sub-problems. One issue is addressed and a problem statement written: How Might I _____?
- Idea Finding—Brainstorming is highlighted and solutions are sought.
- Solution Finding—Ideas are examined. Criteria are established to ascertain which ideas are best.
- Acceptance Finding—A plan of action is developed and includes acknowledgement of positive and negative forces involved in implementing the solution.

Synectics. Gordon (1961) devised a series of strategies that use metaphor and analogy to promote thinking that allows students to use the world around them to make their own connections. By observing the way nature solves problems, individuals can gain insight into how to solve other challenges. Gordon uses three types of analogies to stretch thinking.

Direct Analogy (simple comparison).
How is a pickle like a pain?

Personal Analogy (empathic involvement).
I am the . . . I am a candle about to be lit.

Symbolic Analogy (compressed conflict, an oxymoron).
What is an example of a selfish generosity?

In *The Art of the Possible*, Gordon and Poze (1976) use metaphorical thinking to solve problems. The five steps involved in describing the problem are:

Paradox. What compressed conflict (two words that oppose each other) describes your problem?

Analogue. What do you observe in nature that presents an analogy for your problem? How is the problem solved?

Unique Activity. Description of how the analogy works or acts.

Equivalent. What are the parallel elements of the unique activity and the elements of your problem?

New Idea. You now have produced a new idea that solves your problem. If not, your paradox is at fault.

One group of students was guided through a synectics exercise to assist in outlining appropriate disciplinary procedures in the classroom. After analyzing the problem, they decided that their compressed conflict would be "Controlled Freedom." As their analogy, they chose to compare their challenge to a baseball game. They defined the roles of the players and compared them with those of the students and the teacher in the room. They analyzed the structure of the game and what made a good team. They thought about fair play and cooperation. They concluded that they all had freedom to do their best but had to work within a set of rules and needed to exercise control if they were to be successful.

Gordon (1961) and Gordon and Poze (1976) have produced a variety of very useful materials that encourage the development of analogy and metaphor in problem solving.

De Bono's (1982) Heuristics Situations are presented and ideas are evaluated using such mnemonic devices as a PMI:

P - Plus—Ideas are viewed in terms of plus or positive
M - Minus—Ideas are seen in terms of negative aspects
I - Interesting—Ideas are evaluated as to how interesting they appear

In his *Six Thinking Hats*, De Bono encourages using different colored hats to see challenges from a variety of perspectives:

White—Facts
Red—Emotions and feelings
Black—Negative thoughts
Yellow—Positive constructive thoughts
Green—Creativity
Blue—Metacognition

Task Orientation and Motivation

To achieve eminence in a field, one must develop a passion for one's work, be intrinsically motivated, and be willing to take chances. In the classroom, students can be exposed to topics of interest that allow them to become totally immersed in learning. When observing children at work, it is important to note whether individual children are always task oriented or whether they are motivated only when involved in a particular domain. Interest in a domain can be evidence of a gift.

Parents often complain that their children become so completely absorbed that it is difficult to tear them away. This is a behavior, however, that we wish to reward when present and cultivate if not evident.

Teacher Support for Behaviors Indicative of Task Orientation

Rendfrey, Frayer, and Quilling (1971, p. 10) adapt the work of Klausmeier, Schwenn, and Lamal (1968) to report on behaviors that indicate task commitment:

A. The student starts promptly and completes self-, teacher-, or group-assigned tasks that together comprise the minimum requirements related to various curriculum areas:

1. Attends to the teacher and other situational elements when attention is required.
2. Begins tasks promptly.
3. Seeks feedback concerning performance on tasks.
4. Returns to tasks voluntarily after interruption or initial lack of progress.
5. Persists at tasks until completed.

B. The student assumes responsibility for learning more than the minimum requirements without teacher guidance during school hours and outside school hours. In addition to behaviors 1-5, listed above, the student:

6. Continues working when the teacher leaves the room.
7. Does additional work during school hours.
8. Works on school-related activities outside school hours.
9. Identifies activities that are relevant for class projects.
10. Seeks suggestions for going beyond minimum amount or quality of work.

Independent study, allowing children to select topics that interest them, is one avenue that is often rewarding. Another is observing students as they work in all of the content areas; teachers can note which ones capture their interest. What happens in an interdisciplinary unit? Does the child exhibit a passion for history or is it science that is appealing?

Intrinsic motivation is an inner driving force that moves one to devote one's life to a particular profession and achieve prominence. Teachers should be keen observers of students who demonstrate the ability to be task oriented and provide them with opportunities that tap into their innate abilities and allow task orientation to flourish.

When individuals find their passion, task orientation and intrinsic motivation become a part of the creative process (Amabile, 1983). Exposure to all of the domains of intelligence, independent study, and interdisciplinary study have become a part of the Cline Model so that giftedness can emerge and interest and enjoyment can follow.

Background Experience and Opportunity

Foundations Supporting Background of Experience and Opportunity

It has been shown that exceptional performance usually is based on an extremely rich knowledge base acquired through a long period of motivated learning (Schneider, 1993, p. 321). In his interviews with 120 men and women who had reached eminence in their fields, Bloom (1985) reported on the years of commitment (a minimum of a dozen) that were central to the development of talent. He highlights the support and instruction that were provided by teachers and parents. Subotnik's (1995) conversations with masters in the arts and science provide examples of how individuals have been shaped by their background and experiences. Both Angela Goethals and Midori Goto were raised in families where there was a deep appreciation of the arts. As a young child Angela Goethals accompanied her mother when she worked in a children's Shakespeare company. A family friend took her on some auditions for stage productions. When she was nine she was offered a role and began her career as a professional actress. Midori grew up in a household of violinists. She practiced from the age of four and was featured in a concert at the New York Philharmonic at age ten.

Sunil Weeramantry grew up in a family where chess was played as a recreation. At the age of six, when his family in Sri Lanka was restricted for long periods of time he played chess with his grandfather. At age seven he could beat him. He was enrolled in a chess club and began his competitive career.

Fran Wilczek engaged in conversation with his father about his interest in objects that move. At six he asked for a telescope; at eleven his passion for science became evident.

Knowledge and background experience provide the grist for creative insights. Gruber and Davis (1988) compare the occurrence of creative insights to bolts of lightning:

> A bolt of lightning is by no means a unitary event. It has inner structure and temporal development. There is a period of preparation in which electrical charge is built up; the charge is not a "trait" of the thundercloud, but a relationship between cloud and ground below, or

between cloud and cloud. The buildup of potential difference involves a positive feedback mechanism in which myriad collisions of ice pellets or water drops produce the charge; these earlier events, though of low intensity, prepare the way for intensification later on. . . . This upward stroke is the brilliant event that we normally see as lightning—the rest of all that preceded it. (p. 243)

Many behaviors are genetically determined. Blakeslee (1990) reported on the connection between genetics and perfect pitch in music. Genetic predispositions will emerge only with the appropriate environmental triggers or supports. For giftedness to surface, students should be exposed to each of the intelligence domains so that precocity can be noted.

Ericsson and Charness (1994) studied the performance of the best practitioners, deemed to be "experts, in their fields." (An expert is defined as one who consistently exhibits superior performance on a specified set of representative tasks for the domain.) They found that superior performance reflects extreme adaptations, accomplished through life-long effort, to demands in restricted, well-defined domains. Skills involved in encoding are specific to given domains, and the effects of deliberate practice in a given domain have a far greater effect than previously believed. In order for an individual to achieve eminence in a field, he must be introduced to the prerequisite skills. Opportunities for growth and advancement must be provided.

External Environment

The external environment that encourages the development and expression of creativity includes the atmosphere provided for students in the classroom, the home environment, the field of judges that evaluate products, and the values of society at a given time.

The Home Environment

In the Abecedarian Project (Ramey & Campbell, 1984), more than a hundred low-income black infants whose parents' average IQ was 85 were provided with good nutrition and intellectual stimulation in a preschool where specially-trained teachers talked and interacted with the children. Teachers were also sent to the home where they met with parents regularly to help them understand the value of talking and reading to their babies and to suggest appropriate strategies. By the age of three, the experimental group of children tested 17 points higher on IQ tests than the children in the control group. A follow-up study reported that gains were sustained.

Moss (1990) investigated the metacognitive development of the gifted during preschool years and examined the exchanges between mothers and children during a joint play problem-solving situation. Mothers of gifted preschoolers were significantly more likely to model metacognitive strategies and initiate metacognitive exchanges. As a result, it was suggested that "differences between gifted and average-ability children in metacognitive skills may, in part, be rooted in social interaction" (p. 19).

The Impact of the Environment on the Anatomy of the Brain. Marian Diamond is another important contributor to the field. In her work, *Enriching Heredity* (1988), she studied the impact of the environment on the anatomy of the brain. She draws upon 27 years of research in her laboratory dealing with environmental influences on the anatomy of the mammalian forebrain, primarily that of the rat. She focussed on the effects of aging and of enrichment and impoverishment on the brain. The question is raised whether the results of her studies are applicable to humans. She claims that, whether one is dealing with rats, cats, dogs, monkeys, or human beings, the brain consists of nerve cells and glial cells. In all species, most nerve cells have branches that are called axons and dendrites. It is the pattern and quantity of the branches that account for some of the differences among species. She believes that her findings may have wide application to mammalian nerve cells in general.

> There are many reasons to believe that data collected from rat brains can be useful in establishing guidelines for studying events occurring in the human brain. Accepting the vast complexity of the human brain, I only hope that this collection of information from controlled rat experiments and from a few studies on human brains will eventually serve in directing others toward a better understanding of the potential of the human brain . . . and thus, to greater efforts to improve upon the human condition. (p. 10)

Diamond has been successful in illustrating the detailed anatomical changes that occur in the brain with modifications to the environment. She wished to determine whether multisensory environmental conditions altered the cortical thickness of one hemisphere differently from that of the other. Male and female laboratory animals were exposed to enriched or impoverished conditions for similar periods of time. Her experiments indicated that enriched environmental settings produced anatomical changes in the cerebral cortex. Nutrition plays a critical role in human brain development and in the development of intellectual prowess. In her work she noted that the deprived brain can change if enriched living conditions are provided. Enriched diets and enriched living conditions could overcome some of the deficiencies in the brains of offspring whose mothers were exposed to protein deficits during pregnancy and lactation. She concluded that "Environmental enrichment can mitigate the impact of a range of deprivations and stressful situations" (p. 139).

How to Provide a Positive Classroom Environment

For the classroom teacher, the emphasis is on a classroom environment that is positive and that allows students to take risks. Levinthal (1988) describes the relationship between a positive environment and endorphin levels:

For the human species, the experience of social attachment and comfort becomes inevitably bound up with the euphoria of human affection, intimacy, and love. There is also a behavioral dependency that becomes built into our relationships with people we care about. The slogan "Hugs are better than drugs" may be something you find on a car bumper, but it tells a basic truth of our evolution. You can feel the release of an opiate system through the acts of social comfort and love or by exogenous opiates from the outside.

Teacher Attitudes. Attitudes of teachers and parents can play an important part in the development of children's gifts. Bloom (1985) found that the positive attitudes of initial teachers proved to be more important in the development of talent than did their expertise. Torrance (1964) reported that destructive criticism had a negative impact on idea production. His study involved two groups. One was instructed to read previous research reports with a constructive attitude. The second was to read the same reports with a critical, fault-finding attitude. After the readings, the students were asked to list new ideas for research suggested by their readings. The number of high-quality ideas produced by the group who had been instructed to be constructive in their attitude exceeded those produced by the critical reading group.

Positive and negative thoughts and attitudes impact the energy that is transmitted in the classroom and affect the students. In her work on integrative education, Barbara Clark (1986) recognizes the importance of a positive classroom atmosphere. At the National Association for Gifted Children convention in Cincinnati, Clark (1989) involved the participants in the following demonstration of the power of positive energy and how teachers' attitudes can have an impact on positive and negative classroom behaviors. This exercise can be done with two individuals or with a large group. Instructions to the group were given as follows:

With two people facing each other in the center of the group, one will be designated the leader and the other the participant. Ask all members in the room to center themselves and begin thinking about a pleasant memory. It can be a person who brings a smile to your face, an event, or an object that you truly love. Have the participant raise his or her stronger arm straight out to shoulder height. The leader informs that person that he or she is going to press on the arm to force it down. The participant is to resist and prevent the leader from pulling it down. While all the others in the room are thinking positive thoughts, the leader will attempt to force the arm down. The participant will feel the strength in the arm and be able to resist.

The participant then rests the arm, and the group is instructed to think negative thoughts. They might remember a person or happening that was painful for them. The participant is then asked to raise the arm once again, and to resist and prevent the leader from pushing the arm down. As the leader presses down once again, both the leader and participant will note that the arm is noticeably weaker.

In workshops, this writer extended the demonstration further. After the participant noted the difference in the energy field, the participant was instructed to leave the room. The group then established a pattern of energy that would be sent to the participant: first the group would think positive thoughts, then they would think negative thoughts, and the third time, positive thoughts once more. The participant is asked back into the room. The leader asks that the participant not think of anything other than resisting. The same task will be required, that of raising the arm to shoulder level and resisting the pressure. Without the participant's knowledge, the group is given a signal to think positive thoughts. The leader exerts pressure on the arm of the participant. The strength in the arm is obvious as the participant resists. The group is then given a signal to think negative thoughts, and the leader exerts pressure once again. This time, the weakness in the arm is noted. When thoughts are positive, the strength returns to the arm.

Non-surprisingly, positive thoughts and attitudes are enabling; while negative thoughts and attitudes are disabling. In *The Role of Confirmation, Negation and Functionalization in the Classroom*, Cline (1989) categorizes statements made in classrooms as follows:

> *Confirming Statements.* To be effective, praise should be specific; it can take more than one form. The stance, tone of voice, or facial expression can speak louder than the words being said.
> *Negation.* Negative statements also take many forms and can traumatize forever; sarcasm can be cutting. Body language communicates negative feelings as well.
> *Functionalization.* Functionalizing statements reduce acts and behaviors to the function being preformed. These statements that often take the form of requests neither enable nor disable but serve to give directions. It is also possible to change a functionalizing statement into a confirming one by accompanying the statement with a gesture or a smile and positive eye contact. Purkey and Novak (1984) in *Inviting School Success*, and Cline (1989) in *What Would Happen If I Said Yes?* offer creative suggestions for establishing the desired atmosphere. Creating a positive atmosphere in the classroom involves not only the attitude of the teacher but also the attitudes of the students toward one another. If the teacher models the appropriate behavior and does not support negative behavior among the students, the classroom atmosphere will be greatly enhanced. Teachers need to make conscious efforts to remain positive and avoid negative statements.
> *Relaxation and Imagery.* Based on Ghiselin's (1952) reports that many creative breakthroughs in art, science, and mathematics included relaxed states and visual images, Sisk and Shallcross (1986) suggest using relaxation exercises and visual imagery exercises to enhance the creative process in the classroom. Such activities can be incorporated into any part of the curriculum.

One of the approaches Cline (1989) suggests is:

Close your eyes. Following these instructions will allow your body to relax.

Imagine a place that you find very peaceful; for instance, picture yourself on a beautiful, warm summer day lying in the sun on a beach by an ocean or lake. Feel yourself lying on the soft, soft sand, or on a beach towel that is soft and comfortable. Let yourself feel the sun, pleasantly warm, and feel the gentle breeze touching your neck and face. Picture the beautiful clear blue sky with fluffy little white clouds drifting lazily by. Let yourself feel the soothing, penetrating warmth of the sun, and tell yourself that your mind and body feel completely relaxed and perfectly at ease…peaceful, relaxed, comfortable, calm, so at ease, at peace with the universe…completely relaxed…calm, peaceful, tranquil. Now as you open your eyes, let yourself continue to feel relaxed and yet perfectly alert…peaceful and normal again…Open your eyes. (p. 107)

Another approach to relaxation is allowing each part of the body to tense…and then relax. When using relaxation techniques, teachers can incorporate visualization exercises that enhance learning. For example, students might be involved in identifying challenges they might face in the future. During a relaxation exercise, they might be asked to visualize solutions to the problem. In addition, students might become apprised of the times of day when they are in a relaxed state that allows them to key into creative insights involving all areas of their lives.

Summary

Many factors contribute to and influence the development of human potential. Teachers can control many of them. Using the multiple intelligence philosophy in the classroom will enable the identification and nurturance of possible giftedness. Teachers can establish a positive atmosphere in the classroom as they weave critical and creative thinking skills into all aspects of the curriculum.

Teachers are key figures in the development of potential in students. As they design environments that allow giftedness to surface, they will become advocates for providing special opportunities. Administrators can support them in their efforts and plan creatively, enlisting all members of the educational community. The school becomes a community working together with the interests of talent development in its center.

Additional References:

Barell, J. (1955). *Teaching for thoughtfulness: Classroom strategies to enhance intellectual development.* White Plains, New York: Longman Publishing.

Baron, J. B., & Sternberg, R. J. (1987). *Teaching thinking skills: Theory and practice.* New York: W. H. Freeman and Company.

Bynum, T. W., and Lipman, M. (1976). *Philosophy for children.* Oxford, England: Metaphilosophy Foundation.

Costa, A. (Ed.) (1985). *Developing minds: A resource book for teaching thinking.* Alexandria, Virginia: Association for Supervision and Curriculum Development.

Costa, A. (Ed.) (1991). *Developing minds: Programs for teaching thinking.* Alexandria, Virginia: Association for Supervision and Curriculum Development.

Link, F. R. (Ed.) (1985). *Essays on the intellect.* Alexandria, Virginia: Association for Supervision and Curriculum Development.

Paul, R. W. (1995). *Socratic questioning and role-playing.* Santa Rosa, California: Foundation for Critical Thinking.

Paul, R. W. (1995). *The logic of creative and critical thinking.* Santa Rosa, California: Foundation for Critical Thinking.

Paul, R. W. (1995). *Making critical thinking intuitive.* Santa Rosa, California: Foundation for Critical Thinking.

Paul, R. W. (1995). *Why students and teachers don't reason well.* Santa Rosa, California: Foundation for Critical Thinking.

Paul, R., Binker, A. J. A., & Weil, D. (1995). *Critical thinking handbook: K-3rd grades: A guide for remodelling lesson plans in language arts, social studies and science.* Santa Rosa, California: Foundation for Critical Thinking.

Paul, R., Binker, A. J. A., Jensen, K., & Kreklau, H. (1990). *Critical thinking handbook: 4th-6th grades: A guide for remodelling lesson plans in language arts, social studies and science.* Rohnert Park, California: Foundation for Critical Thinking, Sonoma State University.

Odyssey—*A Curriculum for Thinking Series* (1986). Watertown: Mastery Education Corp.
Adams, M J., Buscaglia, J., de Sanchez, Margarita, Swets, J. A.
Foundations of reasoning.
Herrnstein, R., Adams, M J., Huggins, A. W. F., Starr, B. J.
Understanding language.
Nickerson, R. S.
Verbal reasoning.
Grignetti, M. C.
Problem solving.
Feehrer, C. E., Adams, M. J.
Decision making.
Perkins, D. N. Laserna, C.
Inventive thinking.

Strasser, B. B., Babcock, R. W., Cowan, R., Dalls, G. T., Gothold, S. E., & Rudolph, S. E. (1971). *Teaching toward inquiry.* National Education Association of the United States. Developed in association with the Office of the Los Angeles County Superintendent of Schools

For Further Investigations in Creativity:

Briggs, J. (1990). *Fire in the crucible.* Los Angeles: Jeremy P. Tarcher.

Callahan, C. (1978). *Developing creativity in the gifted and talented.* Reston, Virginia: Council for Exceptional Children.

De Bono, E. (1982). *De Bono's thinking course.* New York: Facts on File.

De Bono, E. (1985). *Six Thinking Hats.* Boston, Mass: Little Brown.

Glover, J. A., Ronning, R. R., & Reynolds, C. R. (1989). *Perspectives on individual differences—Handbook of creativity.* New York: Plenum.

Gordon, J. J. (1961). *Synectics.* New York: Harper and Row.

Ochse, R. (1990). *Before the gates of excellence.* Cambridge: Cambridge University Press.

Parnes, S. J. (Ed.) (1992). *Source book for creative problem solving.* New York: Creative Education Foundation.

Rubenzer, R. L. (1982). *Educating the other half: implications of left/right brain research.* Reston, Virginia: Council for Exceptional Children.

Schlichter, C. L., & Palmer, W. (Eds.) (1993). *Thinking Smart: A primer of the talents unlimited model.* Mansfield, CT.: Creative Learning Press.

Sternberg, R. (Ed.) (1988). *The nature of creativity.* Cambridge: Cambridge University Press.

Photo by Carole Meyers

Faculty members can work together as they assess and report student progress.

Chapter 5
Teaching Tools: Lessons,
Records, Reports

Typical questions a classroom teacher might ask:

- How might I begin to design lessons that include creative and critical thinking skills?
- How might I record possible markers of potential giftedness?
- What is the best way to report student progress?
- What is the best way to conduct parent conferences?

To answer these questions, this chapter includes:

- How to analyze and assess existing units of instruction to provide for creative and critical thinking
- How teachers can include activities helpful in the assessment of multiple intelligences
- Sample forms to assist in gathering data on the child
    From the point of view of the student
    From the point of view of the parent
- How teachers can record markers of giftedness
- Suggestions for conducting parent conferences

Designing Lessons to Assist in the Identification of Potential Gifts

Steps in Designing Lessons: A Place to Begin

To integrate the education of the gifted into the fabric of the school, classrooms must reflect an intelligence-friendly environment. Classroom design, lectures, and lessons should integrate opportunities for the expression and development of multiple intelligences. As teachers observe student interactions with the curriculum and record those observations, they can gather data that are valuable both for ongoing curriculum development and for reporting to parents and administrators.

Teachers can begin by analyzing existing lessons or units. Analyze the questions included at the end of the unit or those used for test purposes. Classify and categorize the questions using Bloom's Taxonomy. Are they challenging for your gifted students? Are there opportunities for students to apply knowledge across domains, using complex thought processes, as prescribed by Taba? Are there opportunities for creative responses?

Examine the kinds of tasks that students are asked to perform at the completion of the unit. How many of the intelligences does the lesson or unit tap into? What primary intelligence will be evidenced? What secondary intelligences will surface? Modify units to include opportunities for all of the intelligences to be expressed (i.e., language, math, leadership, music, drama, dance, or art). Add questions that address creative and cognitive thinking skills, using the models provided in Chapter 4. Evaluate student interactions with all aspects of the curriculum and note areas that demonstrate potential gifts in students' folders. Record all of the results—both written and observed. Begin accumulating a portfolio for each student. Concentrate on the individual strengths of each child.

Gather data in a student file that can be shared with parents, administrators, and other teachers.

Differentiating the Curriculum and Integrating Cognitive Processes

Following is a guide for teachers when designing lessons or evaluating existing lessons:

What Levels of Thinking Have I Used in My Lesson/Unit or Exam?

- *What questions address Level 1*—Knowledge base (Recall of specific information). List, write, enumerate, relate, recall, recollect, retrace, recite.
- *What questions address Level 2*—Understanding (Shows understanding of material communicated). Explain in your own words, compare contrast, examine, translate, demonstrate.
- *What questions address Level 3*—Application (Uses ideas, principles, methods, or concepts and applies them to new situations). Demonstrate, use it to solve, where does it lead, how can you use it?
- *What questions address Level 4*—Analysis (Breaks down or sees parts of information). Uncovers, dissects, probes, how, why, what are the causes, what are the consequences, what are the steps in the process?
- *What questions address Level 5*—Synthesis (Putting together elements or parts to form a whole). Invent, create, make, devise, originate, establish, compose, design.
- *What questions address Level 6*—Evaluation (Judging the value of materials and methods. Applying standards and criteria). Are con-

cepts or broad-based themes involved in the lesson/unit? (Is there an underlying theme, i.e., change or systems?)
- What relationships exist?
- Can generalizations be drawn from studying change/systems?
- What else can this be related to?
- How might these ideas be transferred to other situations?

Have I Included Creative Thinking Activities in the Lesson/Unit?
- Have I included opportunities for divergent thinking (e.g., mapping or brainstorming) in the lesson/unit?
- Do the questions include statements such as:
    How might I?
    What if?
    How many ways can I?

Observing students as they respond to lessons/units or tests, will allow profiles to emerge that can be used in determining the kind of differentiation warranted. Observations need to be systematically noted and recorded.

Using Multiple Intelligence Theory in Designing Lessons or Units

Teachers can modify existing curricula and modify units to identify students who have specific gifts. When designing or evaluating lessons, decisions can be made about the primary and secondary abilities being tapped. In an assignment that requests students to compile a memory book that includes drawings and anecdotes, the primary skill in question would be intrapersonal intelligence, but verbal/linguistic skills would also surface as might spatial abilities. Interdisciplinary curriculum units allow many intelligences to surface. Cooperative learning strategies highlight the personal intelligences and leadership skills. The teacher becomes a keen observer and notes "markers" of strength. In each of the areas of intelligence, students should be introduced to the prerequisite skills involved. This will not only assist teachers in the identification of gifts and talents but also lay the foundation for mastering the skills in all of the content areas that are delineated in the school curriculum. Teachers should design their lessons around the abilities they wish to assess.

The following guide for teachers is designed to assist them to design/redesign lessons so that opportunities for all of the multiple intelligences are present.

Lesson: Title (Teachers may choose to highlight one or more of the following options.)

Verbal/Linguistic: What opportunities have been provided so that my students can demonstrate superior writing abilities?
Triggers or words associated with verbal linguistic abilities include:

Tell	Compose	Journals	Interpret
Report	Retell	Videotapes	Question
Narrate	Write a Poem	Autobiographies	Brainstorm
Write	Fable	Myths	Communicate
Fantasize	Prose	Facts	Summarize
Explain	Stories	Big Books	Interview
Name	Reports	Describe	Read
Debate	Fiction	Imagine	

Mathematical/Logical: Do some components of the lesson/unit require logical or mathematical connections? Triggers or words that indicate mathematical connections include:

Compare	Equal	Distribute	Weigh
Sets	Link	Pair	Justify
Graph	Estimate	Solve	Balance
Survey	Predict	Experiment	Map
Multiply	Enlarge	Write an equation	Number
Divide	Between	Deductive	Reorder
Add	Enumerate	Inductive	Predict
Subtract	Numerate	Trial and error	Approximate
Join	Sequence	Pattern	Guesstimate
Manipulate	Display	Hypothesize	Value
Weigh	Chart	Formulate	Infer
Measure	Plot	Restate	Justify
Notation	Diagram	Formula	Label
Same/Like	Shape	Compare	Check
Different/Unlike	Design	Contrast	Round-off
Length	Calculate	Categorize	Invert
Order	Compute	Approximate	Analogies
Identify	Direction	Multiple	Storyboard
Match	Associate	Measure	Observe change

Musical: Do the students have an opportunity to demonstrate musicality during the lesson/unit or in a concluding project?
Triggers or words associated with musical skills include:

Rhythm	Gallop	Orchestrate	Scale
Tap	Conduct	Tone	Snap
Express	Tonality	Vocalize	Mood
Timbre	Tune	Perform	Bass
Falsetto	Illustrate	Treble	Soprano
Invent	Loud	Baritone	Classical
Soft	Tenor	Percussion	Range
Create	Pitch	Clap	Compose
Melody	Sing	Notation	Movements

Hum	Quarter	Listen	Whistle
Harmony	Sing	Beat	Chant
Instruments	Choral Singing	Stamp	Solo

Visual/Spatial: Does the lesson/unit include a component that allows my students to express themselves in ways that demonstrate visual/spatial abilities (e.g., three-dimensional projects, drawings, sculptures)? Triggers or words to express visual/spatial ability include:

Design	Model	Create	Imprint
Build	Three-dimensional	Visualize	Medium
Draw	Geometric	Photograph	Spectrum
Above	Abstract	Below	Illustrate
Between	Carve	Frame	Diagram
Construct	Graph	Sculpt	Contour
Tactile			

Bodily/Kinesthetic: Does the lesson or unit lend itself to physical expression?
Triggers or words associated with bodily/kinesthetic expression include:

Movement	Interpret	Ballet	Create a dance
Sports	Move to music	Dance	March
Mime	Charades	Parts of body	Relay race
Muscles	Pantomime	Jump rope	Hula Hoop
Animal movement	Skip	Hop	Body language
Throw	Catch	Tapdance	

Inter./Intrapersonal Skills: How are personal skills demonstrated in this lesson/unit?
Triggers or words that indicate personal skills include:

Communicate	Lead	Cooperate	Value
Understand	Decide	Feel	Emulate
Know	Model	Interpret	Congratulate
Empathize	Evaluate	Internalize	Appreciate
Substantiate	Elaborate	Assist	Mentor
Tutor	Aid	Host	

After the lessons have been designed, determine:
The primary intelligence the lesson/unit focuses on:
The secondary intelligences that may surface:

Creative Thinking: Does the lesson or unit include opportunities for divergent thinking?
Trigger words that encourage creative production include:

Create	Eliminate	Design	Rearrange
Elaborate	Fantasize	Brainstorm	Daydream
In what ways might I…	Relax	Invent	Imagine
Build	Visualize	Substitute	Combine
Adapt	Minify	Modify	Maximize
Put to other uses			

Following is a sample unit that was taken from a fourth grade unit that provides an example of how a unit can be modified.

Sample Unit

Winslow Press has developed books that encourage reading and that guide teachers in providing activities that address critical and creative thinking. Here is a section from the Teacher Curriculum Guide to the novel *Water Rat* by Marnie Laird.

SYNOPSIS (A Brief Overview)
This historical novel depicts the harsh realities of life in Colonial Delaware for Matt, an orphan who courageously meets life's challenges. There is mystery and adventure galore, as Matt helps capture menacing pirates and then defeats his archenemy, Eli, the wicked tavern-keeper. In the course of his adventures Matt earns the right to a bright future and earns the esteem of the people he meets and cares about.

PRE-READING ACTIVITIES (Motivate and Involve)
Discuss the Colonial period with students to determine their understanding of the times during which the story takes place. Encourage them to discuss other books they have read about this period.

THEME: Life in Colonial America

RELATED CURRICULUM AREAS
Social Studies: historical events and circumstances
Science: waterways and salt marshes in the Mid-Atlantic States
Math: economics of trade, barter, and money during Colonial times
Careers: occupations and professions common to the period (cooper, blacksmith, etc.)
Language Arts: listening and discussion skills, research skills, report writing, use of technology, drama, and creative writing
CRITICAL THINKING QUESTIONS (Stimulate Thought and Discussion)
Knowledge: List all the events you can think of that led to Matt's seeking refuge with the Campbell family.
Comprehension: In this story, Matt both fears and hates Eli, yet continues to stay with him. Why is this so?

Application: How does Matt demonstrate to Tom his superior knowledge of the creek and the marsh area?

Analysis: How does the author's description of the pirate captain make him appear so menacing that you can feel Matt's terror?

Synthesis: Matt struggles with his feelings throughout the story. His relationships affect him deeply. Describe one such relationship.

Evaluation: Suppose you were Matt. What would you consider your greatest triumph in this story?

CONCEPTS (Ideas to Consider)

Understanding that the time and place in which people live often dictate the circumstances of their lives.

The economy and culture of a region are related to land, climate and natural resources.

Many occupations contribute to economic growth and social welfare. There are inequities in economic and social relationships.

FOLLOW-UP ACTIVITIES (Develop Learning Skills and Creativity)

Fluency: Imagine you are traveling back in time to the year 1747 and that your designated place of arrival is near Eli's tavern. What things will you see when you land? Tape an account of your arrival.

Flexibility: Pick one object that you brought with you. List all the ways it might be useful to you.

Originality: Upon landing, you become a character in *Water Rat*. How would you fit into the story? How would your arrival change the story? Prepare a brief skit that demonstrates the personality of your character.

Elaboration: Make up a story to explain to the inhabitants of Fast Landing how you arrived, and why you do or do not fit in.

Risk Taking: What would you do and think about if you couldn't get back to the present? Prepare an entry for your personal diary.

Complexity: List some of the problems that Matt had to deal with. How would you tackle these problems? Ask members of your family (or class) to discuss and react to the problem situations. Record their solutions. How do they compare?

Curiosity: If you could stay in that time for a day, a week, or a month as a reporter, how would you go about gathering data for an article? Outline your plans.

Imagination: Pick one character from the story *Water Rat* and have him or her land in the present. How might today's world seem to him or her? Conduct a TV interview with the time traveler. (Ask a friend to help.)

Look for students who demonstrate a great deal of originality in their responses.

Responses might be written, drawn, or verbalized. Teachers will begin to appreciate students who are exceptionally creative and who might not be performing in traditional ways in assigned tasks.

A well-designed curriculum becomes the identifier of talents and abilities. Teachers can then plan appropriate follow-up in and out of the classroom.

Gathering Data, Recording and Reporting Student Progress

As teachers work with students in regular classrooms, profiles of giftedness will emerge. Keeping records that assist in assessing progress and establishing a profile becomes an important task. It enables teachers to plan for students, to provide valuable information for future teachers, and to communicate with parents.

Gathering information. In the beginning of the school year, classroom teachers can use prepared inventories to gather information about the students and their parents. Appendix A can assist in the process:

- Student interest inventory (the student inventory may reveal areas of giftedness)
- Parent inventory (seeing the child from the parent's perspective can provide wonderful insights into a student's potential gifts. Often students are involved at home in endeavors that teachers might never know about). Parents can provide valuable information that will assist teachers in identifying possible areas of giftedness. The form can be completed early in the school year so that teachers can be "on the lookout" for special strengths. Observations in the classroom will often corroborate parent observations.
- Resource development questionnaire (professions, interests, and hobbies) may divulge clues as to the student's proclivities and allow teachers to begin a data base of individuals that might serve as mentors to students.

Recording Markers of Giftedness Using a Matrix. Teachers can use a matrix to identify possible giftedness (Appendix C). The matrix provides a place for teachers to list the names of the students in the room on one side and behaviors that might indicate potential giftedness on the other. As teachers note behaviors exhibited during lessons, they can put a check next to the student's name, or describe an interaction. As time goes on, profiles of student performance will emerge. It may become evident that a student is gifted in one domain or in many. Gifted thinkers will also evidence themselves.

How to Use Portfolios in the Identification of Gifts. Portfolios provide authentic assessments of students' abilities over time. Certain decisions should be made before beginning to establish student portfolios. Questions that will assist in the decision-making include:

- How often will data be gathered?
- Who will decide what is to be collected?
- What criteria will be used to make the selection (e.g., samples which illustrate a skill or talent in a domain—show evidence of higher levels of thinking—show evidence of unusual interests—show evidence of unusual creativity)? As each piece is selected, the following should be recorded:

> Date of collection
> Person who selected it (e.g., student, teacher, parent)
> Reason for selection (e.g., level of thinking demonstrated, creativity, presentation)

Wright and Borland (1992) used early childhood developmental portfolios in the identification and education of young economically-disadvantaged children. They included the following in their assessment, which can serve as guidelines:

- *Standard Sample*—Teachers collect examples of students' work in response to one or more activities in which all students have participated. The activity is curriculum based and grounded in work being done in the classroom, is developmentally appropriate, and is representative of a specific domain.
- *Teacher-selected sample*—Teachers select samples to demonstrate a student's ability, potential, or growth in a domain. This is especially helpful for children whose test scores do not reflect their abilities.
- *Child-selected sample*—Students are asked to select work that has a special meaning for them. Children are asked to complete a sentence as to why this work has been selected.
- *Notable moment cards*—Teachers capture special moments that are recommended for, but not exclusively for, affective and social development.
- *Let-Me-Tell-You-About-My-Child Cards*—Teachers send letters home encouraging parents to share information about their child's interests and activities.

Information gathered can take a variety of forms:

- Written samples
- Photographs (e.g., pictures of artwork, sculptures or structures)
- Audiotapes
- Videotapes
- Anecdotes
- Awards received
- Computer discs—portfolios can be compiled over time using computer disks that can incorporate photographs with written and spoken words

Establishing appropriate guidelines sets a positive atmosphere in the classroom. Other than the standard sample, emphasis in the portfolio should be on the identification of areas of strength. It should include samples and anecdotes that catch children at their best. Teachers graduating from teacher training institutes today often have portfolios of their own. Sharing portfolios with students sets an excellent example. Students can see what a portfolio is as a teacher models it for them.

The students' portfolio will provide the data necessary for appropriate curriculum differentiation to take place.

Conducting Parent Conferences. Parent conferences provide wonderful opportunities for teachers to learn about their students as they share pertinent information. Teachers need to establish a rapport with parents so that teacher and parent can work together in the best interests of the student. Teachers need to be good listeners when they meet with parents. At the beginning of the conference, it is best for the teacher to ask the parent to tell about the child before sharing information from classroom observations. As the teacher listens carefully, a profile of the child at home emerges. Information that should be sought at the outset:

- Tell me about your child.
- How is your child enjoying this year?
- What do you see as your child's strengths?

When sharing information with parents, teachers need to stress strengths. When deficits are noted, share them after positive comments have been made. Frame them as "How might we help _____?" Common complaints from parents or teachers are that the child is forgetful or disorganized. Very often the nature of the child is such that he or she begins exhibiting signs of being "an absent-minded professor" at a young age. Children should not be penalized but assisted, even if there are no great improvements. Students can be shown ways to help themselves, such as keeping material in folders and using calendars.

Any information shared with parents should be substantiated with supporting data. Reporting to parents can include any and all of the following:

- A report card that is already in place
- Review of the student portfolio
- Anecdotal comments to apprise parents of special abilities or gifts as they have been noted

Teachers can create their own "report card" and list and include a list of characteristics that might be indicators of giftedness. The form in Appendix C, "Authentic Assessment of Student Ability," offers a sample that might be used for this purpose.

If students exhibit talents or abilities that are not accommodated in the school setting, teachers may make recommendations as to how students' gifts may be realized in after-school or summer programs. Teachers and parents need to work together to support the best interests of the child.

Conferences also provide opportunities for teachers to "fact find," to see how parent support might be elicited for the student and the school. Parents can be powerful partners in supporting teachers and administrators in establishing programs for the gifted.

Developing a Differentiated Educational Plan or Profile (DEP)

As teachers note special domains of potential giftedness, teachers may wish to establish DEPs. This can assist them in pulling together an individual profile and determine future educational planning. A sample DEP is presented in Table 5-1.

Table 5-1. Sample DEP (Differentiated Education Plan).

Name & Grade	Student Needs	Evidence	Recommended Differentiation	Programming Alternative
Mary Dep Grade 4	Mary needs to have her language arts curriculum expanded.	The attached examples of Mary's writing indicate her ability to use language.	Mary is an independent learner who finishes her class work quickly and easily. Mary needs to be provided with opportunities to read and compare different types of writing and focus on the works of fine poets. She has a natural affinity to use language which should be encouraged. She should be allowed time to develop her skills.	Time will be provided in class. Professional writers will be brought in from the community to mentor her. Outside audiences will be sought for her work. When deemed suitable, her work will be sent for possible publication.

Other Comments:

How Teachers Can Record Information to Be Passed on to Future Teachers

As teachers observe gifts in their students, they will want to provide next year's teacher with relevant information so that student growth can continue. The "Student Growth" form in Appendix C can be used for this purpose.

Summary

Implementation of the Cline Model is facilitated by using the following steps to foster the development of human potential in students:

- Step I—Design lessons so as to expose children to the basic skills involved in each and every one of the talent areas.
- Step II—Incorporate higher cognitive processes into lessons.

- Step III—Record markers and/or establish portfolios for all students to note areas of strength.
- Step IV—Once areas of possible of giftedness are noted, outline an instructional plan that denotes areas where the curriculum should be differentiated.
- Step V—Determine appropriate programming.
- Step VI—Communicate with parents, informing them of potential gifts and enlisting their support.

When properly designed, the curriculum can reveal information currently available through testing. The curriculum must be the identifier of special abilities. Ongoing assessment needs to take place as students are observed in all domains of accomplishment.

Looking to the Future

Integrating programs for the gifted into the school requires communication between:

- Classroom teachers
- Administrators
- Parents
- Students
- Community

As a society, we need to be concerned with providing all students with an education that gives them the tools for success. Creative and critical thinking skills are not reserved for students identified as gifted but need to be taught to all students, so that those needing a challenge will identify themselves. We need to expand our definition of potential giftedness and view intelligence as multi-dimensional. Children need to be introduced to all domains of intelligence. Opportunities for students' strengths to be expressed and celebrated need to be provided. IQ and achievement tests can provide additional information important for individual students so that appropriate plans can be devised. Tests should be used as a device for helping students and teachers redesign the teaching-learning objectives. New tests should be used to evaluate progress rather than for selection or special treatment. In addition to tests, evaluation of abilities should involve operant, lifelike situations. Schooling needs to address occupational and social outcomes, such as leadership and interpersonal skills. Both verbal and non-verbal communication skills are important. Patience, moderate goal setting, and ego development are also meaningful skills.

As all members of the community join together, the world becomes the laboratory and encyclopedia for the gifted child, and learning is extended beyond the walls of the classroom.

Appendices

Appendix A:
Inventories and Questionnaires

Student Interest Inventory

Student Name _____ Date_____

What subjects do you enjoy most in school?

What do you get your best grades in?

Are there any topics that you would like to find out more about that are not part of the school program?

Do you attend any special class?

Do you collect anything?

Have you won any special awards?

What career would you like to pursue when you begin to work?

Do you have any hobbies?

When you visit a library, what section of the library do you usually find yourself in?

What are your favorite books?

What do you do in your leisure time?

Parent Inventory

Child's Name_____ Date_____

Parent's or Guardian's Name _____

Your child's hobbies or interests:

Projects your child enjoys working on at home:

Interests when alone:

Interests with friends:

Interests with family members:

Books your child enjoys reading:

Unusual accomplishments, past or present:

Competitions entered:

Special talents (music, art, athletics, etc.):

Private lessons:

Aspirations:

Relationships with others:

Special needs:

Work and study habits:

General description of your child:

Resource Development Questionnaire
For Parents and Community Members

Name _____Date_____

Occupation:

Hobbies:

General interests:

Travel.

Vacations:

Special classes or training:

Past work experience:

Unusual experiences:

Contests or competitions:

Collections:

Address _____

Telephone Number _____

I would be willing to meet with a child or a group of children once _____
regularly _____

Student Evaluation of an Independent Study Project

Name _____Date_____

Project:

Rate each of the items according to the following scale:

        0—Not observed at all
        1—Fair—Could be improved
        2—Very good
        3—Excellent

1. _____ The project is attractive.

2. _____ The project demonstrates in-depth knowledge of the topic.

3. _____ The project is well organized.

4. _____ The project shows use of extended resources.

5. _____ The bibliography demonstrates a wide selection of books
and periodicals.

6. _____ The project is clear, meaningful, interesting, and understandable.

7. _____ The project is imaginative and creative.

The best part of the project was:

The following could be improved in the following ways:

Appendix B:
Lesson Designs

**Designing Lessons
Using Multiple Intelligence Theory**

Lesson:

Students have opportunities to demonstrate abilities in the following ways:

Mathematical/Logical:

Verbal/Linguistic:

Musical:

Spatial:

Bodily/Kinesthetic:

Personal Skills:

The primary intelligence the lesson focussed on:

Secondary intelligences that may surface:

Designing Lessons
to Assess Cognitive Processes

Lesson:

Can I use brainstorming or mapping in the lesson
to exercise divergent thinking?

Check to see that questions to be asked orally
and in written exams assess all levels.

Level 1—Knowledge base

Level 2—Understanding

Level 3—Application

Level 4—Analysis

Level 5—Synthesis

Level 6—Evaluation

What concepts were involved in the lesson:

How might they be transferred to other situations:

Appendix C:
Gift Identification and Assessment

Matrix for Identifying Special Gifts

Student Name	Skill in Specific Domain (Specify)	Store of Knowledge	Divergent Thinker	Unusual Interests	Curious Desire to Know	Task Oriented	Independent Learner	Makes Connections in Thinking	Other

Authentic Assessment of Student Ability

Name _____

Description of Student Performance in Activities related to:

Music

Dance

Drama

Leadership Ability

Task Orientation and Motivation

Ability to Make Connections in Thinking

Creativity

Topics of Special Interest to the Student

To the Parent:

You can help by

Student Growth

Name _____

Grade_____Classroom Teacher _____

This last year this student excelled in:

Mathematics—Level Reached _____

Language Arts—Areas in which the student demonstrated advanced abilities included, e.g., writing, speaking, foreign language, debating _____ _____

Music—Ability was noted, e.g., in activities that contained a musical component, special classes, performances _____

Art—Ability was noted, e.g., in activities that contained an artistic component, special classes, exhibits _____

Drama—Ability was noted, e.g., in activities that contained a dramatic component, performances, special classes_____

Leadership—Ability was exhibited when _____

Student undertook an independent study in _____

Special opportunities, e.g., advanced curriculum, mentors, computer programs etc. were provided for this student in following ways: _____
_____
_____

Recommendations for next year:_____

Signed _____

Suggestions for Recording Gifted Behaviors

Characteristic	Formal Test	Objective Self-Report	Written Report	Discussion or Questioning	Planned Observation	Product or Performance Observed	Incidental Observation	Anecdotal Record	Photograph
Independent Learner									
Makes Connections in Thinking									
Exceptional Motivation									
Exceptional Memory									
Highly Creative									
Problem Solver									
Natural Leader									
Self-Directed									
Curious Intense Desire to Know									
Sense of Humor									

Bibliography

AEGIS. (1998, Winter). Policy 2510. Testing out for credit. *Newsletter of the WVAGT (West Virginia Association for the Gifted and Talented).*

Amabile, T. (1983). *The social psychology of creativity.* New York: Springer-Verlag.

Archambault, F., Westberg, F., Brown, S., Hallmark, B., Zhang, W., & Emmons, C. (1993). Classroom practices used with gifted third and fourth grade students. *Journal for the Education of the Gifted, 16,* 103–119.

Arieti, S. (1976). *Creativity: The magic synthesis.* New York: Basic Books, Inc.

Armstrong, T. (1994). *Multiple intelligences in the classroom.* Alexandria, VA: Association for Supervision and Curriculum Development.

Barell, J. (1995). *Teaching for thoughtfulness: Classroom strategies to enhance intellectual development.* White Plains, NY: Longman Publishing.

Baron, J. B., & Sternberg, R. J. (1987). *Teaching thinking skills: Theory and practice.* New York: W. H. Freeman and Company.

Barron, F. (1988). Putting creativity to work. In R. Sternberg (Ed.) *The nature of creativity.* (pp. 76–98). Cambridge: Cambridge University Press.

Baum, S. M., Owen, S. V., & Oreck, B. A. (1996). Talent beyond words: Identification of potential talent in dance and music in elementary students. *Gifted Child Quarterly, 40*(2), 93–101.

Bellanca, J., Chapman, C., & Swartz, E. (1994). *Multiple assessments for multiple intelligences.* Palatine, IL: IRI/Skylight Publishing.

Benbow, C. P., & Minor, L. L. (1986). Mathematically talented males and females and achievement in high school sciences. *American Educational Research Journal, 23,* 425–436.

Benbow, C. P., Stanley, J. C. (1982). Consequences in high school and college of sex differences in mathematical reasoning ability: A longitudinal perspective. *American Educational Research Journal, 19,* 598–622.

Bentley, J. E. (1937). *Superior children.* New York: W. W. Norton & Company, Inc.

Blakeslee, S. (1990, November 20). Perfect pitch: The key may lie in the genes. *The New York Times,* p. C1.

Blakeslee, S. (1995, February 3). Scientists find place on left side of the brain where perfect pitch is heard. *The New York Times,* p. A16.

Blakeslee, S. (1997, April 17). Studies show talking with infants shapes basis of ability to think. *The New York Times,* p. D21.

Bloom, B. S. (Ed.). (1956). *Taxonomy of educational objectives: Cognitive and affective domains.* New York: David McKay.

Bloom, B. S. (Ed.). (1985). *Developing talent in young people.* New York: Ballantine Books.

Briggs, J. (1990). *Fire in the crucible—The self-creation of creativity and genius.* Los Angeles: Jeremy P. Archer.

Brigham, C. C. (1923). *A study of American intelligence.* Princeton, NJ: Princeton University Press.

Broadwin, J., Lenchner, G. & Rudolph, D. J. (1998). *AP Calculus problems AB and BC, Part II.* Bellmore, NY: Mathematical Olympiads.

Burks, B. S., Jensen, D. W., & Terman, L. M. (1930). *Genetic studies of genius: Vol. III. The promise of youth.* Stanford, CA: Stanford University Press.

Burns, D. E. (1985). The land of opportunity. *GCT, 37,* 14–15.

Burt, C. (1949). The structure of the mind: A review of the results of factor analysis. *British Journal of Educational Psychology, 19,* 100–111.

Bynum, T. W., & Lipman, M. (1976). *Philosophy for children.* Oxford, England: Metaphilosophy Foundation.

Callahan, C. (1978). *Developing creativity in the gifted and talented.* Reston, VA: Council for Exceptional Children.

Callahan, C. M. (1997, March). *When a bull's-eye is not in the middle: The challenge of learning to respond to academic and cultural diversity in heterogeneous settings.* Paper presented at the Annual Meeting of the American Educational Research Association Chicago.

Campbell, F. A., & Ramey, C. T. (1994). Effects of early intervention on intellectual and academic achievement: A follow-up study of children from low income families. *Child Development, 65,* 684–698.

Campbell, F. A., & Ramey, C. T. (1995). Cognitive and school outcomes for high risk African-American students at middle adolescence: Positive effects of early intervention. *American Educational Research Journal, 32,* 743–772.

Cattell, R. B. (1971). *Abilities: Their structure, growth, and action.* New York: Houghton Mifflin.

Cattell, R. B. (1987). *Intelligence: Its structure, growth and action.* Amsterdam; Oxford: North-Holland.

Chall, J. S., & Conrad, S. S. (1991). *Should textbooks challenge students?: The case for easier or harder textbooks.* New York: Teachers College Press.

Chambers, J. A. (1973). College teachers: Their effect on creativity. *Journal of Educational Psychology 65, 3,* 326–334.

Chapman, C. (1993). *If the shoe fits: How to develop multiple intelligences in the classroom.* Palatine, IL: IRI/Skylight Publishing.

Clark, B. 1986). *Optimizing learning.* Columbus, OH: Merrill Publishing.

Clark, B. (1989, November). *Integrative Education.* Paper presented at the National Association for Gifted Children Conference, Cincinnati, Ohio.

Clark, G. A., & Zimmerman, E. (1992). *Issues and practices related to identification of gifted and talented students in the visual arts.* Storrs, CT: The National Research Center on the Gifted and Talented.

Cline, S. (1986). *The independent learner.* New York: D.O.K. Publishers.

Cline, S. (1989). *What would happen if I said yes?... A guide to creativity for parents and teachers.* New York: D.O.K. Publishers.

Colangelo, N., Assouline, S. G., Cole, V., Cutrona, C., Maxey, J. E. (1996). Exceptional academic performance: Perfect scores on the PLAN. *Gifted Child Quarterly, 40*(2), 102–110.

Cole, M., John-Steiner, V., Scribner, S., & Souberman, E. (1978). *Mind in society.* London, England: Harvard University Press.

Coleman, L. (1994). Portfolio assessment: A key to identifying hidden talents and empowering teachers of young children. *Gifted Child Quarterly, 38* (2), 65–69.

Collins, N. D., & Parkhurst, L. (1996). Teaching strategies for gifted children in the regular classroom—The writing process: A tool for working with gifted students in the regular classroom. *Roeper Review, 18* (4), 277–280.

The Columbus Group. (1991, July). [Unpublished transcript of the meeting of the Columbus Group]. Columbus, OH: Author.

Costa, A. L. (1981). Teaching for intelligent behavior. *Educational Leadership, 39*(1), 29–32.

Costa, A. L. (1984a). Mediating the metacognitive. *Educational Leadership, 42*(3), 57–62.

Costa, A. L. (1984b). Thinking: How do we know students are getting better at it? *Roeper Review, 6*(4), 197–199.

Costa, A. L. (1985, Autumn). Teacher behaviors that enable student thinking. In A. Costa (Ed.), *Developing Minds. A Resource Book for Teaching Thinking* (pp. 125–137). Alexandria, VA: Association for Supervision and Curriculum Development.

Costa, A. L. (Ed.). (1985). *Developing Minds. A Resource Book for Teaching Thinking.* Alexandria, VA: Association for Supervision and Curriculum Development.

Costa, A. L. (Ed.). (1991). *Developing Minds. Programs for Teaching Thinking.* Alexandria, VA: Association for Supervision and Curriculum Development.

Council of State Directors of Programs for the Gifted. (1991). *The 1990 State of the States Gifted and Talented Education Report* [Results of survey conducted by the Council of State Directors of Programs for the Gifted].

Council of State Directors of Programs for the Gifted. (1994). *The 1994 State of the States Gifted and Talented Education Report* [Results of survey conducted by the Council of State Directors of Programs for the Gifted].

Council of State Directors of Programs for the Gifted. (1996). *The 1996 State of the States Gifted and Talented Education Report* [Results of survey conducted by the Council of State Directors of Programs for the Gifted].

Cox, D. N., Daniel, N., & Boston, B. (1985). *Educating able learners.* Austin: University of Texas Press.

Cox, Gillian, et al. (1926) *The early mental traits of three hundred geniuses, Vol. II of genetic studies of genius.* Stanford: Stanford University Press.

Csikszentmihalyi, M. (1990). *Flow: The psychology of optimal experience.* New York: Harper & Row.

D'Amico, V. (1942). *Creative teaching in art.* Scranton, PA: International Textbook Company.

Davies, I. K. (1981). *Instructional techniques.* New York: Hill Publishing.

Davis, S., & Johns, J. (1989, November/December). Gifted students get published. *Gifted Child Today*, pp. 21–22.

De Bono, E. (1982). *De Bono's thinking course.* New York: Facts on File.

De Bono, E. (1985). *Six thinking hats.* Boston, MA: Little Brown.

Dehaene, S. (1998). *The number sense.* New York: Oxford University Press.

Deno, E. (1970). Special education as developmental capital. *Exceptional Children, 37*, 123–130.

Detterman, D. K., & Sternberg, R. J. (Eds.). (1982). *How and how much can intelligence be increased.* Norwood, NJ: Ablex Publishing.

Diamond, M. C. (1988). *Enriching heredity: The impact of the environment on the anatomy of the brain.* New York: The Free Press, a division of Macmillan.

Dixon, J. P. (1983). *The spatial child.* Springfield, IL: Charles C. Thomas.

Draze, D. (1987). *Winners' circle: A guide for achievement.* San Luis Obispo, CA: Dandy Lion Publications.

Draze, D. (1991). *Roundtable: Discussion questions for independent growth.* San Luis Obispo, CA: Dandy Lion Publications.

Eberle, R. F. (1971). *SCAMPER.* Buffalo, NY: D.O.K.

Elias, M. J., Zins, J. E., Weissberg, R. P., Frey, K. S., Greenberg, M. T., Haynes, N. M., Kessler, R., Schwab-Stone, M. E., & Shriver, T. P. (1997). *Promoting social and emotional learning: Guidelines for educators.* Alexandria, VA: Association for Supervision and Curriculum Development.

Ennis, R. H. (1986). A taxonomy of critical thinking dispositions and abilities. In J. B. Baron & R.S. Sternberg (Eds.). *Teaching thinking skills: Theory and practice* (pp. 9–26). New York: W. H. Freeman.

Ericsson, K. A., & Charness, N. (1994). Expert performance. Its structure and acquisition. *American Psychologist, 49*(8), 725–747.

Faculty of the New City School, St. Louis, MO. (1994). *Celebrating multiple intelligence: Teaching for success: A practical guide created by the faculty of the New City School.* St. Louis, MO: Author.

Falvey, M. A., Givner, C. C., & Kimm, C. (1995). What is an inclusive school? In R. A. Villa & J. S. Thousand (Eds.), *Creating an inclusive school* (pp. 1–12). Alexandria, VA: Association for Supervision and Curriculum Development.

Feldhusen, J. F. (1992). *TIDE: Talent identification and development in education.* Sarasota, FL: Center for Creative Learning.

Feldhusen, J. F. (1994). Leadership curriculum. In J. VanTassel-Baska (Ed.), *Comprehensive curriculum for gifted learners* (pp. 347–398). Boston: Allyn & Bacon.

Feldhusen, J. F. (1997). *Talent identification and development in education; The basic tenets.* Paper presented at The First Annual Summer Institute—Integrating Gifted Education into the Fabric of the School, Garden City, Long Island.

Feuerstein, R. (1979). *The dynamic assessment of retarded performers: The learning potential assessment device, theory, instruments, and techniques.* Baltimore, MD: University Park Press.

Feuerstein, R. (1980). *Instrumental enrichment: An intervention program for cognitive modifiability.* Baltimore, MD: University Park Press.

Feuerstein, R., Hoffman, M. B., Egozi, M., & Shachar-Segev, N. (1994). Intervention programs for low performers: Goals, means, and expected outcomes. In M. Ben-Hur (Ed.), *On Feuerstein's instrumental enrichment* (pp. 3–50). Palatine, IL: IRI/Skylight Publishing.

Fischer, K. W. (1988, May–June). Cognitive development in real children: Levels and variations [Excerpted from a paper presented at the Cross-Laboratory Conference on Teaching Thinking and At-Risk Students, Research for Better Schools, Philadelphia, November 1987]. *Teaching Thinking and Problem Solving, 10*(3), 1–4.

Flynn, J. R. (1984). The mean IQ of Americans—massive gains 1932–1978. *Psychological Bulletin, 98,* 29–51.

Frasier, M. (1992, March). Ethnic/minority children: Reflections and directions. *Challenges in gifted education: Developing potential and investing in knowledge for the 21st century.* ED 344 407 EC 301 136.

Frasier, M., Garcia, J., & Passow, A. H. (1995). *A review of assessment issues in gifted education and their implications for identifying gifted minority students.* Storrs, CT: National Research Center on the Gifted and Talented.

Freud, S. (1908). The relation of the poet to day-dreaming. In *Collected Papers.* Vol. II. London: Hogarth.

Gagné, F. (1995). From giftedness to talent: A developmental model and its impact on the language of the field. *Roeper Review, 18* (2), 103–111.

Gagné, F. (1997, July). *The multigifts of multitalented individuals.* Paper presented at the First Annual Institute Integrating Gifted Education into the Fabric of School, Garden City, NY.

Gailbraith, R. E., & Jones, T. M. (1976). *Moral reasoning: A teaching handbook for adapting Kohlberg to the classroom.* Minneapolis: Greenhaven Press.

Gallagher, J., Herradine, C. C., & Coleman, M. R. (1997). Challenge or boredom? Gifted students' view on their schooling. *Roeper Review, 19*(3), 132–136.

Gallagher, J. J., Oglesby, K., Stern, A., Caplow, D., Courtright, R., Fulton, L., Guiton, G., & Langenbach, J. (1982). *Leadership unit: The use of teacher-scholar teams to develop units for the gifted.* New York: Trillium.

Galler, J. R. (Ed.). (1984). *Human nutrition: A comprehensive treatise: Vol. 5. Nutrition and behavior.* New York: Plenum Press.

Galton, F. (1925). *Hereditary genius: An inquiry into its laws and consequences.* London: Macmillan Publishing Co., Inc.

Gardner, H. (1975). *The shattered mind: The person after brain damage.* New York: Knopf.

Gardner, H. (1983). *Frames of mind: The theory of multiple intelligences.* New York: Basic Books.

Gardner, H. (1989). *To open minds: Chinese clues to the dilemma of contemporary education.* New York: Basic Books.

Gardner, H. (1993). *Creating minds: An anatomy of creativity seen through the lives of Freud, Einstein, Picasso, Stravinsky, Eliot, Graham, and Gandhi.* New York: Basic Books.

Garrett, C. (1991). *Novel Ties Study Guide. Annie and the Old One.* New Hyde Park, NY: Learning Links.

Gesell, A., & Ilg, F. L. (1943). *The infant and child in the culture of today: The guidance of development in home and nursery school.* London: Hamilton.

Getzels, J. W., & Jackson, P. W. (1962). *Creativity and intelligence: Explorations with gifted students.* London: John Wiley & Sons.

Ghiselin, B. (1952). *The creative process, a symposium.* Berkeley: University of California Press.

Glover, J. A., Ronning, R. R., & Reynolds, C. R. (1989). *Perspectives on individual differences—Handbook on creativity.* New York: Plenum.

Goddard, H. H. (1913). The Binet tests in relation to immigration. *Journal of Psycho-Asthetics, 18,* 105–107.

Goddard, H. H. (1917). Mental tests and the immigrant. *Journal of Delinquency, 2,* 271.

Goddard, H. H. (1920). *Human efficiency and levels of intelligence.* Princeton, NJ: Princeton University Press.

Goldman, L. (1984). Warning: The Socratic method can be dangerous. *Educational Leadership, 42,* 1, 57–62.

Goldstein, D. & Wagner, R. (1993). After School Programs, Competitions, School Olympics and Summer Programs. In K. A. Heller, F. Mönks & A. H. Passow (Eds.), *International handbook of research and development of giftedness and talent* (pp. 593–604). Oxford: Pergamon Press.

Goleman, D. (1995). *Emotional intelligence.* New York: Bantam Books.

Gordon, E. E. (1998). *Introduction to research and the psychology of music.* Chicago: GIA Publications.

Gordon, W. J. J. (1961). *Synectics.* New York: Harper and Row.

Gordon, W. J. J., & Poze T. (1976). *The art of the possible.* Cambridge, MA: Porpoise Books.

Gowan, J. C. (1979). The development of the creative individual. In J. C. Gowan, J. Khatena, & E. P. Torrance (Eds.) *Educating the Ablest* (pp. 58–79) Itasca, Ill.: F. E. Peacock.

Gregorc, A. (1982). *Gregorc style indicator.* Maynard, MA: Gabriel Systems.

Grenough, M., Marshall, B., McGuire, L., Orourke, K. & Spector, P. (1980). *Bananas and fifty-four other varieties.* Stratford, CT: Center for Theatre Techniques in Education.

Griggs, S., & Dunn, R. (1984). Selected case studies of the learning style preferences of gifted students. *Gifted Child Quarterly, 28*(3), 115–119.

Gruber, H. E., & Davis, S. N. (1988). Inching our way up Mount Olympus: The evolving systems approach to creative thinking. In R. Sternberg (Ed.), *The nature of creativity* (pp. 243–270). Cambridge, England: Cambridge University Press.

Guilford, J. P. (1959). Three faces of intellect. *American Psychologist 14,* 469–479.

Guilford, J. P. (1964). Progress in the discovery of intellectual factors. In C. W. Taylor (Ed.), *Widening horizons in creativity* (pp. 282–297). New York: Wiley.

Guilford, J. P. (1967). *The nature of human intelligence.* New York: McGraw-Hill.

Guildford, J. P. & Merrifield (1960). The structure of intellect model: Its uses and implications. *Report from the Psychological Laboratory, No. 24.* Los Angeles: University of Southern California.

Haavind, H. & Hartmann, H. (1977). *Mothers as teachers and their children as learners.* Paper to the XXIst Congress of Psychology, Paris, June 1976.

Hacker, A. (1995). *Two nations: Black and white, separate, hostile, unequal.* New York: Ballantine Books.

Haensly, P. A. & Reynolds, C. R. (1989). Creativity and intelligence. In J.A. Glover, R.R. Ronning & C.R. Reynolds (Eds.) *Handbook of creativity.* New York: Putnam.

Hallahan, D. P. & Kauffmann, J. M. (1997). *Exceptional children.* Boston: Allyn & Bacon.

Halsted, J. W. (1994). *Some of my best friends are books: Guiding gifted readers from pre-school to high school.* Dayton, OH: Ohio Psychology Press.

Hamachek, D. E. (1978). Psychodynamics of normal and neurotic perfectionism. *Psychology, 15,* 27–33.

Hanninen, G. (1988, March). A study of teacher training in gifted education. *Roeper Review, 10,* (3), 139–144.

Hargreaves, D. (1996). The development of artistic and musical competence. In I. Deliege and J. Sloboda (Eds.) *Musical beginnings.* New York: Oxford University Press.

Haris, C. R. (1993). *Identifying and serving recent immigrant children who are gifted.* ERIC Clearinghouse on Disabilities and Gifted Education. Reston, VA. ED 358676.

Harootunian, B., & Yarger, D. (1981, February). *Teacher's conceptions of their own success.* Washington, DC: ERIC Clearinghouse on Teachers Education, SP017 372.

Hegeman, K. (1997, August). *The moral development of young gifted children.* Paper presented at the 12th World Conference of the World Council for Gifted and Talented Children. Seattle, Washington.

Heller, K. A., Mönks, F. J., & Passow, A. H. (Eds.). (1993). *International handbook of research and development of giftedness and talent.* Oxford: Pergamon Press.

Henderson, K. (1993). *Market guide for young readers.* Cincinnati, OH: Writers Digest Books.

Herrnstein, R. J., & Murray, C. (1994). *The bell curve: Intelligence and class structure in American life.* New York: Free Press.

Hollingworth, L. S. (1926). *Gifted children: Their nature and nurture.* New York: Macmillan Publishing Co., Inc.

Hoover, S. M., Sayler, M. & Feldhusen, J. F. (1993). Cluster grouping of gifted students at the elementary level. *Roeper Review, 16*(1), 13–15.

Horn, J. L., & Cattell, R. B. (1967). Age differences in fluid and crystallized intelligence. *Acta Psychologica, 26,* 107–129.

Hyatt, C., & Gottlieb, L. (1987). *When smart people fail.* New York: Simon & Schuster.

Jarwan, F. A., & Feldhusen, J. F. (1993). *Residential schools of mathematics and science for academically talented youth: An analysis of admission programs.* Storrs, CT: The National Research Center on the Gifted and Talented.

Jensen, A. R. (1969). How much can we boost IQ and scholastic achievement? *Harvard Educational Review, 39,* 1–123.

John-Steiner, V. (1985). *Notebooks of the mind.* New York: Harper & Row.

Johnson-Laird, P. N. (1988). Freedom and constraint in creativity. In R.J. Sternberg (Ed.), *The nature of creativity,* (pp. 202–219). Cambridge: Cambridge University Press.

Jung, C. G. (1971). Psychological types. In *Collected works.* Vol. 6. Princeton, NJ: Princeton University Press.

Karnes, F. A., & Chauvin, J. C. (1985). *Leadership skills inventory.* NY: D.O.K.

Karnes, F. A., & McGinnis, J. C. (1995, January/February). Looking for leadership. Students' perceptions of leaders for the next millennium. *Gifted Child Today Magazine, 18*(1), 30–35.

Karnes, F. A., & Whorton, J. E. (1996). Teacher certification and endorsement in gifted education: A critical need. *Roeper Review, 19*(1), 54–56.

Kay, S. (1982, February). The gifted and the arts: A prismatic view. *School Arts, 81*(6), 44–45.

Khatena, J. (1992). *Gifted: Challenge and response for education.* Itaska, IL: F.E. Peacock Publishers.

Klausmeier, H. J., Schwenn, E. A., & Lamal, P. A. (1968). *A system of individually guided motivation* [Practical paper from the Wisconsin Research and Development Center for Cognitive Learning]. Madison: The University of Wisconsin-Madison.

Krathwohl, D. R., Bloom B. S., & Masia, B. B. (1956). Taxonomy of educational objectives. The classification of educational goals. Handbook II: Affective domain. In B. Bloom (Ed.), *Taxonomy of educational objectives.* New York: David McKay.

Krutetskii, V. A. (1976). *The psychology of mathematical abilities in school children.* J. Teller, Trans., J. Kilpatrick & I. Wioszup (Eds.). Chicago: University of Chicago Press.

Lazar-Morrison, C. and Others (1980). *A review of the literature on test use.* Los Angeles: Center for the Study of Evaluation.

Lazear, D. G. (1991). *Seven ways of knowing: Teaching for multiple intelligences* (2nd ed.). Palatine, IL: IRI/Skylight Publishing.

Lazear, D. G. (1994). *Multiple intelligence approaches to assessment: Solving the assessment conundrum.* Tucson, AZ: Zephyr Press.

Lenchner, G. (1983). *Creative problem solving in school mathematics.* Boston, MA: Houghton Mifflin Company.

Levinthal, C. F. (1988). *Messengers of paradise: Opiates and the brain. The struggle over pain, rage, uncertainty, and addiction.* New York: Anchor Press.

Lilly, M. S. (1971). A training based model for special education. *Exceptional Children, 37*, 745–749.

Lindsay, B. (1988, October). A lamp for Diogenes: Leadership giftedness and moral education. *Roeper Review, XI*(l), 8–11.

Link, F. R. (Ed.). (1985). *Essays on intellect.* Alexandria, VA: Association for Supervision and Curriculum Development.

Lowenfeld, V. (1957). *Creative and mental growth* (3rd ed.). New York: Macmillan.

Lozoff, B. (1989). Nutrition and behavior. *American Psychologist, 44*, 231–236.

MacKinnon, D. W. (1978). *In search of human effectiveness.* Buffalo, NY: The Creative Education Foundation, Inc.

Marek-Schroer, M. F., & Schroer, N. A. (1993). Identifying and providing for musically gifted young children. *Roeper Review, 16*(1), 33–36.

Marland, S. P., Jr. (1972). *Education of the gifted and talented* (Vols. 1–2). Washington, DC: U.S. Government Printing Office.

Martin, C. E. (1984). Why some gifted children do not like to read. *Roeper Review, 7*(2), 72–78.

McAlpine, J., Weincek, B., Jeweler, S., & Finkbinder, M. (1994). *I want to be like.* San Luis Obispo, CA: Dandy Lion Publications.

McClelland, D. C. (1973). Testing for competence rather than intelligence. *American Psychologist, 28*, 1–14.

Miller, R. C. (1990). Discovering Mathematical talent. Council for Exceptional Children. Reston, VA: ERIC Clearinghouse on Handicapped and Gifted Children.

Minton, H. L. (1987). Lewis M. Terman and mental testing: In search of the democratic ideal. In M. M. Sokal (Ed.), *Psychological testing and American society 1890–1930* (pp. 95–112). New Brunswick, NJ: Rutgers University Press.

Miserandino, A., Subotnik, R., & Ou, K. (1995, Summer). Identifying and nurturing mathematical talent in urban school settings. *The Journal of Secondary Gifted Education*, 244–247.

Morelock, M. J. (1996). On the nature of giftedness and talent: Imposing order on chaos. *Roeper Review, 19*(1), 4–12.

Morelock, M. J. & Feldman, D. F. (1997). High IQ children, extreme precocity, and savant syndrome in N. Colangelo and G. Davis, eds. *Handbook of gifted education.*

Morelock, M. J., & Feldman, D. H. (1993). Prodigies and savants: What they have to tell us about giftedness. In K. A. Heller, F. J. Mönks, & A. H. Passow (Eds.), *International handbook of research and development of giftedness and talent* (pp.161–181). Oxford: Pergamon Press.

Moss, E. (1990). Social interaction and metacognitive development in gifted preschoolers. *Gifted Child Quarterly, 34*(1), 16–20.

Muscott, H. S. (1991). *Teachers' standards, students' behavior, and the cascade of services model for youth with emotional disturbances: A differential analysis of classroom analogies.* Unpublished doctoral dissertation, Teachers College, Columbia University, New York.

Myers, I. B., & McCaulley, M. H. (1985). *Manual: A guide to the development and use of the Myers Briggs Type Indicator.* Palo Alto, CA: Consulting Psychologists Press.

Nisbet, R. E. (Ed.) (1993). *Rules for reasoning.* Hillsdale, New Jersey: Erlbaum.

Ochse, R. (1990). *Before the gates of excellence—The determinants of creative genius.* Cambridge, England: Cambridge University Press.

Osborn, A. F. (1979). *Applied Imagination.* New York: Charles Scribner's Sons.

O'Tuel, F. S. & Rawl (1985, November). *Sex differences in school variables for gifted students.* Paper presented at the annual meeting of the National Association for Gifted Children, Denver.

P. L. 94-142 (1975). Education for all handicapped children act, S. 6, 94th Congress (See 613 (a) (4) 1st session, June. Report No. 94-168.

Palincsar, A. S. (1986). The role of dialogue in providing scaffolded instruction. *Educational Psychologist, 21* (1 & 2), 73–98.

Palincsar, A. S. & Brown, A. L. (1984). The reciprocal teaching of comprehension-fostering and comprehension-monitoring activities. *Cognition and Instruction, 1* (2), 17–175.

Palincsar, A. S. & Brown, A. L. (1988). Teaching and practicing thinking skills to promote comprehension in the context of group problem solving. *Remedial and Special Education, 9* (1), 53–59.

Parker, W. D. & Adkins, K. K. (1995). Perfectionism and the gifted. *Roeper Review, 17,* 173–176.

Parnes, S. J. (1985). *A facilitating style of leadership.* NY: Bearly Limited.

Parnes, S. J. (1992). *Source book for creative problem solving.* New York: Creative Education Foundation.

Parsons, J. Adler, T. & Kaczala, C. (1982). Socialization of achievement attitudes and beliefs. Parental influences. *Child Development, 53,* 310–321.

Paschitti, M. S. (1988). An investigation of the success and processes used to solve mathematical insight by SAT identified 7th and 8th grade students. Unpublished doctoral dissertation, State University of New Jersey-Rutgers. Dissertation Abstracts 1989 – DEW 8827359.

Passow, A. H. (Ed.) (1979). *The gifted and the talented: Their education and development. The 78th yearbook of the National Society for the Study of Education.* Chicago: University of Chicago Press.

Passow, A. H. (1982a, March). *Differentiated curricula for the gifted/talented: A point of view. Curricula for the Gifted.* Selected Proceedings of the First National Conference for the Gifted/Talented, National State Leadership Training Institute, Ventura, California.

Passow, A. H. (1982b). *The gifted disadvantaged: Some reflections.* In *Identifying and educating the disadvantaged gifted and talented.* Selected proceedings from the Fifth National Conference on Disadvantaged Gifted and Talented, Los Angeles, CA, sponsored by The National/State Leadership Training Institute on the Gifted and Talented.

Passow, A. H. (1986). Reflections on three decades of education of the gifted. *Gifted Child Quarterly, 8*(4), 223–226.

Passow, A. H., & Rudnitski, R. A. (1993). *State policies regarding education of the gifted as reflected in legislation and regulation.* Storrs, CT: The National Research Center on the Gifted and Talented.

Paul, R. W. (1984, September). The Socratic spirit: An answer to Louis Goldman. *Educational Leadership, 42,* 1, pp. 63–64.

Paul, R. W. (1995a). *The logic of creative and critical thinking.* Santa Rosa, CA: Foundation for Critical Thinking.

Paul, R. W. (1995b). *Making critical thinking intuitive.* Santa Rosa, CA: Foundation for Critical Thinking.

Paul, R. W. (1995c). *Socratic questioning and role-playing.* Santa Rosa, CA: Foundation for Critical Thinking.

Paul, R. W. (1995d). *Why students and teachers don't reason well.* Santa Rosa, CA: Foundation for Critical Thinking.

Paul, R., Binker, A. J. A., Jensen, K., & Kreklau, H. (1990). *Critical thinking handbook: 4th–6th grades. A guide for remodeling lesson plans in language arts, social studies, and science.* Rohnert Park, CA: Foundation for Critical Thinking, Sonoma State University.

Paul, R., Binker, A. J. A., & Weil, D. (1995). *Critical thinking handbook: K–3rd Grades. A guide to remodeling lesson plans in language arts, social studies, and science.* Santa Rosa, CA: Foundation for Critical Thinking.

Perkins, D. N. (1995). *Outsmarting IQ.* New York: The Free Press.

Phenix, P. H. (1964). *Realms of meaning: A philosophy of the curriculum for general education.* New York: McGraw-Hill.

Phillips, J. L. (1975). *The origins of intellect: Piaget's theory* (2d ed.). San Francisco: W.H. Freeman.

Piaget, J. & Inhelder, B. (1967). *The child's conception of space.* New York: W.W. Norton.

Plucker, J. A., Callahan, C. M., & Tomchin, E. M. (1996). Wherefore art thou, multiple intelligences? Alternative assessments for identifying talent in ethnically diverse and low income students. *Gifted Child Quarterly*, 4(2), 81–89.

Polya, G. (1945). *How to solve it: A new aspect of mathematical method* (2nd ed.). Garden City, New York: Doubleday.

Porath, M. (1993). Gifted young artists: Developmental and individual differences. *Roeper Review*, 16(1), 29–33.

Postman, L. S. (1962). *Psychology in the making: Histories of selected research problems.* New York: Alfred Knopf.

Presseisen, R., & Kozulin, A. (1994). Mediated learning: The contributions of Vygotsky and Feuerstein in theory and practice. In M. Ben-Hur (Ed.), *On Feuerstein's instrumental enrichment* (pp. 51–82). Palatine, IL: IRI/Skylight Publishing.

Price, G., Dunn, K., Dunn, R., & Griggs, S. (1981). Studies in students' learning styles. *Roeper Review*, 4(2), 38–40.

Pulaski, M. A. S. (1980). *Understanding Piaget: An introduction to children's cognitive development* (Rev. ed.). New York: Harper & Row.

Purkey, W. W., & Novak, J.M. (1984). *Inviting school success.* Belmont, CA: Wadsworth Publishing Co.

Pyryt, M. (1997). *Enhancing divergent thinking: A meta-analytic review.* Paper presented at the meeting of the American Educational Research Association, Chicago.

Pyryt, M., Masharov, Y., & Feng, C. (1993). Programs and strategies for nurturing talents/gifts in science and technology. In K. A. Heller, F. Mönks, & A. H. Passow (Eds.), *International handbook of research and development of giftedness and talent* (pp. 453–472). Oxford: Pergamon Press.

Ramey, C. T., & Campbell, F. A. (1984). Preventive education for high-risk children: Cognitive consequences of the Carolina Abecedarian Project. *American Journal of Mental Deficiency*, 88(5), 515–523.

Ramos-Ford, V., & Gardner, H. (1997). Giftedness from a multiple intelligence perspective. In N. Colangelo & G. Davis (Eds.), *Handbook of gifted education* (pp. 54–66). Boston, MA: Allyn & Bacon.

Raths, L., Harmin, M., & Simon, S. (1966). *Values and teaching.* Columbus, OH: Charles Merrill.

Reed, J. (1987). Robert M. Yerkes and the mental testing movement. In M. M. Sokal (Ed.), *Psychological testing and American society 1890–1930* (pp. 75–94). New Brunswick, NJ: Rutgers University Press.

Reis, S. M., Burns, D. E., & Renzulli, J. Z. (1992). *Curriculum compacting.* Mansfield Center, CT: Creative Learning Press.

Reis, S. M., & Gavin, M. K. (1997). *Why Jane Can Do Math: How Teachers Can Encourage Talented Girls in Mathematics.* Paper presented at the annual conference of AGATE (Advocacy for Gifted and Talented Education), New York.

Rendfrey, K., Frayer, A., & Quilling, M. (1971, January). *Individually guided motivation: Setting goals for learning* [Practical paper from the Wisconsin Research and Development Center for Cognitive Learning]. Madison: The University of Wisconsin-Madison.

Renzulli, J. S. (1977). *The enrichment triad.* Wethersfield, CT: Creative Learning Press.

Renzulli, J. S. (1994). *Schools for talent development: A practical plan for total school improvement.* Mansfield Center, CT: Creative Learning Press.

Renzulli, J. S., & Gable, R. K. (1979). A factorial study of the attitudes of gifted students toward independent study. *Gifted Child Quarterly, 20,* 91–99, 104.

Renzulli, J. S., & Smith, L. H. (1978). *The learning styles inventory: A measure of student preference for instructional techniques.* Mansfield Center, CT: Creative Learning Press.

Reynolds, M. C. (1962). A framework for considering some issues in special education. *Exceptional Children, 28,* 367–379.

Robinson, A. (1986). Elementary language arts for the gifted: Assimilation and accommodation in the curriculum. *Gifted Child Quarterly, 130*(4), 178–181.

Roe, A. (1953). *The making of a scientist.* Westport, CT: Greenwood Press.

Rogers, C. (1959). Toward a theory of creativity. In H.H. Anderson (Ed.), *Creativity and its cultivation* (pp. 69–82). New York, Harper & Row.

Rubenzer, R. L. (1982). *Educating the other half: Implications of left/right brain research.* Reston, VA: Council for Exceptional Children.

Samelson, F. (1987). Was early mental testing: (a) racist inspired; (b) objective science; (c) a technology for democracy; (d) the origin of the multiple choice exam; (e) none of the above? (Mark the right answer). In M. M. Sokal (Ed.), *Psychological testing and American society* (pp. 113–127). New Brunswick, NJ: Rutgers University Press.

Sapon-Shevin, M. (1994). *Playing favorites: gifted education and the disruption of community.* Albany, NY: State University of New York Press.

Sattler, J. M. (1974). *Assessment of children's intelligence.* Philadelphia: W.B. Saunders Co.

Sattler, J. M. (1992). *Assessment of children* (Rev. ed.). San Diego, CA: Jerome M. Sattler Publisher, Inc.

Schlichter, C. L. (1993). Talents unlimited: Implementing the multiple talent approach in mainstream and gifted programs. In C. L. Schlichter & W. R. Palmer (Eds.), *Thinking smart: A primer of the Talents Unlimited model.* Mansfield Center: Creative Learning Press.

Schlichter, C. L., & Palmer, W. (Eds.). (1993). *Thinking smart: A primer of the Talents Unlimited model.* Mansfield, CT: Creative Learning Press.

Schneider, W. (1993). Acquiring expertise: Determinants of exceptional performance. In K. A. Heller, F. Mönks, & A. H. Passow (Eds.), *International handbook of research and development of giftedness and talent.* Oxford: Pergamon Press.

Scruggs, T. E., Mastropieri, M., Monson, J., and Jorgensen, C. (1985). Maximizing what gifted students can learn: Recent findings of learning strategy research. *Gifted Child Quarterly*, 29 (4), 181–185.

Seiger, S. D. (1984, April). Reaching beyond thinking skills to thinking strategies for the academically gifted. *Roeper Review*, 6(4), 185–188.

Sergent, D., & Roche, S. (1973). Perceptual shifts in the auditory information processing of young children. *Psychology of Music*, 1(2) 39–48.

Sheffield, L. (1994). *The development of gifted and talented mathematics students and the national council of teachers of mathematics standards.* Storrs, CT: The National Research Center on the Gifted, The University of Connecticut.

Shuter, R. (1968). *The psychology of musical ability.* London: Methuen & Co., Ltd.

Shuter-Dyson, R. (1982). Musical ability. In D. Deutsch (Ed.), *The psychology of music* (pp. 391–412). New York: Academic Press.

Silverman, L. K. (1993). The gifted individual. In L. K. Silverman (Ed.), *Counseling the gifted and talented* (pp. 51–78). Denver, CO: Love Publishing.

Simon, S. B., Howe, L. W., & Kirschenbaum, H. (1972). *Values clarification.* New York: Hart Publishing Co.

Simpson, E. (1966). *The classification of educational objectives, psychomotor domain: Final report* (U.S. Office of Education Contract # 5-85-104). Urbana, IL: College of Education, University of Illinois.

Sisk, D. A., & Shallcross, D. J. (1986). *Leadership—Making things happen.* New York: Bearly Limited.

Sisk, D. (1993). Leadership education for the gifted. In K. A. Heller, F. Mönks, & A. H. Passow (Eds.), *International handbook of research and development of giftedness and talent* (pp. 491–506). Oxford: Pergamon Press.

Sokal, M. M. (1987). James McKeen Cattell and mental anthropometry: Nineteenth-century science and reform and the origins of psychological testing. In M. M. Sokal (Ed.), *Psychological testing and American society 1890–1930* (pp. 21–45). New Brunswick, NJ: Rutgers University Press.

Spearman, C. E. (1927). *The abilities of man: Their nature and measurement.* New York: Macmillan.

Stanley, J. C. (1991). An academic model for educating the mathematically talented. *Gifted Child Quarterly*, 35(1), 36–41.

Sternberg, R. J. (1988a). *The nature of creativity.* Cambridge, England: Cambridge University Press.

Sternberg, R. J. (1988b). *The triarchic mind: A new theory of human intelligence.* New York: Viking Press.

Stevens, K. C. (1980). The effect of topic interest on the reading comprehension of high ability students. *Journal of Educational Research, 7*(3), 365–368.

Strasser, B. B., Babcock, R. W., Cowan, R., Dalls, G. T., Gothold, S. E., & Rudolph, S. E. (1972). *Teaching Toward Inquiry.* Washington, DC: National Education Association.

Subotnik, R. (1995) Talent developed: Conversations with masters in arts and science. *Journal for the Education of the Gifted.* Vol. 18, 4, pp. 440–466.

Taba, H. (1966, February). *Teaching strategies and cognitive functioning in elementary school children.* San Francisco: San Francisco State College, Cooperative Research Project No. 2040 supported by the Office of Education, U.S. Department of Health, Education and Welfare.

Tangherlini, A. E., & Durden, W. G. (1993). Strategies for nurturing verbal talents in youth: The word as discipline and mystery. In K. A. Heller, F. Mönks, & A. H. Passow (Eds.), *International handbook of research and development of giftedness and talent* (pp. 427–442). Oxford: Pergamon Press.

Tannenbaum, A. J. (1979). Pre-Sputnik to post-Watergate: Concern about the gifted. In A. H. Passow (Ed.), *The gifted and the talented: Their education and development. The 78th yearbook of the National Society for the Study of Education* (pp. 5–27). Chicago: University of Chicago Press.

Tannenbaum, A. J. (1983). *Gifted children: Psychological and educational perspectives.* New York: Macmillan.

Tannenbaum, A. J. (1986). Giftedness: A psychosocial approach. In R. J. Sternberg & J. E. Davidson (Eds.), *Conceptions of giftedness* (pp. 21–52). New York: Cambridge University Press.

Tannenbaum, A. J. (1993). History of giftedness and "gifted education" in world perspective. In K. A. Heller, F. Mönks, & A. H. Passow (Eds.), *International handbook of research and development of giftedness and talent* (pp. 3–28). Oxford: Pergamon Press.

Tannenbaum, A. J., & Baldwin, L. J. (1983). Giftedness and learning disability: A paradoxical combination. In L. H. Fox, L. Brody, & D. Tobin (Eds.), *Learning-disabled gifted children—identification and programming* (pp. 11–36). Baltimore, MD: University Park Press.

Tanner, D., & Tanner, L. N. (1980). *Curriculum development: Theory into practice* (2d ed.). New York: Macmillan Publishing Co., Inc.

Taylor, C. W. (1967). Questioning and creating: A model for curriculum reform. *Journal of Creative Behavior, 1*(1) 22–23.

Teplov, B. M. (1966). *Psychologie des aptitudes musicales* [The psychology of musical aptitude]. Paris, France: Presses Universitaires de France.

Terman, L. M. (1926). *Genetic studies of genius: Vol. I. Mental and physical traits of a thousand gifted children* (2nd ed.). Stanford, CA: Stanford University Press.

Terman, L. M., & Oden, M. H. (1947). *Genetic studies of genius: Vol. IV. The gifted child grows up: Twenty-five year follow-up of a superior group.* Stanford, CA: Stanford University Press.

Terman, L. M., & Oden, M. H. (1959). *Genetic studies of genius: Vol. V. The gifted group at midlife: Thirty-five year follow-up of the superior child.* Stanford, CA: Stanford University Press.

Thompson, M. C. (1994). *Inspecting own ideas: A grammar self-study program for high ability students.* Williamsburg, VA: College of William and Mary.

Thurstone, L. L. (1947). *Multiple-factor analysis: A development and expansion of "The vectors of the mind."* Chicago: University of Chicago Press.

Tomlinson, C. A. (1995). *How to differentiate instruction in mixed ability classrooms.* Alexandria, VA: Association for Supervision and Curriculum Development.

Torrance, E. P. (1964). Ebb and flow of creativity. In C. W. Taylor (Ed.), *Creativity: Progress and potential* (pp. 49–128). New York: McGraw-Hill.

Torrance, E. P. (1967). *Understanding the fourth grade slump in creative thinking: Final Report.* Athens, GA: Georgia University.

Torrance, E. P. (1969). *Creativity.* Belmont, Calif.: Dimensions Publishing Company.

Torrance, E. P. (1988). *Style of learning and thinking.* Bensenville, IL: Scholastic Testing Service.

Tref, R. (1996). *Maximizing your classroom time for authentic science: differentiating science curriculum for the gifted.* Global Summit on Science and Science Teaching, San Francisco, CA.

Treffinger, D. J., & Feldhusen, J. F. (1996). Talent recognition and development: Successor to gifted education. *Journal for the Education of the Gifted, 19*(3), 181–193.

U. S. Department of Education, Office of Educational Research and Improvement. (1993). *National excellence: A case for developing America's talent.* Washington, DC: U.S. Government Printing Office.

VanTassel-Baska, J. (1988). *Comprehensive curriculum for gifted learners.* Boston: Allyn & Bacon.

VanTassel-Baska, J. (1993). Theory and research on curriculum development for the gifted. In K. A. Heller, F. Mönks, & A. H. Passow (Eds.), *International handbook of research and development of giftedness and talent* (pp. 365–386). Oxford: Pergamon Press.

Vernon, P. E. (1950). *The structure of human abilities.* New York: John Wiley & Sons.

Vernon, P. E. (Ed.) (1970). *Creativity.* England: Penguin Books.

Vernon, P. E. (1979). *The structure of human abilities.* Westport, CT: Greenwood Press.

Villa, R. A., Van der Klift, E., Udis, J., Thousand, J. S., Nevin, A. I., Kunc, N., & Chapple, J. W. (1995). Questions, concerns, beliefs, and practical advise about inclusive education. In R. A. Villa & J. S. Thousand (Eds.), *Creating an inclusive school* (pp. 136–161). Alexandria, VA: Association for Supervision and Curriculum Development.

Vygotsky, L. S. (1978). *Mind in society: The development of higher psychological processes,* M. Cole, V. John-Steiner, S. Scribner, & E. Souberman (Eds.). Cambridge: Harvard University Press.

Wagner, P. A. & Penner, J. (1984, April). A new approach to teaching forms of reasoning to the gifted. *Roeper Review, 6,* 4, pp. 188–190.

Wallas, G. (1926). *The art of thought.* New York: Harcourt Brace.

Walters, J., Krechevsky, M., & Gardner, H. (1985). *Development of musical, mathematical, and scientific talents in normal and gifted children* (Report No. 31). Cambridge, MA: Harvard Project Zero.

Waxman, B., Robinson, N. M., & Mukhopadhayay, S. (1996). *Teachers Nurturing Math-Talented Young Children.* (Available from the Halbert Robinson Center for the Study of Capable Youth, Box 351630, University of Washington, Seattle, WA 98195-1630).

Wechsler, D. (1958). *The measurement and appraisal of adult intelligence* (4th ed.). Baltimore, MD: Williams and Wilkins.

Weil, M. & Joyce, B., (1976). *Academic models of teaching.* Omaha, Nebraska: Center for Urban Education.

Westberg, K., Archambault, F., Dobyns, S., & Slavin, T. (1993). The classroom practices observational study. *Journal for the Education of the Gifted, 16,* 120–146.

Whitfield, J. (1994). *Getting kids published.* Waco, TX: Prufrock Press.

Wieczerkowski, W., & Prado, T. M. (1993). Programs and strategies for nurturing talents/gifts in mathematics. In K. A. Heller, F. Mönks, & A. H. Passow (Eds.), *International handbook of research and development of giftedness and talent* (pp. 443–452). Oxford: Pergamon Press.

Winebrenner, S. (1992). *Teaching gifted kids in the regular classroom.* Minneapolis, MN: Freespirit Publishing.

Winner, E., & Martino, G. (1993). Giftedness in the visual arts and music. In K. A. Heller, F. Mönks, & A. H. Passow (Eds.), *International handbook of research and development of giftedness and talent* (pp. 253–282). Oxford: Pergamon Press.

Winter, G. W. (1987). *Identifying children in grades 1–3 who are gifted and talented in visual and performing arts using performance rated criterion.* South Carolina: ERIC ED 289 330.

Wright, L., & Borland, J. H. (1992, March). A special friend: Adolescent mentors for young economically disadvantaged, potentially gifted students. *Roeper Review, 14(3),* 124–129.

Yoakum, C. S., & Yerkes, R. M. (1920). *Army mental tests* (Published with the authorization of the War Department). New York: Henry Holt & Co.

York, J. (1994, Spring/Summer). *What's working.* Minneapolis, MN: Institute on Community Integration, University of Minnesota.

Zorman, R. (1993). Mentoring and role modeling programs for the gifted. In K. A. Heller, F. Mönks, & A. H. Passow (Eds.), *International handbook of research and development of giftedness and talent* (pp. 727–742). Oxford: Pergamon.

Index

ability grouping, 8, 9, 39–40
acceleration, 45–46
    and curriculum compacting, 37
    early use of, 7, 8
    and flexible grouping, 39
    in mathematics, 34, 43
    See also grade skipping
adding on, 37
Advanced Academy of Georgia, 102
advanced placement, 46
advanced readers. *See* readers, gifted
AEGIS, 47
aesthetic talent. *See* artistic ability
after-school activities. *See* extracurricular
        activities
Aliferis Music Achievement Test, 73
Alper, Ted, 48
AltaVista, 43
Amabile, T., 6, 120, 122, 120
analysis, in Bloom's Taxonomy, 113
Anthropometric Laboratory, 13
application, in Bloom's Taxonomy, 113
Archambault, F., 49, 50
Arieti, S., 120
Armstrong, T., 98, 100
Army, U.S., mental tests, 14
art, 30–31
    schools specializing in, 47
    See also artistic ability
The Art of the Possible (Gordon & Poze), 127
artistic ability, 3, 5, 22, 24, 62, 69, 100, 161
    visual/spatial abilities and, 84–87
    See also visual/spatial intelligence
assessment
    in Bloom's Taxonomy, 114
    of cognitive skills, 158
    and creativity, 122, 124
    and curriculum design, 7, 19, 25, 29, 53,
        107, 118, 140
    of independent study, 156
    of logical/mathematical intelligence,
        61–62
    of multiple intelligences, 139
    of musicality, 74–75
    of verbal/linguistic intelligence, 69
    of visual/spatial intelligence, 87, 88
athletic ability. *See* kinesthetic intelligence
audiences, finding appropriate, 29, 45, 48
Authentic Assessment of Student Ability, 160

background of experience, 6, 7, 21, 105, 111,
        129–130
Baldwin, L. J., 5
Bananas and Fifty-Four Other Varieties
        (Grenough et al.), 99
Baron, J. B., 118, 121
basic skills
    and ability grouping, 39
    expansion of, 36
    exposure to, 27
    and lesson design, 149
Baum, S. M., 78
The Bell Curve (Herrnstein & Murray), 16
Bellanca, J., 100
Benbow, C. P., 25
Bentley, J. E., 7, 8, 73
Bentley Measures of Musical Ability, 73
bibliotherapy, 96, 99
Binet, Alfred, 3, 14
Blakeslee, S., 3, 73, 106, 130
Bloom, B. S., 15, 32, 112, 129, 132
Bloom's Taxonomy, 36, 112–114, 140
bodily/kinesthetic intelligence. *See* kinesthetic
        intelligence
*The Bookfinder, A Guide to Children's
        Literature About the Needs*

and Problems of Youth Aged 2 and Up, 96
Borland, J. H., 147
boundary breaking, 97
breadth, as element of curricular modification, 35
Brigham, Carl, 14
Broadwin, J., 61
Brown, S., 50
Burks, B. S., 15
Burns, D. E., 37, 41
Burt, C., 3

Callahan, C. M., 24, 26, 30, 136
Campbell, F. A., 3, 15, 130
Caplow, D., 31
Cardinal Principles of Secondary Education, 8
Carolina Abecedarian Project, 15
cascade model, 12
Cattell, James McKeen, 13
Cattell, R. B., 4, 13, 15
CD-ROMs, 40, 41, 48, 88
Celebrating Multiple Intelligence: Teaching for Success, 100
Chall, J. S., 34
Chambers, J. A., 122
Chapman, C., 100
Chapple, J. W., 11, 12
Charness, N., 130
The Chocolate Caper, 61
Clark, Barbara, 132
Clark, G. A., 86, 120
class discussions, 94, 117
The Classification of Educational Objectives, Psychomotor Domain (Simpson), 71, 72
Classroom Connect, 44
classroom environment, 19, 22, 131–134, 139
Cline, S., 6, 7, 19, 20, 44, 54, 105, 133, 134
Cline Model for Developing Curriculum for the Gifted, xi, 7, 13, 19–50, *23*, 105, 112, 129
    content, 25, 26, *28*, 29–33

art, 30–31
dance, 25, 31, 48, 49, 74–80, *80*, 98, 140, 143
drama, 31, 48, 49, 67, 96, 98, 140, 144
language arts, 30, 65
leadership, 31–33, 47, 95, 99, 101–102, 141, 150
mathematics, 30
music, 31, 71–78. *See also* musicality
physical education, 30
science, 30, 41, 44, 47, 49, 62
social studies, 30, 34, 135
curricular modifications, 7, 19, 22, 25, 26, 33–37, 149–150
    adding on, 37
    breadth, 35
    compacting, 36–37, 44, 61
    complex cognitive processes, 36
    content, 25, 26, *28*, 29–33, 34
    depth, 27, 35, 37, 40–42, 44
    expansion of basic skills and comprehension, 36
    independent study, 29, 33, 36, 42, 44–47, 128–129
    process, 34
    product, 34–35
    telescoping, 36–37
    tempo, 35–36
    implementing, 149–150
    programming alternatives, 25, 26, 28, 37–38, *38*
cluster grouping, 39
cognitive development, 105–109, *108*
cognitive processes, complex, 33, 36
cognitive skills
    assessing, 158
    teaching, 106–111, 115
Cohen, Don, 44
Cole, M., 15, 107, 109
Coleman, L., 6
Coleman, M. R., 33
College for Younger Scholars (Mass.), 102
College Gifted Programs (N.J.), 102

College of William and Mary School of
Education, 68
Collins, N. D., 67
Columbus Group, 5, 6
combined classes, 47
combining opportunities, 48
Commission of Reorganization of Secondary
Education, 8
communication patterns, 94
community residents, 37, 47
compacting, 36–37, 44, 61
competitions
logical/mathematical, 62–63, 119
musical, 69
science, 49
comprehension
in Bloom's Taxonomy, 112
compared to analysis, 113
compared to application, 113
defined, 112
expansion of, 36
reading, 67
verbal, 15
computers, 29, 36, 40, 43–44, 48, 88, 147
concept formation, 114, *115*
confirming statements, 133
conflict resolution, 114–115
Conrad, S. S., 34
contracts. *See* learning contracts
cooperative grouping, 39
correspondence courses, 47–48
Costa, A. L., 106, 107
Council of State Directors of Programs for
the Gifted, 8
Courtright, R., 31
Cox, Gillian, 15
Creating Minds (Gardner), 100
creative writing, 65, 66, 144
creativity, 119–127
assessing, 124
and brainstorming, 124–125
in the classroom, 121, 124–127
defining, 119
ebb and flow of, 121
and the external environment, 130

and giftedness, 4, 6, 7, 20, 21, 105
and hemispheric preference, 98
identifying, 86, 143–144
impediments to, 122
influences upon, 105, 122–123
linking to curriculum, 123–124
theories of, 119, 120
thinking abilities associated with, 123
credit by examination, 47, 61
critical thinking skills, 42, 98, 116–117, 139,
144, 150
criticism, destructive, 124, 132–133
Csikszentmihalyi, M., 19
CTY program, 62
curricula
as assessment tools, 7, 19, 25, 53, 107,
118
compacting, 36–37, 44, 61
core, 28, 30, 31, 32, 41
and creativity, 123–124
differentiated. *See* curricular
differentiation
for the gifted, 23, 27–28
and independent study, 44, 46–47
for language arts, 65–66, 65
for leadership and values education,
31–32, 47
for mathematics, 59–61, 59
modifying. *See* curricular differentiation
for moral education, 31–33
for music and dance identification, *80*
for personal skill development, 99
planning, 28–29
self-selection, 36, 67
curricular differentiation, 33–49, *35*
academic foundations for, 19
and the Cline Model, 7, 19, 22, 25, 26,
33–37, 149–150
foundations for designing, 26–27
through self-selection, 67
strategies for, 26, 34, 53, 101
teachers as designers of, 28–29
variations in, 19
Cushing, Harvey, 82

D'Amico, V., 84, 85
dance, 25, 31, 48, 49, 74–80, 98, 140, 143
    curriculum for, *80*
    identifying talent in, 77–78, 79, *80*
Dandy Lion Publications, 61
data gathering, 48, 95, 139, 140, 146–149
Davies, I. K., 93, 94
Davis, S., 69
Davis, S. N., 129
De Bono, E., 127
deductive reasoning, 59, 60, 61, 116, 117
Dehaene, S., 3
Deno, E., 12
DEP (Differentiated Educational Plan
        or Profile), 149
depth, 27, 35, 37, 40–42, 44
Detterman, D. K., 109
development, proximal, 15, 33, 39, 107–109
Diamond, M. C., 16, 106, 109, 131
differentiated curriculum. *See* curricular dif-
    ferentiation
Differentiated Educational Plan or Profile
        (DEP), 149, *149*
dioramas, 88, 96
disabilities, xi, 1, 2, 10, 11, 12, 24, 25, 40
disadvantaged students, 8, 10, 11, 106, 147
Dixon, J. P., 82, 83, 84
Dobyns, S., 50
Dogpile, 43
Drake Musical Aptitude Tests, 73
drama, 31, 48, 49, 67, 96, 98, 140, 144
Draze, D., 98, 99
Dunn, K., 98
Dunn, R., 98
Durden, W. G., 65

Eberle, R. F., 125
Education of the Gifted and Talented, 8
educators. *See* teachers
Edwin Gordon Musical Aptitude Profile, 73
Egozi, M., 107, 110
Einstein, Albert, 56
elaboration, 120, 124
Elias, M. J., 90, 92

Eliot, T. S., 63, 64
Emmons, C., 50
emotional intelligence. *See* intelligence:
        emotional
Emotional Intelligence (Goleman), 32
Ennis, R. H., 116
Enriching Heredity (Diamond), 131
environment
    classroom, 22, 131–134, 139
    external, 6, 14, 16, 21, 33, 105, 106,
        130–134
    home, 3, 130–131
EPGY program, 48
ERIC, 44
Ericsson, K. A., 130
Euclidean space, 83, 84
evaluation. *See* assessment
Excite, 43
external environment, 6, 14, 16, 21, 33, 105,
        106, 130–134
extracurricular activities, 46–47

Falvey, M. A., 11, 12
Fechner, G. T., 13
Feldhusen, J. F., 22, 39, 62
Feldman, D. F., 21
Feng, C., 62
Feuerstein, R., 15, 33, 106, 107, 109, 110, 111
Finkbinder, M., 99
Fischer, K. W., 106, 107, 108
flexibility, 123–124
flexible grouping, 39
fluency, 3, 15, 120, 123
Flynn, James R., 15
foreign language ability, 30, 65–66
*Frames of Mind: The Theory of Multiple
        Intelligences* (Gardner), 15
Frasier, M., 2
Frayer, A., 128
Freud, Sigmund, 90, 119
Frey, K. S., 90, 92
Fulton, L., 31
functionalization, 133

Gable, R. K., 44
Gagne, F., 6, 22
Gailbraith, R. E., 32
Gallagher, J., 33
Gallagher, J. J., 31
Galler, J. R., 3
Galton, F., 13, 120
Gandhi, Mahatma, 88, 89
Garcia, J., 2
Gardner, H., 5, 6, 15, 21, 22, 24, 25, 27, 30,
        31, 32, 53, 56, 73, 100, 106, 120
Gaston Test of Musicality, 73
Gavin, M. K., 44
Gelfand, I. M., 48
generalizing, 59, 114, 115, *115*
genetic predispositions. *See* heredity
Gesell, A., 71
Getting Kids Published (Whitfield), 69
Getzels, J. W., 121
Ghiselin, B., 133
Gifner, C. C., 11, 12
Gift Identification and Assessment, 159
gifted children, programs for
    criticisms of, 2
    history of, 7–8
    identification procedures in, 10–11, *10*
    inconsistencies in, 8–9
    IQ tests used in, 3, 11
    in mathematics, 62
    selected listing of, 102
    underrepresented groups in, 25–26
    See also programming alternatives
giftedness
    alternative assessments of, 24
    in art, 30–31, *30*
    and career choice, 99
    components of, 20–22
    in dance, 31
    defining, 2–9, *10*, 150
    in drama, 31
    identifying, 9–12, 13, 19, 33, 36, 44–45,
        105–136, 146, 159
    and intelligence, 13, 25, 73
    in language arts, 30
    in leadership, 31–33

    markers of, 27, 28, 30, 42, 53, 61, 126,
        139, 141, 146, 148, 150
    in mathematics, 30
    multidimensionality of, 22–24
    in music, 31, 71, 73
    naturalist, 24
    physical, 30
    in science, 30
    in social studies, 30
    spiritualist, 24
    theories of, 13, 105
    unrecognized, 19
    in the visual arts, 82, 84
    See also intelligence; talent
Goddard, Henry, 14
Goethals, Angela, 129
Goldman, L., 116
Goldstein, David, 62
Goleman, D., 15, 16, 25, 32, 90, 91, 92
Gordon, E. E., 72
Gordon, W. J. J., 126, 127
Goslar, Lotte, 79, 80
Goto, Midori, 129
Gottlieb, L., 25, 32, 56, 91
Gowan, J. C., 120
grade skipping, 7, 45, 47, 61
Graham, Martha, 75, 76
Greenberg, M. T., 90, 92
Gregorc, A., 98
Grenough, M., 99
Griggs, S., 98
grouping, types of, 39
Gruber, H. E., 129
Guilford, J. P., 4, 15, 120, 123, 125
Guiton, G., 31

Hacker, A., 16, 25, 32
Haensly, P. A., 119
Halbert Robinson Center for the Study of
        Capable Youth, 62
Hallmark, B., 50
Halsted, J. W., 69, 99
Handicapped Children's Education Act, 11
handicaps. *See* disabilities

Hargreaves, D., 71
Harmin, M., 32
Harootunian, B., 107
Haynes, N. M., 90, 92
Hegeman, K., 31
Henderson, K., 49, 69
Henderson, Morgan, xv
heredity, 3, 13, 15, 16, 20, 106, 130
Herradine, C. C., 33
Herrnstein, R. J., 16
heuristics, 111, 118–119, 127
high school mentors, 43
Hoffman, M. B., 107, 110
Hollingworth, Leta, 7
home environment, 3, 130–131
honors class, 46
Hoover, S. M., 39
Horn, John, 15
Howe, L. W., 32
Hyatt, C., 25, 32, 56, 91

I Want to Be Like (McAlpine et al.), 99
IDEA (Individuals with Disabilities
        Education Act), 11
*If The Shoe Fits: How to Develop Multiple
        Intelligences in the Classroom*
        (Chapman), 100
Ilg, F. L., 71
imagery, 82, 133
inclusion, 10–12
independent study, 29, 33, 36, 42, 44–45
    in the Cline Model, 129
    credit for, 46–47
    evaluating, 35, 45, 114, 156
    preferred by gifted children, 98
    and task orientation, 128
Indiana Oregon Music Test, 73
Individuals with Disabilities Education Act
        (IDEA), 11
inductive reasoning, 3, 116, 117
inferring, 111, 114, 115
inquiry training, 117
intellectual peers, interaction with, 12,
        42–43, 98, 109, 121

intelligence, 63–69, 106–119
    bodily/kinesthetic, 21, 24, 25, 55, 75–80
    categories of, 24
    as component of giftedness, 20
    crystallized, 15
    definitions of, 2, 106, 107, 111
    development of, 106–118
    domains of, 21, 106
    emotional, 16, 32, 90, 91–92
    environmental influences on, 21, 106
    fluid, 15
    and giftedness, 1
    and heredity, 3, 13, 15, 16, 20, 106, 120
    identification of, 106–118
    improving, 14, 15, 33, 109, 110
    interpersonal, 21, 24, 31, 55
    logical/mathematical, 24, 25, 55, 56–62
    measuring, 2, 3, 13–16
    multifaceted nature of, 2, 3–7, 13, 15, 20
    multiple, 12, 19, 22, 53–102
        assessing, 139
        in the classroom, 134, 139
        education, 99–100
        inventory of, 53–56, *54*
        theory of, 5, 15, 19, 21, 22, 24, 100
            linking to classroom curriculum,
            30–31
            used in lesson design, 141–144,
            157
    musical, 21, 24, 25, 55, 69–75
    personal, 25, 32, 88–99
    spatial, 21, 24
    tests, 14, 15, 16, 25, 49
    verbal/linguistic, 24, 25, 30, 55, 63–69
    visual/spatial, 55, 81–88
intelligence quotient. *See* intelligence;
        IQ tests
interdisciplinary study, 33, 42, 61, 128, 129,
        141
interest centers, 41–42
*International Handbook of Research and
        Development of Giftedness and
        Talent* (Pyryt et al.), 62
Internet, 26, 35, 41–44, 48
internships, 46

interpersonal intelligence, 31, 88–99
intrapersonal intelligence, 31, 88–99
inventories, sample, 153–162
Inviting School Success (Purkey & Novak),
        133
IQ tests, 1, 2, 3, 5, 7, 11, 13, 16, 24, 25, 53,
        57, 59, 73, 82, 84, 106, 107,
        130. *See also* tests

Jackson, P. W., 121
Jacob K. Javits Gifted and Talented Students
        Education Act, 5, 8
Jarwan, F. A., 62
Jensen, A. R., 15, 135
Jensen, D. W., 15
Jeweler, S., 99
John-Steiner, V., 15, 107, 109
Johns, J., 69
Johns Hopkins Talent Search, xi, 66
Johnson-Laird, P. N., 119
Jones, T. M., 32
Jorgensen, C. 118
Joyce, B., 117
Jung, C. G., 120

Karnes, F. A., 50
Kay, S., 87
Kessler, R., 90, 92
Khatena, J., 8
Kimm, C., 11, 12
kinesthetic intelligence, 21, 24, 25, 55,
        75–80, 143
Kirschenbaum, H., 32
Klausmeier, H. J., 128
knowledge, 6, 27, 112. *See also* background
        of experience
Kozulin, A., 109, 110
Krathwohl, D. R., 32
Krechevsky, M., 73
Krutetskii, V. A., 57
Kuhl, P., 106
Kunc, N., 11, 12
Kwalwasser-Dyema Music Tests, 73

Laird, Marnie, 144
Lamal, P. A., 128
Langenbach, J., 31
language arts, 30, 65. *See also* verbal/
        linguistic intelligence
*Language Arts Curriculum for High Ability
        Learners—Exemplary Teaching
        Units*, 68
Lazear, D. G., 100
Lazer-Morrison, C., 107
leadership education, 31–33, 47, 95, 99, 141,
        150
    resources for, 101–102
learning centers, 40–41
learning contracts, 29, 36, 42, 44
Learning Potential Assessment Device
        (LPAD), 111
learning styles, 40, 95, 96, 97–99
Lenchner, C., 60, 61, 119
Leonardo da Vinci, 82
lessons, 157–158
    for assessing cognitive processes, 158
    and curriculum differentiation, 140–141
    to identify giftedness, 139–149
    and integrating cognitive processes,
        140–141
    sample unit, 144–146
    steps in designing, 139–140, 141–144, 157
Levinthal, C. F., 131, 132
Lilly, M.S., 11
Lindsay, B., 31, 32
linguistic intelligence. See verbal/linguistic
        intelligence
Logic Countdown, 61
logical/mathematical intelligence, 56–62
    activities promoting, 59–61
    assessing, 61–62
    competitions, 62–63, 119
    identifying, 58–59, 142
    structure of, 58
Lowenfeld, V., 85, 86
Lozoff, B., 3
LPAD (Learning Potential Assessment
        Device), 111
Lycos, 43

Mackinnon, D. W., 15, 120
Madison Music Tests, 73
Magellan, 43
Mainwaring Tests of Musical Ability, 73
"Manifesto for Children" (Torrance et al.), xv
Marek-Schroer, M. F., 71
markers of giftedness, 42, 61, 126
    recording, 27, 28, 30, 53, 139, 141, 146,
        148, 150
*Market Guide for Young Writers: Where and
    How to Sell What You Write*
    (Henderson), 49, 69
Marland, S. P., Jr., 4, 5, 8
Marland Report, 4
Marshall, B., 99
Martin, C. E., 67
Martino, G., 71, 73, 82, 84, 87
Masharov, Y., 62
Masia, B. B., 32
Mastropieri, M., 118
Math Olympiad, 119
mathematics, 30. *See also* logical/mathemati-
    cal intelligence
MathMagic Project, 44
matrix
    to identify giftedness, 29, 78, 146, 159
    Tannenbaum, 22, 24
McAlpine, J., 99
McCaulley, M. H., 98
McClelland, D. C., 15
McGuire, L., 99
mediated learning, 33, 107, 109–111
mentors, 22, 33, 36, 43, 46, 48, 146
Merlyn's Pen, 48, 49
Merrifield, P., 120
metacognition, 33, 106–107, 111, 117,
    130–131
Miller, R. C., 58, 59
Minor, L. L., 25
minorities, ethnics, 2, 10, 11, 14, 15, 16
Minton, H. L., 15
mirror game, 96
Miserandino, A., 58
mnemonic devices, 125, 127

"The Model of Human Potential" (Cline),
    20, 105
Modern Language Aptitude Test, 66
Monson, J., 118
moral education, 31–33
Morelock, M. J., 21, 22
Moss, E., 130
motivation, 92, 128–129
    characteristics of, 7
    intrinsic, 122, 128, 129
    provided by curriculum, 19
    provided by environment, 21
    role in giftedness, 6, 7, 105
    teacher support for, 128–129
Mozart, Wolfgang Amadeus, 120
Mukhopadhayay, S., 62
*Multiple Assessments for Multiple Intelli-
    gences* (Bellanca et al.), 100
multiple intelligence. *See* intelligence:
    multiple
*Multiple Intelligence Approaches to
    Assessment* (Lazear), 100
Multiple Intelligence Inventory, 53–56, *54*
Murray, C., 16
Muscott, H. S., 12
musical intelligence, 5, 21, 24, 25, 55, 69–75.
    See also musicality
musicality, 71–72, 77–78
    activities promoting, 41, 49, 69, 73–74,
        78–79, 142–143
    assessing, 74–75
    genetic predisposition for, 130
    identifying, 72–73, 80, 142
    See also dance
Myers, I. B., 98

National Assessment of Educational Progress
    (NAEP), 10
National Association for Gifted Children, 132
National Council of Teachers of
    Mathematics, 44
*National Excellence: A Case for Developing
    America's Talent* (Riley), 9

National Javits Language Arts Curriculum Project, 68
National Science Foundation Mathematics Forum, 44
National Science Teachers Association, 44
National/State Leadership Training Institute, 8
The Nature of Human Intelligence (Guilford), 15, 123
negation. *See* criticism: destructive
Nevin, A. I., 11, 12
Newton, Isaac, 82
Nisbet, R. E., 118
No Problem! Taking the Problem out of Mathematical Problem Solving, 61
Novak, J. M., 133
numerical ability. *See* logical/mathematical intelligence
nutrition, 3, 130–131

Oden, M. H., 15
Office of Gifted and Talented, 8
Oglesby, K., 31
omnibus prodigy, 21
One-Hour Mysteries, 61
opportunities, 2–3, 5, 10, 129–130
orators, 24, 65
Oreck, B. A., 78
originality, 80, 120, 123–124. *See also* creativity
Orourke, K., 99
Osborn, Alex, 124, 125
Otis, Arthur S., 14
Ou, K., 58
Owen, S. V., 78

Pantomime Circus dance company, 79
parents
    role of, 6, 12, 15, 28, 29, 43–44, 46, 58, 129, 132, 146
    sharing information with, 9, 28, 80, 88, 139, 148–150
Parkhurst, L., 67

Passow, A. H., 2, 10, 26
Paul, R. W., 116
"pedology," 107,
peer nominations, 94
Penner, J., 117
perceptual speed, 3, 15
perfect pitch, 71, 73, 130
Perkins, D. N., 118
personal intelligences, 25, 32, 88–99, 143
Phenix, P. H., 32
Phillips, J. L., 15
physical education, 30
Piaget, Jean, 15, 83, 84, 106, 107, 109
Picasso, Pablo, 81, 82
Plucker, J. A., 24
PMI (mnemonic device), 127
poetic ability, 66. *See also* verbal/linguistic intelligence
Policy 2510 Testing Out for Credit, 47
Polya, G., 118
Porath, M., 85
portfolios, 27, 29, 61, 69, 86–87, 140, 150, 146–148
Postman, L. S., 13
Poze, T., 127
Prado, T. M., 57, 62
Presbury, Jack, xv
pre-schematic stage of artistic ability, 85–86
Presseisen, R., 109, 110
Price, G., 98
Primarily Logic, 61
problem-solving, 34, 45, 60, 111, 119, 123, 126
Professionals at the Arts Connection, 78
Program for Exceptionally Gifted (Va.), 102
Program in Mathematics for Young Scientists (PROMYS), 62
programming alternatives, 25, 26, 28, 37–38, 38. *See also* gifted children, programs for
projective space, 83
PROMYS (Program in Mathematics for Young Scientists), 62
provisional augmentation, 47
pseudorealistic stage of artistic ability, 86

psychomotor domain, 71, 72
Publish a Book Contest, 48
Pulaski, M. A. S., 15, 106
pull-out programs, 48
puppets, 68, 96
Purkey, W. W., 133
Pyryt, M., 62, 123, 124, 125

questionnaires, sample, 153–162
Quilling, M., 128

Ramey, C. T., 3, 15, 130
Ramos-Ford, V., 27
Raths, L., 32
readers, gifted, 65, 67, 69
Reagan Administration, 8
reasoning ability, 3, 21, 22
records and reports, 139–150, 146–149
Reed, J., 14
Reis, S. M., 37, 44
relaxation, 133, 134
Rendfrey, K., 128
Renzulli, J. S., 4, 6, 22, 24, 37, 44, 45, 98, 105
Resource Development Questionnaire for
        Parents and Community
        Members, 155
resource rooms, 12, 45
Rey, Andre, 109
Reynolds, C. R., 119
Reynolds, M. C., 12, 136
Riley, Richard W., 9
Robinson, A., 67
Robinson, N. M., 62
Rodin, Auguste, 82
Roe, Ann, 15
Rogers, C., 120
*The Role of Confirmation, Negation and
        Functionalization in the
        Classroom* (Cline), 133
Ross Young Scholars Program, 62
*Roundtable: Discussion Questions for
        Independent Growth*
        (Draze), 98

Rudnitski, R. A., 10

Samelson, F., 14
Sapon-Shevin, M., 2
Sattler, J. M., 3, 13, 14, 15
Sayler, M., 39
Scale for the Group Measurement of
        Intelligence (Otis), 14
SCAMPER (mnemonic), 125
Schachar-Segeu, N., 107
schematic stage of artistic ability, 86
Schlichter, C. L., 125
Schneider, W., 129
Schroer, N. A., 71
Schwab-Stone, M. E., 90, 92
Schweitzer, Harriet, 48
Schwenn, E. A., 128
science
        competitions, 44, 49, 62
        learning centers, 41
        schools specializing in, 47
        See also logical/mathematical intelligence
Science, Mathematics and Language Arts,
        Center for Gifted Education
        (Williamsburg, Virginia), 102
scribbling stage of artistic ability, 85
Scribner, S., 15, 107, 109
Scruggs, T. E., 118
Seashore Measures of Musical Talents, 73
Seashore Test of Musical Talents, 73
Seiger, S. D., 111
self-paced instruction, 44
self-selected topics. *See* independent study
*Seven Ways of Knowing: Teaching for Multiple
        Intelligences* (Lazear), 100
Shachar-Segev, N., 110
Shallcross, D. J., 32, 133
Sharp, F. C., 13, 14
Sheffield, L., 59, 60, 61
Shriver, T. P., 90, 92
Shuter, R., 71, 73
Silverman, L. K., 5
Simon, S., 32
Simon, S. B., 32

Simon, T., 14
Simpson, Elizabeth, 71
Sisk, D. A., 32, 133
Six Thinking Hats (De Bono), 127
Slavin, T., 50
Smith, L. H., 45, 98
Snap Online, 43
social studies, 30, 34, 135
sociograms, 93–94, *93, 94*
Socratic method, 36, 116–117
software, 29, 43
Sokal, M. M., 13
Some of My Best Friends Are Books
          (Halsted), 69
Souberman, E., 15, 107, 109
spatial intelligence. *See* visual/spatial
          intelligence
Spearman, C. E., 14
special schools, 7, 12, 47–48
Spector, P., 99
sports. *See* kinesthetic intelligence
Sputnik, 8
Stanford-Binet Intelligence Scale, 3, 7
Stanley, J. C., 25, 34, 66
States Gifted and Talented Education
          Reports, 8
Stern, A., 31
Sternberg, Robert, 6, 16, 22, 32, 109, 121,
          134, 136
Stevens, K. C., 67
Stravinsky, Igor, 69
"The Structure of the Intellect" model
          (Guilford), 4
Student Evaluation of an Independent Study
          Project, 156
Student Growth form, 161, *161*
Student Interest Inventory, 153–154
Subotnik, R., 58, 129
Suggestions for Recording Gifted Behaviors,
          162
Swartz, E., 100
synectics, 126–127
synthesis, in Bloom's Taxonomy, 113–114,
          140, 145, 158

Taba, H., 36, 112–116, *115*, 140
talent
     in dance, *79, 80*
     definitions of, 3, 9
     development of, 15, 22, 129, 132, 134
     domains of, 22
     and giftedness, 5, 6, 7, 25
     kinesthetic, 65–66, 65, 76–77
     logical/mathematical, 57–59
     musical, 71–73
     verbal/linguistic, 63–69
     visual/spatial, 82–84
     See also giftedness; intelligence
Talents Unlimited program, 125–126
Tangherlini, A. E., 65
Tannenbaum, A. J., 4, 5, 6, 8, 24, 34, 36, 47,
          49, 120, 121
Tannenbaum Matrix, 22
Tanner, D., 8
Tanner, L. N., 8
task orientation, 2, 6, 7, 21, 33, 44, 105, 128–
          129, 160. *See also* motivation
Taylor, C. W., 125
teachers
     attitudes of, 12, 132–134
     and the Cline Model, 13, 19, 22, 25–26
     as curriculum designers, 28–29, 38
     role in promoting creativity, 122–123
     tools for, 139–150
     training of, 8–9, 10, 148
*Teachers Nurturing Math-Talented Young
          Children* (Waxman et al.), 62
teaching tools, 139–150
technology, 26, 37, 43–44
telecommunications, 43–44
telescoping, 36–37
tempo of learning, 35–36
Teplov, B. M., 71
Terman, Lewis, 3, 14, 15
testing out. *See* credit by examination
tests
     achievement, 59, 62, 65, 72, 86, 150
     aptitude, 59, 73, 86
     civil service, 13
     creativity, 86

IQ, 1, 2, 3, 5, 7, 11, 13–16, 24, 25, 49, 53,
        57, 59, 73, 82, 84, 106, 107, 130
    performance on, 84, 107
    spatial, 84
    standardized, 106, 107
    See also specific tests
Tests of Primary Abilities (Thurstone), 15
Texas Academy for Leadership in the
        Humanities, 102
Texas Academy of Math and Science, 102
Thackray Tests of Rhythmic Aptitude, 73
thinking
    abstract, 58
    creative, 4, 29, 33, 34, 36, 58, 106, 120,
        123, 134, 139, 143, 144, 150
    critical, 42, 98, 116–117, 139, 144, 150
    divergent, 123–124, 141, 143, 158
    higher-order, 3, 27, 30, 34, 36, 38, 112,
        116, 123, 147
    levels of, 112–113
    logical, 30, 60, 61
    metaphorical, 127
    operational, 84
    scientific, 30, 60
    skills, defined, 111–112
    strategies, 36, 111, 114, 115. *See also*
        heuristics
    teaching and modeling, 111–116
Thousand, J. S., 11, 12
Thurstone, L. L., 3, 15
tiered assignments, 29, 38–39
TIP program, 62
*To Open Minds: Chinese Clues to the
        Dilemma of Contemporary
        Education* (Gardner), 100
Tomchin, E. M., 24
Tomlinson, C. A., 50
topological space, 83
Torrance, E. P., xv, 98, 121, 132
Treffinger, D. J., 22
Triarchic Theory of Intelligence (Sternberg),
        16
*Two Nations: Black and White, Separate,
        Hostile, Unequal* (Hacker), 16

Udis, J., 11, 12
underachievement 2, 19, 25
U.S. Army, 14
U.S. Department of Education, 19
University of Washington Transition School
        and Early Entrance Program,
        102

values, 31–33
Van der Klift, E., 11, 12
VanTassel-Baska, J., 26, 34, 65
verbal/linguistic intelligence, 3, 24, 25, 30,
        55, 63–69
    activities promoting, 66–69
    assessing, 69
    identifying, 141–142
    recognizing, 65–66
Vernon, P. E., 3, 15, 120
Vietnam War, 8
Villa, R. A., 11, 12
visual/spatial intelligence, 55, 81–88
    activities promoting, 87
    and the arts, 84–86
    assessing, 88
    coordination of perspectives, 83–84
    and Euclidean space, 83, 84
    identifying, 86–87, 143
    and projective space, 83
    and topological space, 83
Vygotsky, L. S., 15, 33, 39, 107, 109, 110, 111

Wagner, Robert, 62
Wagner, P. A., 117
Wallas, G., 119
Walters, J., 73
Water Rat (Laird), 144
Waxman, B., 62
Webcrawler, 43
Weber, E. H., 13
Wechsler, David, 15
Wechsler Scale, 15
Weeramantry, Sunil, 129
Weil, M., 117

Weincek, B., 99
Weissberg, R. P., 90, 92
Westberg, F., 50
Westberg, K., 50
Westgard, Lance, 79, 80
Westinghouse Awards, 49
What Would Happen If I Said Yes? (Cline), 133
When Smart People Fail (Hyatt & Gottlieb), 32, 56
Whistler and Thorpe Musical Aptitude Test, 73
Whitfield, J., 69
Who's Who Among American High School Students, 10
Whorton, J. E., 50
Wieczerkowski, W., 57, 62
Wilczek, Fran, 129
Winebrenner, S., 42
Wing Standardized Tests of Musical Intelligence, 73
Winner, E., 71, 73, 82, 84, 87
Winners' Circle: A Guide for Achievement (Draze), 99
Winter, G. W., 88
Wissler, C., 13, 14
working style, 27
World War I, 14
World Wide Web, 43–44
Wright, L., 147
Written and Illustrated By (contest), 48
WSWHE BOCES, 68

Yahoo!, 43
Yarger, D., 107
Yerkes, Robert, 14
Yoakum, C. S., 14
York, J., 12
Young Author's Guide to Publishers, 49

"zero reject" philosophy, 11
Zhang, W., 50
Zimmerman, E., 86, 120

Zins, J. E., 90, 92
zone of proximal development, 15, 39, 107–109
Zorman, R., 46